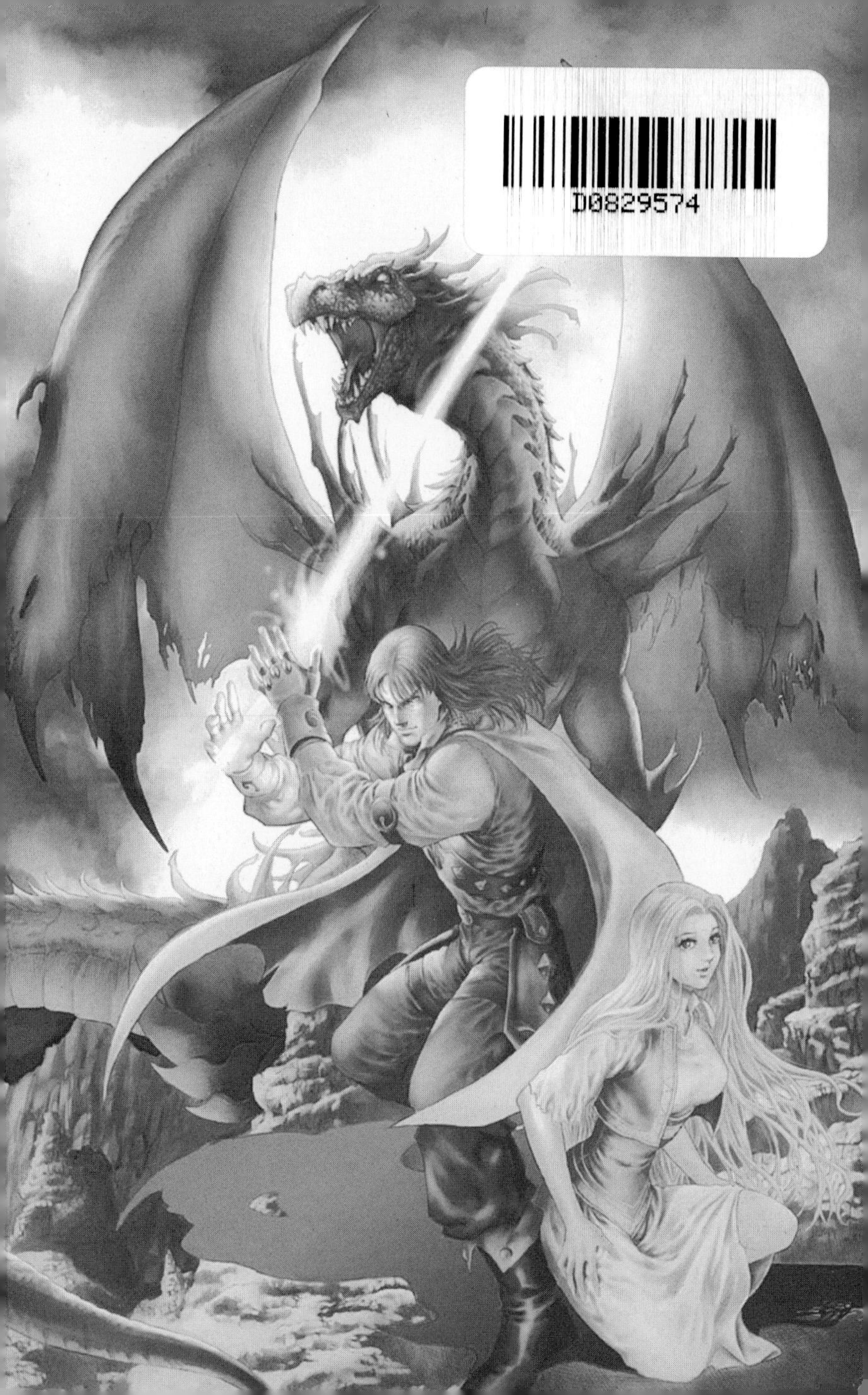

Warcraft®: The Sunwell Trilogy™ Vol. 1
Written by Richard Knaak
Illustrated by Jae-Hwan Kim

Lettering and Layout - Rob Steen
Copy Editor - Peter Ahlstrom
Production Artists - James Lee and James Dashiell
Artist Liaison - Eddie Yu and Studio Ice
Cover Art - Jae-Hwan Kim
Cover Design - Raymond Makowski

Editors - Rob Tokar and Jake Forbes
Digital Imaging Manager - Chris Buford
Production Managers - Jennifer Miller and Mutsumi Miyazaki
Managing Editor - Jill Freshney
VP of Production - Ron Klamert
Publisher and Editor-in-Chief - Mike Kiley
President and C.O.O. - John Parker
C.E.O. - Stuart Levy

A  Manga

TOKYOPOP Inc.
5900 Wilshire Blvd. Suite 2000
Los Angeles, CA 90036

E-mail: info@TOKYOPOP.com
Come visit us online at www.TOKYOPOP.com

Special thanks to Chris Metzen and Elaine Di Iorio for their effort, energy, and enthusiasm.

ISBN: 1-59816-287-X

First TOKYOPOP printing: September 2005
10 9 8 7 6 5 4 3 2
Printed in the USA

WarCraft
The Sunwell Trilogy

Volume 1

Dragon Hunt

Written by
Richard Knaak

Illustrated by
Jae-Hwan Kim

TOKYOPOP®

HAMBURG // LONDON // LOS ANGELES // TOKYO

HISTORY OF THE WORLD OF WARCRAFT

No one knows exactly how the universe began, but it is clear that the Titans--a race of powerful, metal-skinned gods from the far reaches of the cosmos--explored the newborn universe and made it their mission to bring stability to the various worlds and ensure a safe future for the beings that would follow in their footsteps.

As part of their unfathomable, far-sighted plan to create order out of chaos, the Titans shaped the worlds by raising mighty mountains, dredging out vast seas, breathing skies and raging atmospheres into being, and empowering primitive races to maintain their reshaped worlds.

Ruled by an elite sect known as the Pantheon, the Titans brought order to a hundred million worlds scattered throughout the Great Dark Beyond during the first ages of creation. The benevolent Pantheon assigned their greatest warrior, Sargeras, to be the first line of defense against the extra-dimensional demonic beings of the Twisting Nether who sought only to destroy life and devour the energies of the living universe. Sargeras was more than powerful enough to defeat any and all threats he faced…except one.

Unfortunately for the Pantheon, the Titans' inability to conceive of evil or wickedness in any form worked against Sargeras. After countless millennia of witnessing the atrocities of the demonic beings he fought, Sargeras eventually fell into a state of deep confusion, despair and madness.

Sargeras lost all faith in his mission and the Titans' vision of an ordered universe. It wasn't long before he came to believe that the concept of order itself was folly, and that chaos and depravity were the only absolutes within the dark, lonely universe. Believing that the Titans themselves were responsible for creation's failure, Sargeras resolved to form an unstoppable army that would undo the Titans' works throughout the universe and set reality aflame.

Even Sargeras' titanic form became distorted from the corruption that plagued his once-noble heart. His eyes, hair, and beard erupted in fire, and his metallic bronze skin split open to reveal an endless furnace of blistering hate.

In his fury, Sargeras freed the loathsome demons he'd previously imprisoned. These cunning creatures bowed before the dark Titan's vast rage and offered to serve him in whatever malicious ways they could. From the ranks of the powerful Eredar, Sargeras picked two champions to command his demonic army of destruction. Kil'jaeden the Deceiver was chosen to seek out the darkest races in the universe and recruit them into Sargeras' ranks. The second champion, Archimonde the Defiler, was chosen to lead Sargeras' vast armies into battle against any who might resist the twisted Titan's will.

Once Sargeras saw that his armies were amassed and ready to follow his every command, he dubbed them the Burning Legion and launched them into the vastness of the Great Dark. To this date, it is still unclear how many worlds they ravaged on their unholy Burning Crusade across the universe.

Unaware of Sargeras' mission to undo their countless works, the Titans continued to move from world to world, shaping and ordering each planet as they saw fit. Along their journey, they happened upon a small world whose inhabitants would later name Azeroth.

For many ages, the Titans moved and shaped the soil, until at last there remained one perfect continent. At the continent's center, the Titans crafted a lake of scintillating energies. The lake, which they named the Well of Eternity, was to be the fount of life for the world. Its potent energies would nurture the bones of the world and empower life to take root in the land's rich soil. Over time, plants, trees, monsters, and creatures of every kind began to thrive on the primordial continent. As twilight fell on the final day of their labors, the Titans named the continent Kalimdor: "land of eternal starlight."

Satisfied that the small world had been ordered and that their work was done, the Titans prepared to leave Azeroth. However, before they departed, they charged the greatest species of the world with the task of watching over Kalimdor, lest any force should threaten its perfect tranquility. In that age, there were many dragonflights, yet there were five groups that held dominion over their brethren. It was these five flights that the Titans chose to shepherd the budding world. The greatest members of the Pantheon imbued a portion of their power upon each of the flights' leaders. These chosen majestic dragons became known as the Great Aspects, or the Dragon Aspects.

Empowered by the Pantheon, the Five Aspects were charged with the world's defense in the Titans' absence. With the dragons prepared to safeguard their creation, the Titans left Azeroth behind forever. Unfortunately, it was only a matter of time before Sargeras learned of the newborn world's existence.

In time, a primitive tribe of nocturnal humanoids cautiously made their way to the edges of the mesmerizing enchanted lake. Drawn by the Well's strange energies, the feral, nomadic humanoids built crude homes upon its tranquil shores. Over time, the Well's cosmic power affected the tribe, making them strong, wise, and virtually immortal. The tribe adopted the name Kaldorei, which meant "children of the stars" in their native tongue. To celebrate their budding society, they constructed great structures and temples around the lake's periphery.

The Kaldorei--or night elves, as they would later be known--worshipped the moon goddess, Elune, and believed that she slept within the Well's shimmering depths during the daylight hours. The early night elf priests and seers studied the Well with an insatiable curiosity, driven to plumb its untold secrets and power.

As the seemingly endless ages passed, the night elves' civilization expanded and Azshara, the night elves' beautiful and gifted queen, built an immense, wondrous palace on the Well's shore that housed her favored servitors within its bejewelled halls. Her servitors, whom she called the Quel'dorei or "Highborne", doted on her every command and believed themselves to be greater than the rest of their brethren.

Sharing the priests' curiosity towards the Well of Eternity, Azshara ordered the Highborne to plumb its secrets and reveal its true purpose in the world. The Highborne buried themselves in their work and studied the Well ceaselessly. In time, they developed the ability to manipulate and control the Well's cosmic energies. As their experiments progressed, the Highborne found that they could use their newfound powers to either create or destroy at their leisure. The heedless Highborne had stumbled upon primitive magic and they devoted themselves to its mastery.

The Highborne's reckless use of magic sent ripples of energy spiraling out from the Well of Eternity and into the Great Dark Beyond, where they were felt by Sargeras, the Great Enemy of all life. Spying the primordial world of Azeroth and sensing the limitless energies of the Well of Eternity, Sargeras resolved to destroy the fledgling world and claim its energies as his own.

Gathering his vast Burning Legion, Sargeras made his way towards the unsuspecting world of Azeroth. The Legion was composed of a million screaming demons, all ripped from the far corners of the universe, and the demons hungered for conquest.

Corrupted by the magics they wielded, Queen Azshara and the Highborne opened a vast, swirling portal within the depths of the Well of Eternity for Sargeras and his forces. The warrior-demons of the Burning Legion stormed into the world through the Well of Eternity, leaving only ash and sorrow in their wake. Though the brave Kaldorei warriors rushed to defend their ancient homeland, they were forced to give ground, inch by inch, before the fury of the Legion's onslaught.

When the dragons, led by the great red leviathan, Alexstrasza, sent their mighty flights to engage the demons and their infernal masters, all-out warfare erupted. As the battle raged across the burning fields of Kalimdor, a terrible turn of events unfolded. The details of the event have been lost to time, but it is known that Neltharion, the Dragon Aspect of the Earth, went mad during a critical engagement against the Burning Legion. He began to split apart as flame and rage erupted from his dark hide. Renaming himself Deathwing, the burning dragon turned on his brethren and drove the five dragonflights from the field of battle.

Deathwing's sudden betrayal was so destructive that the five dragonflights never truly recovered. Wounded and shocked,

Alexstrasza and the other noble dragons were forced to abandon their mortal allies.

Hatching a desperate plot to destroy the Well of Eternity, a band of Kaldorei freedom fighters clashed with the Highborne at the Well's edge. The ensuing battle threw the Highborne's carefully crafted spellwork into chaos, destabilizing the vortex within the Well and igniting a catastrophic chain of events that forever sundered the world. A massive explosion from the Well shattered the earth and blotted out the skies.

As the aftershocks from the Well's implosion rattled the bones of the world, the seas rushed in to fill the gaping wound left in the earth. Nearly eighty percent of Kalimdor's landmass had been blasted apart, leaving only a handful of separate continents surrounding the new, raging sea. At the center of the new sea, where the Well of Eternity once stood, was a tumultuous storm of tidal fury and chaotic energies. This terrible scar, known as the Maelstrom, would never cease its furious spinning. It would remain a constant reminder of the terrible catastrophe...and the utopian era that had been lost forever.

The few night elves that survived the horrific explosion rallied together on crudely made rafts and slowly made their way to the only landmass in sight. As they journeyed in silence, they surveyed the wreckage of their world and realized that their passions had wrought the destruction all around them. Though Sargeras and his Legion had been ripped from the world by the Well's destruction, the Kaldorei were left to ponder the terrible cost of victory.

Despite the devastation, there were many Highborne who survived the cataclysm--and who wanted to continue using magic. One had even stolen some waters of the Well of Eternity and created a new Well in the night elves' new homeland. Unable to come to terms with their fellow elves, the Highborne, or Quel'dorei, as Azshara had named them in ages past, set out on their own, eventually making their way to the eastern land men would call Lordaeron. They built their own magical kingdom, Quel'Thalas, and rejected the night elves' precepts of moon worship and nocturnal activity. Forever after, they would embrace the sun and be known only as the high elves.

Effectively cut off from the life-giving energies of the Well of Eternity, the high elves discovered that they were no longer immortal or immune to the elements. They also shrank somewhat in height, and their skin lost its characteristic violet hue. Despite their hardships, they encountered many wondrous creatures that had never been seen in Kalimdor…including humans.

Over the course of several thousand years, the high elves developed their society and made alliances with their neighboring human communities. Though the elves had constructed a series of monolithic Runestones at various points around Quel'Thalas to mask their magic from extra-dimensional threats, the humans who had learned magic from the elves were not so cautious. The sinister agents of the Burning Legion, who had been banished when the Well of Eternity collapsed, were lured back into the world by the heedless spellcasting of the human magicians of the city of Dalaran.

Under Sargeras' orders, the cunning demonlord Kil'jaeden plotted the Burning Legion's second invasion of Azeroth. Kil'jaeden surmised that he needed a new force to weaken Azeroth's defenses before the Legion even set foot upon the world. If the mortal races, such as the night elves and dragons, were forced to contend with a new threat, they would be too weak to pose any real resistance when the Legion's true invasion arrived.

Kil'jaeden discovered the lush world of Draenor floating peacefully within the Great Dark Beyond. Home to the shamanistic clan-based orcs, Draenor was as idyllic as it was vast. Kil'jaeden knew that the noble orc clans had great potential to serve the Burning Legion if they could be cultivated properly.

Enthralling the elder orc shaman, Ner'zhul, in much the same way that Sargeras brought Queen Azshara under his control in ages past, the demon spread battle lust and savagery throughout the orc clans. Before long, the spiritual race was transformed into a bloodthirsty people.

Consumed with the curse of this new bloodlust, the orcs became the Burning Legion's greatest weapon. With the aid of a corrupted human mage, a Dark Portal was opened between Draenor and Azeroth, igniting an all-consuming war between the orcs and th humans. Though the human knights of Azeroth found allies in the high elves, the dwarves, and other species, the orcish ogres found allies in trolls, goblins, and more. Many human cities were utterly devastated and the orcs were poised to win the war until they fell victim to their own internal power struggles.

Seizing the opportunity, the humans retook their world and even fought the orcs in Draenor, though many heroic humans lost their lives when Draenor tore itself apart.

Though Ner'zhul was one of the many orcs who escaped Draenor's destruction, the orc shaman's body was torn apart by demons and his spirit was held helpless in stasis by Kil'jaeden. Recklessly agreeing to serve the demon, Ner'zhul's spirit was placed within a specially crafted block of diamond-hard ice gathered from the far reaches of the Twisting Nether. Encased within the frozen cask, Ner'zhul felt his consciousness expand ten thousand-fold. Warped by the demon's chaotic powers, Ner'zhul became a spectral being of unfathomable power. At that moment, the orc known as Ner'zhul was shattered forever, and the Lich King was born.

The Lich King was to spread a plague of death and terror across Azeroth that would snuff out human civilization forever. All those who died from the dreaded plague would arise as the undead, and their spirits would be bound to Ner'zhul's iron will forever.

Though the Lich King fought for the total eradication of human kind, the wealthy and prestigious archmage, Kel'Thuzad, led the city of Dalaran to serve the evil creature. As the ranks of the undead swept across Lordaeron, King Terenas' only son, Prince Arthas, took up the fight against the Scourge. Arthas succeeded in killing Kel'Thuzad, but even so, the undead ranks swelled with every soldier that fell defending the land. Frustrated and stymied by the seemingly unstoppable enemy, Arthas took increasingly extreme steps to conquer them. Finally Arthas' comrades warned him that he was losing his hold on his humanity.

Arthas' fear and resolve proved to be his ultimate undoing. Believing that it would save his people, Arthas took up the cursed runeblade Frostmourne. Though the sword did grant him unfathomable power, it also stole his soul and transformed him into the greatest of the Lich King's death knights. With his soul cast aside and h sanity shattered, Arthas led the Scourge against his own kingdom. Ultimately, Arthas murdered his own father, King Terenas, and crushed Lordaeron under the Lich King's iron heel.

Not long after Arthas and his army of the dead swept across the land, Kel'Thuzad was resurrected and not one living elf remained in Quel'Thalas. The glorious homeland of the high elves, which had stood for more than nine thousand years, was no more. Arthas subsequently led the Scourge south to Dalaran, and then to Kalimdor.

At Kalimdor, the night elves braced themselves and fought the Burning Legion with grim determination. Allied with humans and the orcs (now freed of their savage bloodlust), the night elves severed the Legion's anchor to the Well of Eternity. Unable to draw power from the Well itself, the Burning Legion began to crumble under the combined might of the mortal armies.

By this time, the undead Scourge had essentially transformed Lordaeron and Quel'Thalas into the toxic Plaguelands. The high elves grieved for the loss of their homeland and decided to call themselves blood elves in honor of their fallen people.

Meanwhile, half of the undead forces staged a coup for control over the undead empire. Eventually, the banshee Sylvanas Windrunner and her rebel undead--known as the Forsaken--claimed the ruined capital city of Lordaeron as their own and vowed to drive the Scourge and Kel'Thuzad from the land.

Though weakened, Arthas outmaneuvered the enemy forces that were closing in on the Lich King. Donning Ner'Zhul's unimaginably powerful helm, Arthas' spirit fused with Ner'zhul's to form a single mighty being--the new Lich King--and Arthas became one of the most powerful entities the world had ever known.

Currently, Arthas, the new and immortal Lich King, resides in Northrend; he is rumored to be rebuilding the citadel of Icecrown. His trusted lieutenant, Kel'Thuzad, commands the Scourge in the Plaguelands. Sylvanas and her rebel Forsaken hold only the Tirisfal Glades, a small portion of the war-torn kingdom, while the humans, orcs, and night elves are trying to rebuild their societies on Kalimdor.

AFTER WHAT SEEMED LIKE AGES OF BLOODY CONFLICT, THE WORLD THOUGHT IT HAD AT LAST FOUND PEACE. THE WAR AGAINST THE BRUTISH ORCS HAD COME TO A DEFINITIVE CONCLUSION, AND THE REMNANTS OF THE HORDE HAD BEEN ROUNDED INTO ENCLAVES AND KEPT UNDER GUARD.

SOON AFTER THE LANDS STARTED REBUILDING, A NEW, MONSTROUS EVIL AROSE. THE DEMONIC ARMY OF THE BURNING LEGION, UNITED WITH THE GHOULISH UNDEAD SCOURGE, SWEPT OVER HUMAN AND ORC REALMS ALIKE, FORCING OLD ENEMIES TO BAND TOGETHER.

YET, NOT UNTIL THE COMING OF THE MYSTERIOUS NIGHT ELVES AND THE SACRIFICE OF COUNTLESS LIVES WAS THE BURNING LEGION CRUSHED. NEARLY ALL OF THE ELVEN KINGDOM OF QUEL'THALAS AND THE HUMAN KINGDOM OF LORDAERON LAY IN RUINS, TRANSFORMED INTO FOUL PLAGUELANDS BY THE SCOURGE.

NOW, AN UNSTEADY STALEMATE EXISTS BETWEEN LIVING AND UNDEAD, AND FORCES FROM BOTH SIDES SEEK OUT THAT WHICH WILL DECISIVELY TIP THE SCALES IN THEIR FAVOR.

THUS IS IT THAT A YOUNG BLUE DRAGON WINGS HIS WAY TOWARD WHAT LITTLE REMAINS OF SOUTHERN LORDAERON...

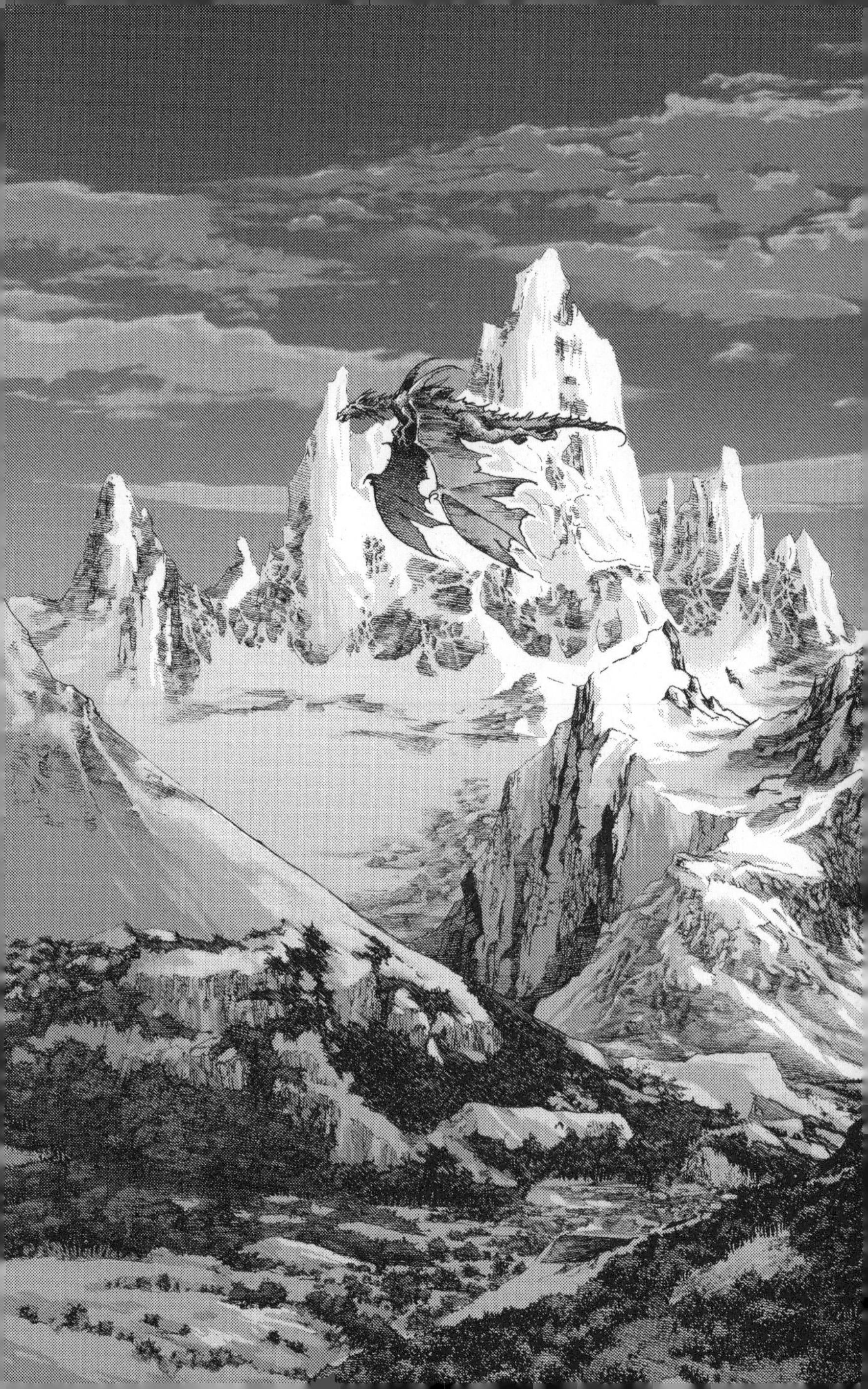

WARCRAFT
THE SUNWELL TRILOGY

DRAGON HUNT

KALIMDOR
EASTERN KINGDOMS

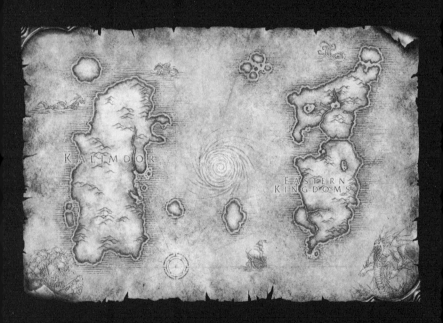

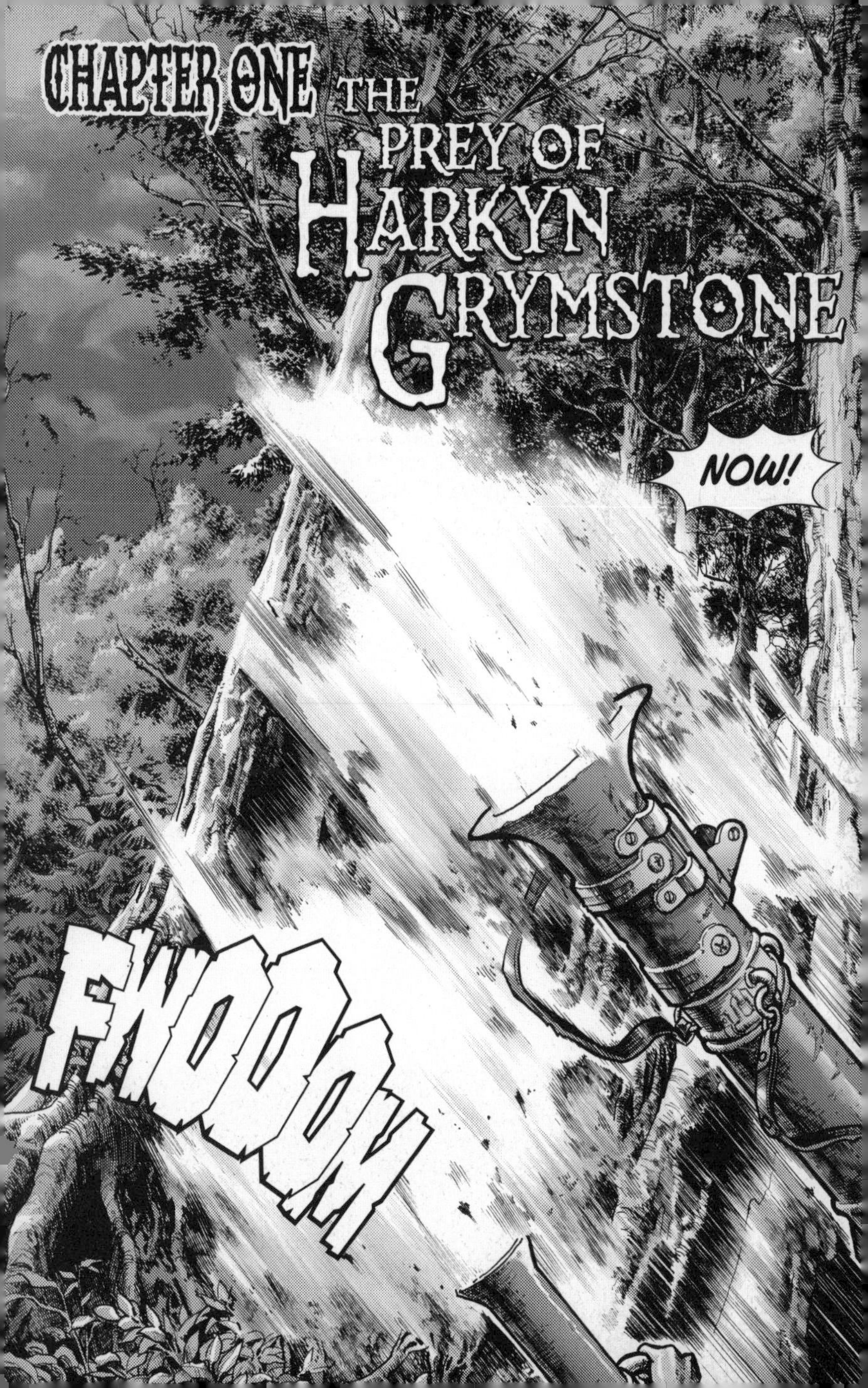
CHAPTER ONE THE PREY OF HARKYN GRYMSTONE
NOW!
FWOOOM

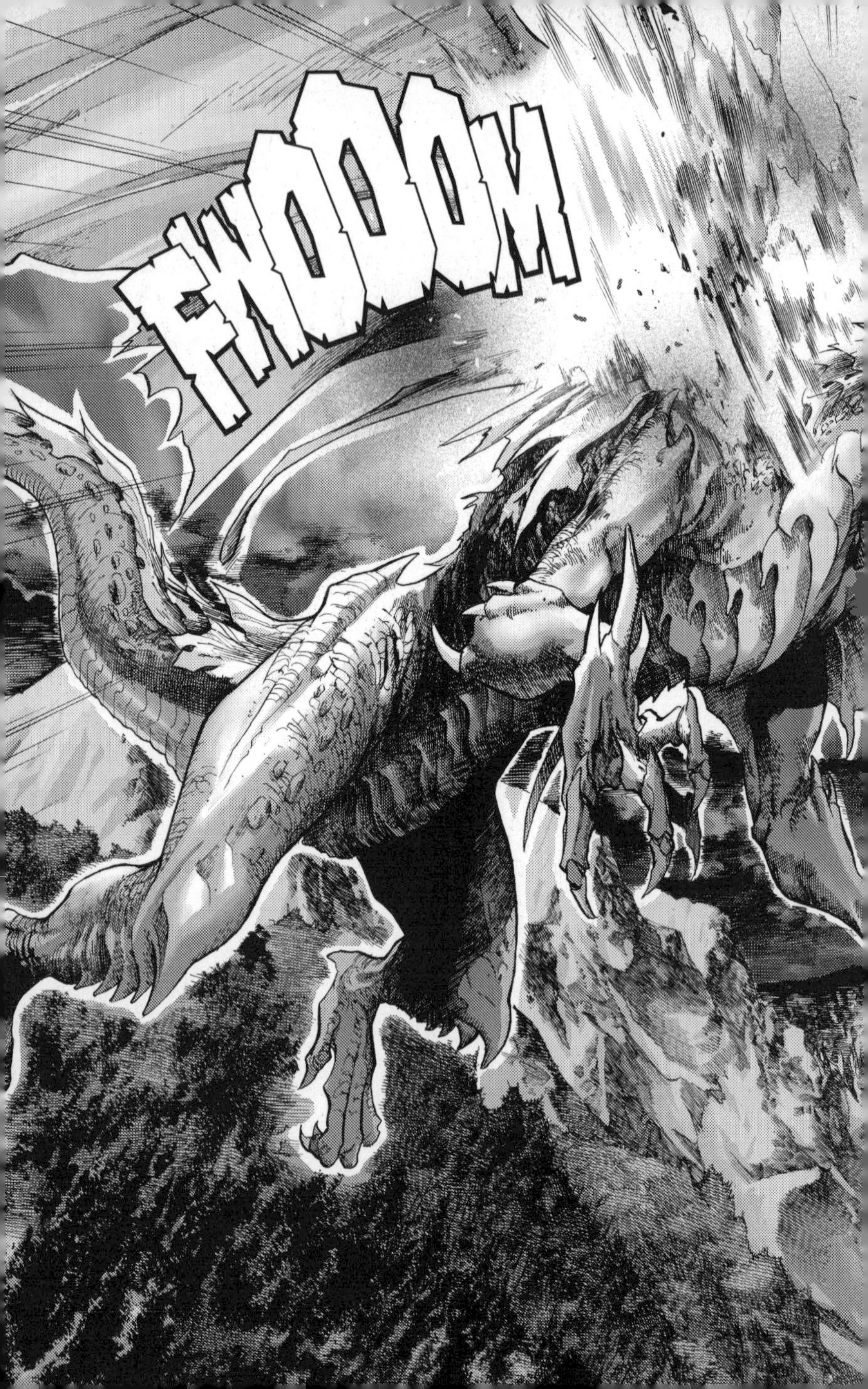
FWOOOM

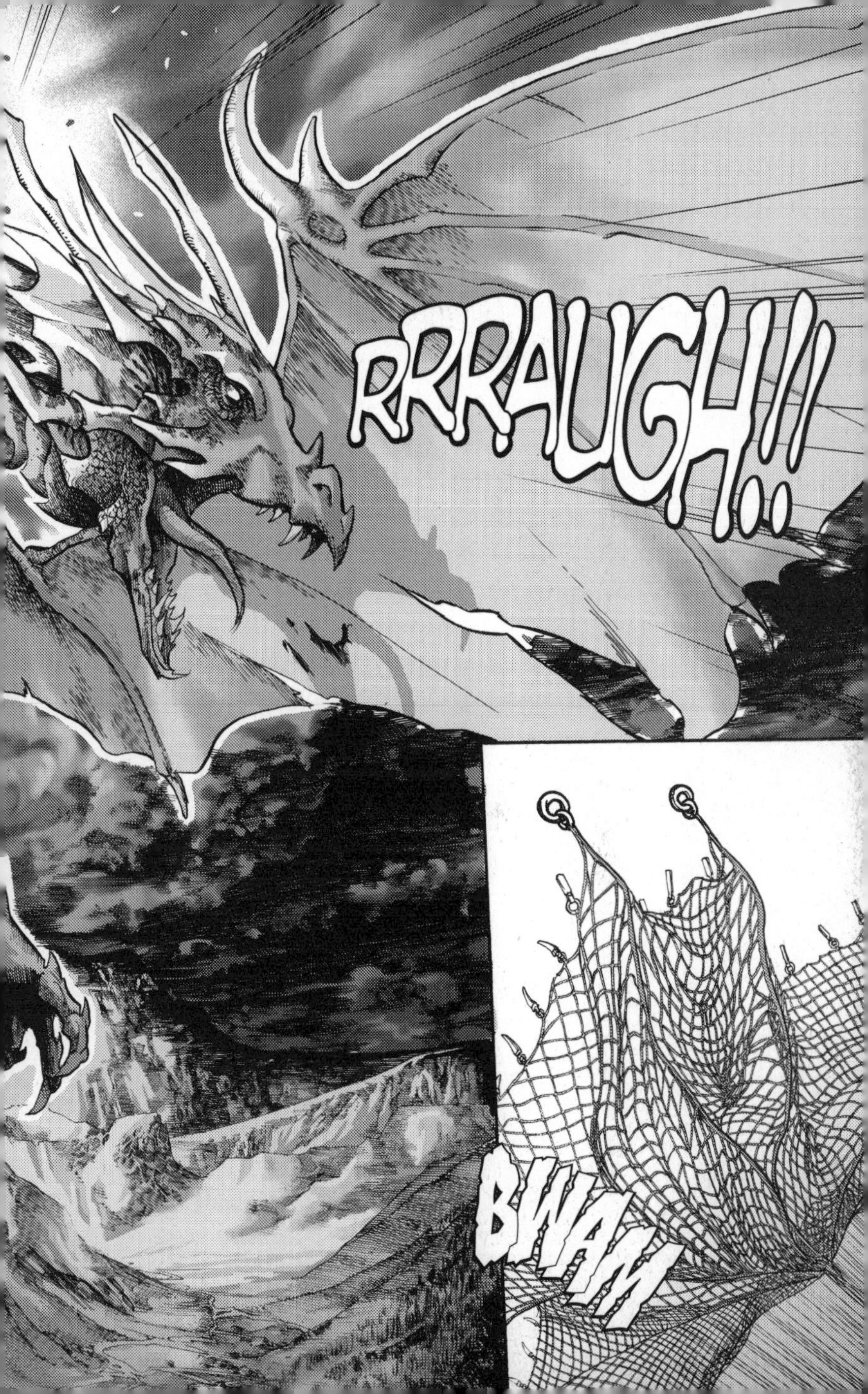
RRRAUGH!!!
BWAM

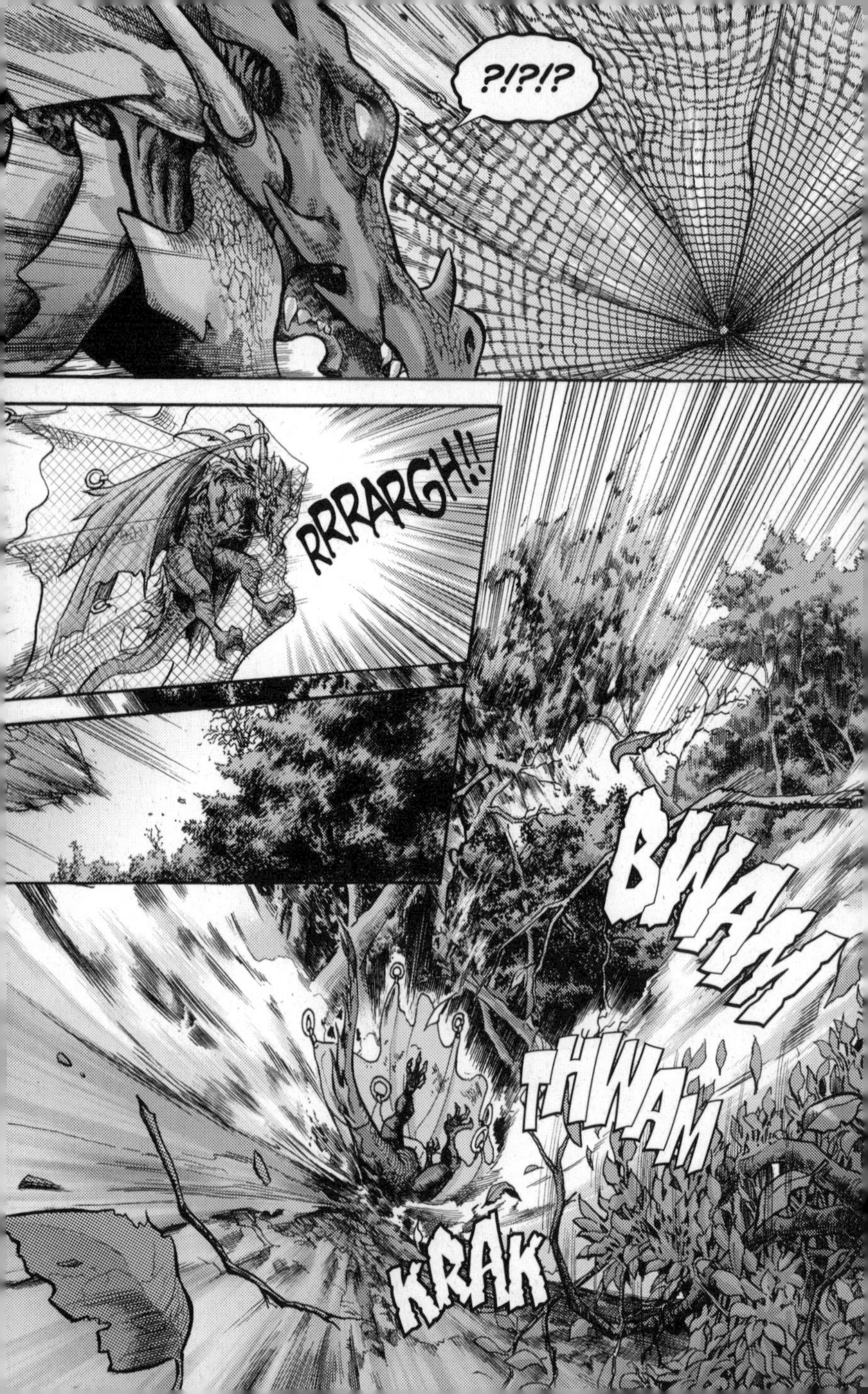
?!?!?
RRRARGH!!
BWAM
THWAM
KRAK

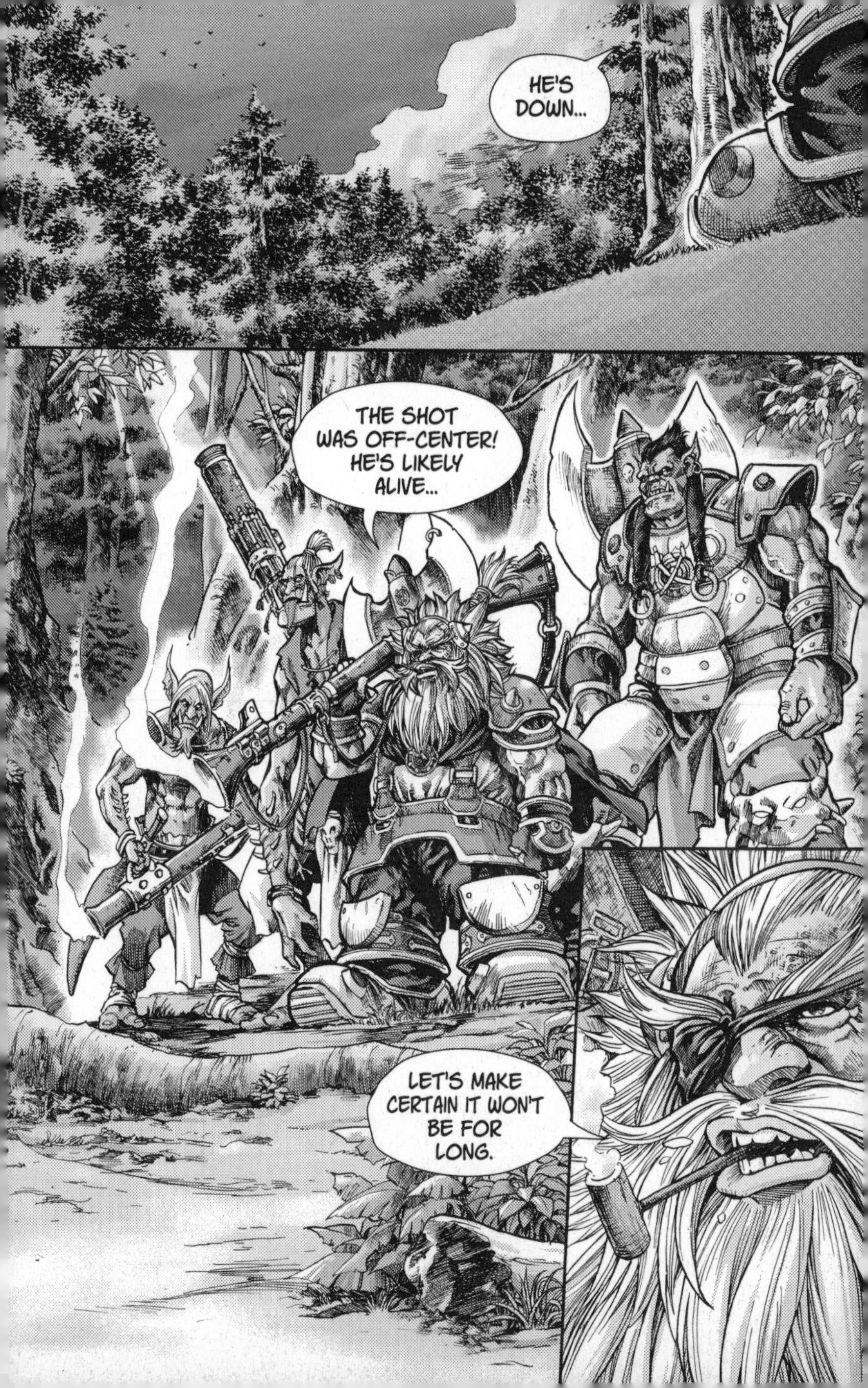
HE'S DOWN...
THE SHOT WAS OFF-CENTER! HE'S LIKELY ALIVE...
LET'S MAKE CERTAIN IT WON'T BE FOR LONG.

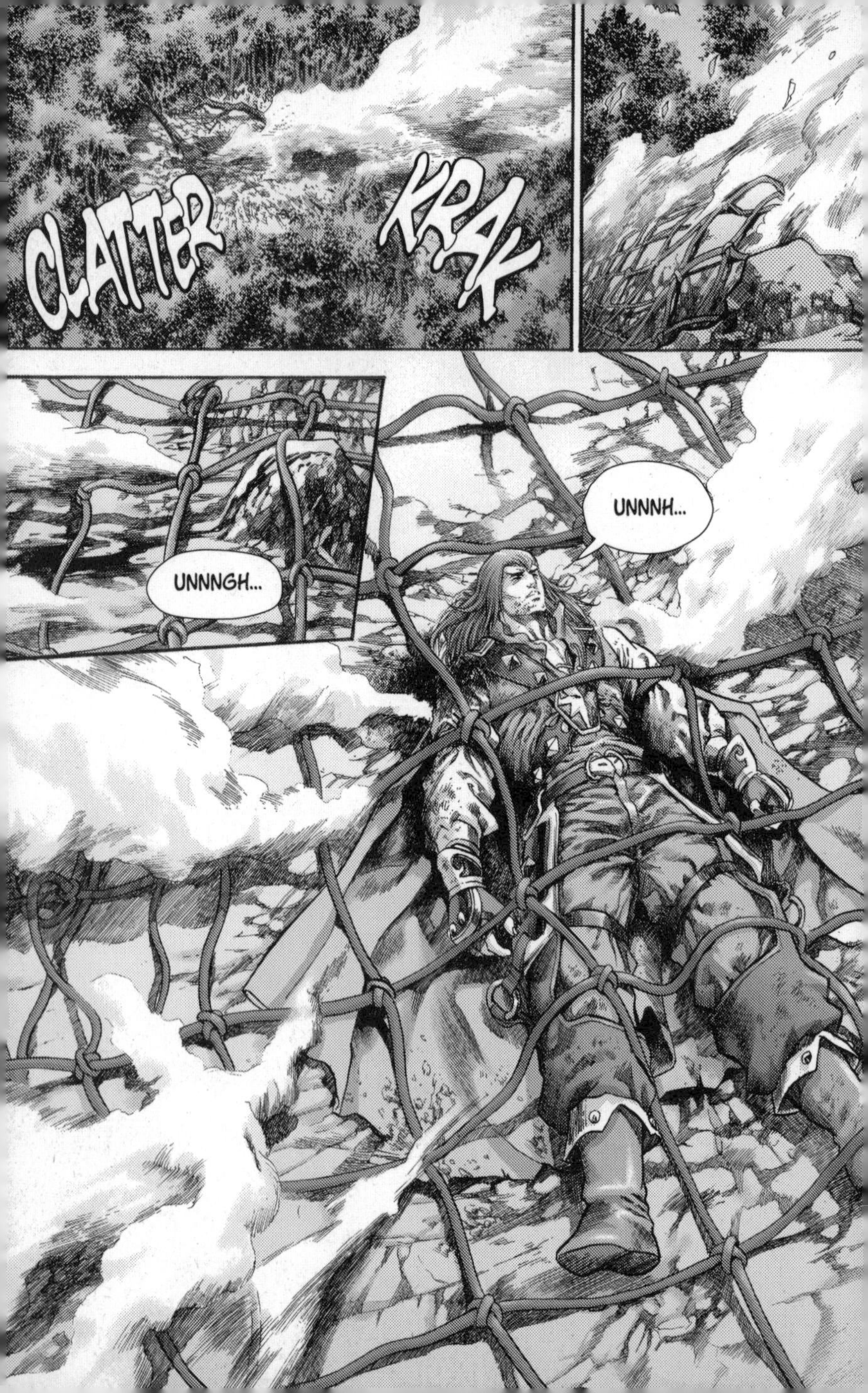
CLATTER
KRAK
UNNNGH...
UNNNH...

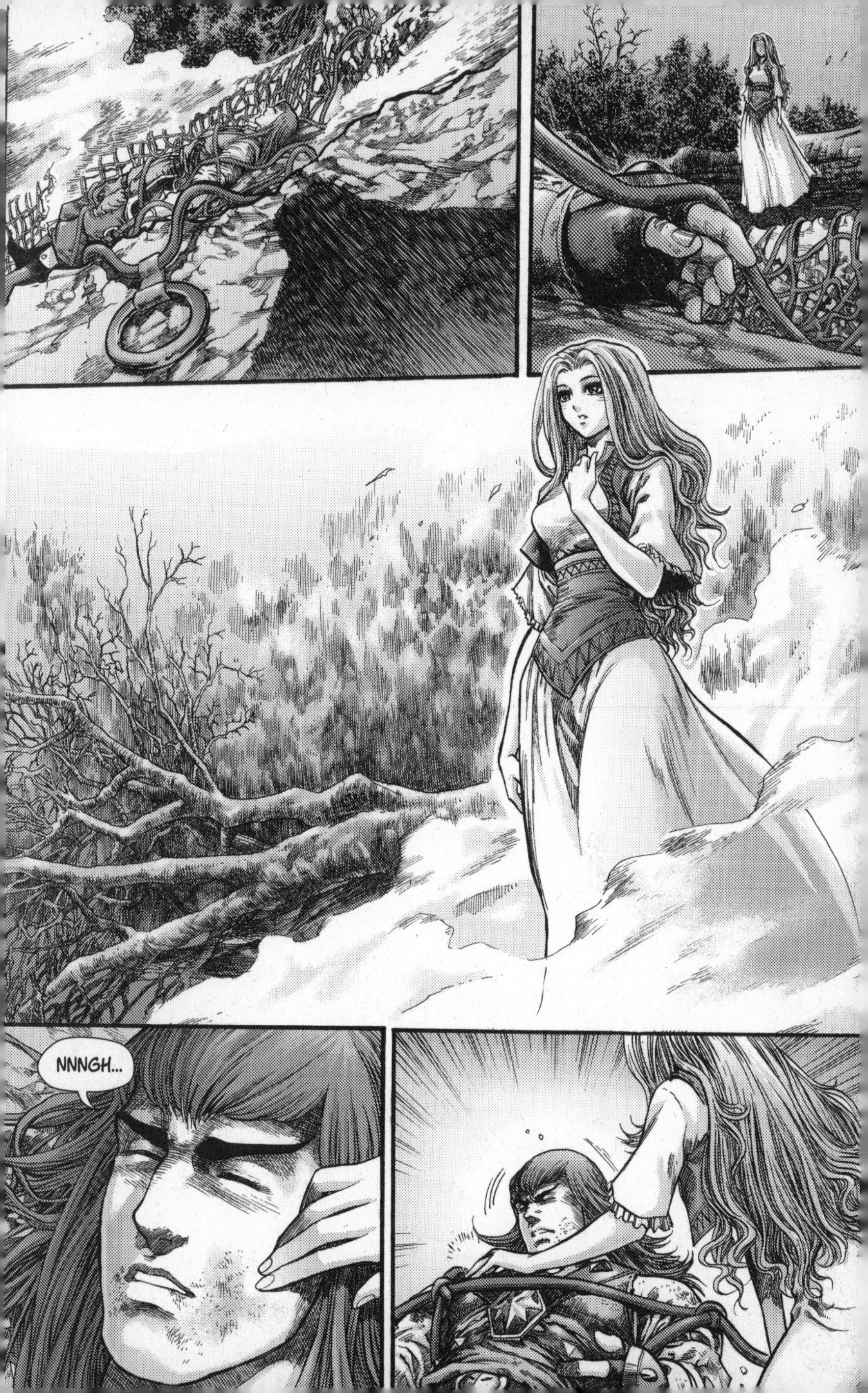
NNNGH...

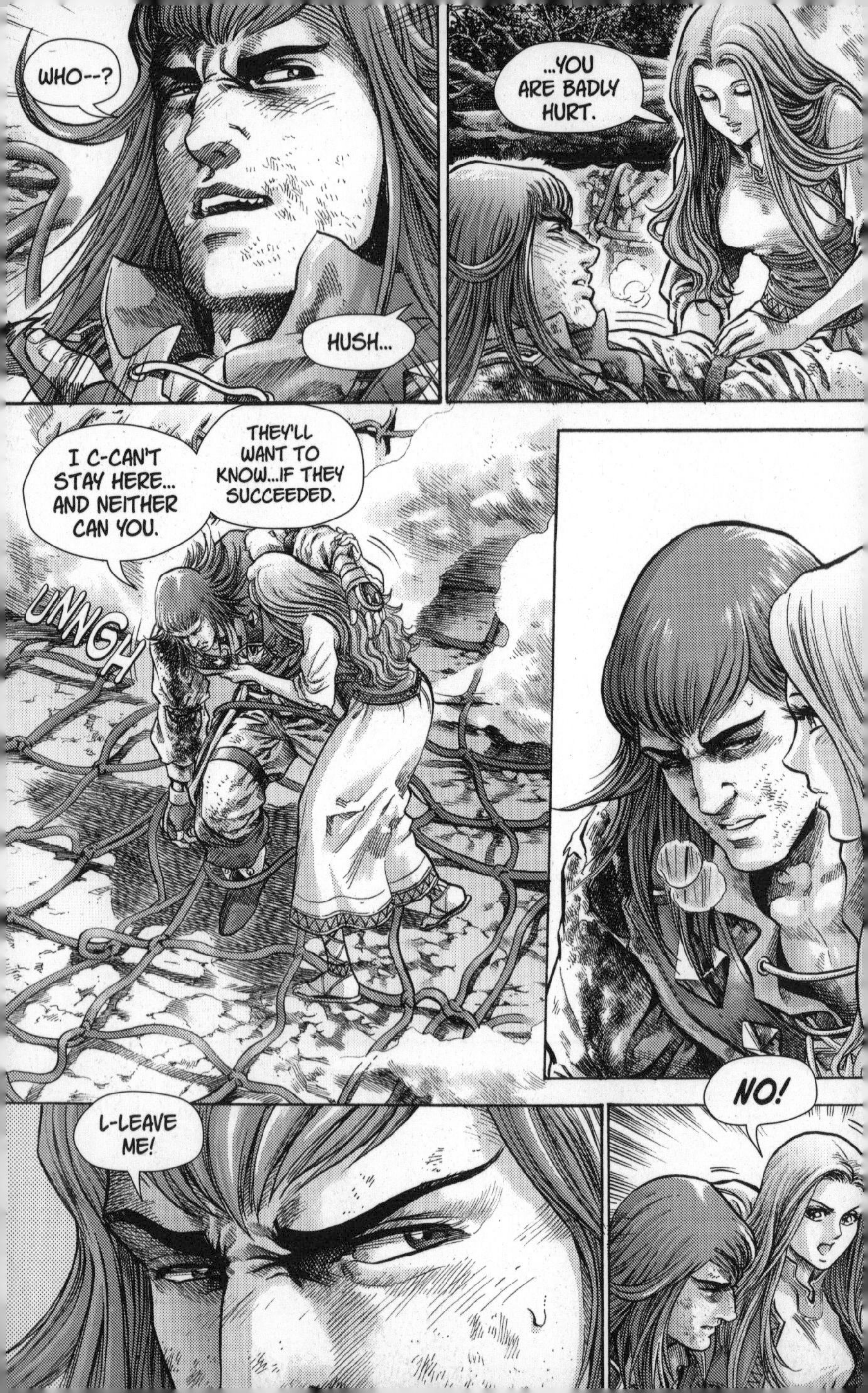
WHO--?
HUSH...
...YOU ARE BADLY HURT.
I C-CAN'T STAY HERE... AND NEITHER CAN YOU.
THEY'LL WANT TO KNOW...IF THEY SUCCEEDED.
UNNGH
L-LEAVE ME!
NO!

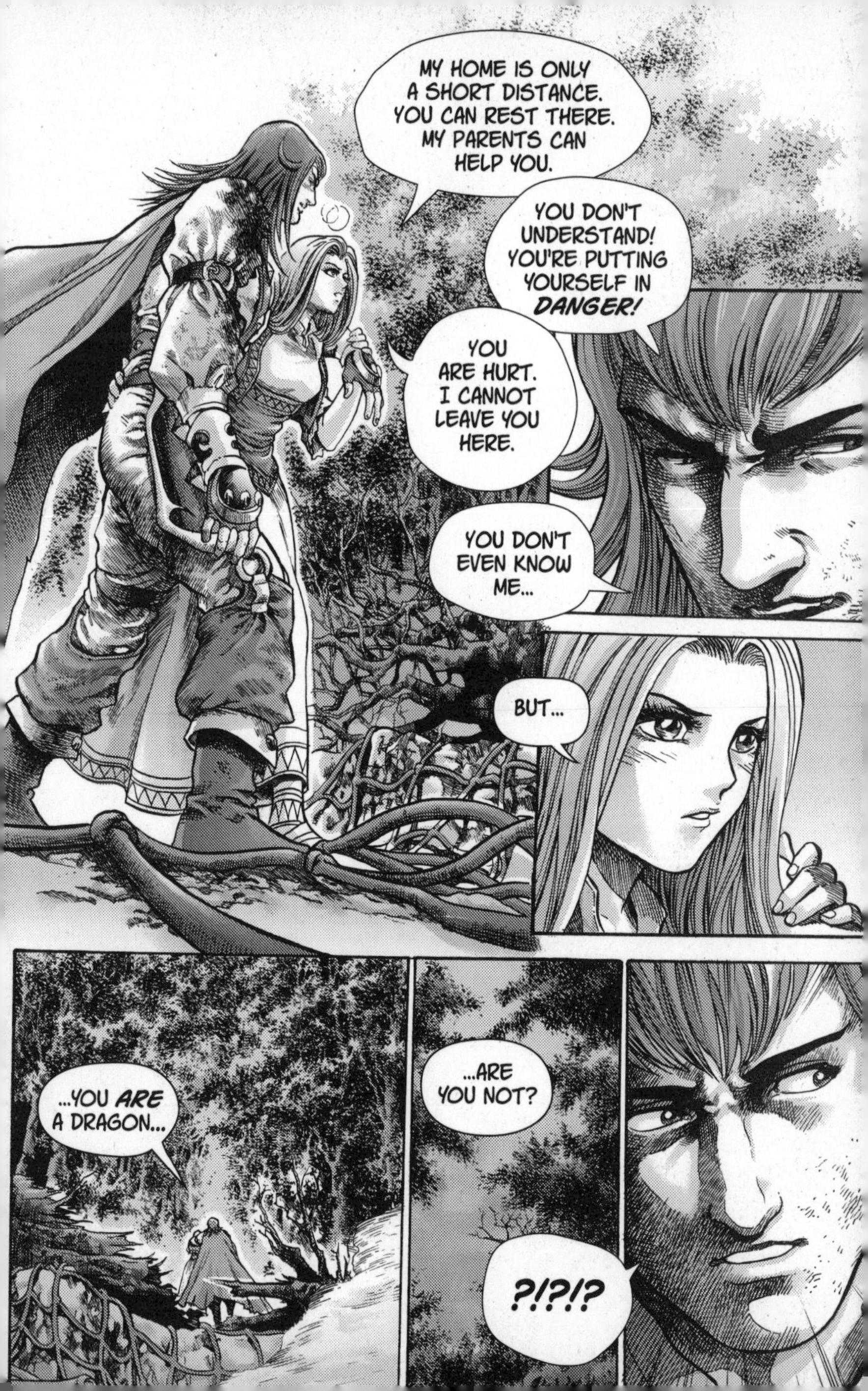
MY HOME IS ONLY A SHORT DISTANCE. YOU CAN REST THERE. MY PARENTS CAN HELP YOU.
YOU DON'T UNDERSTAND! YOU'RE PUTTING YOURSELF IN *DANGER!*
YOU ARE HURT. I CANNOT LEAVE YOU HERE.
YOU DON'T EVEN KNOW ME...
BUT...
...YOU *ARE* A DRAGON...
...ARE YOU NOT?
?!?!?

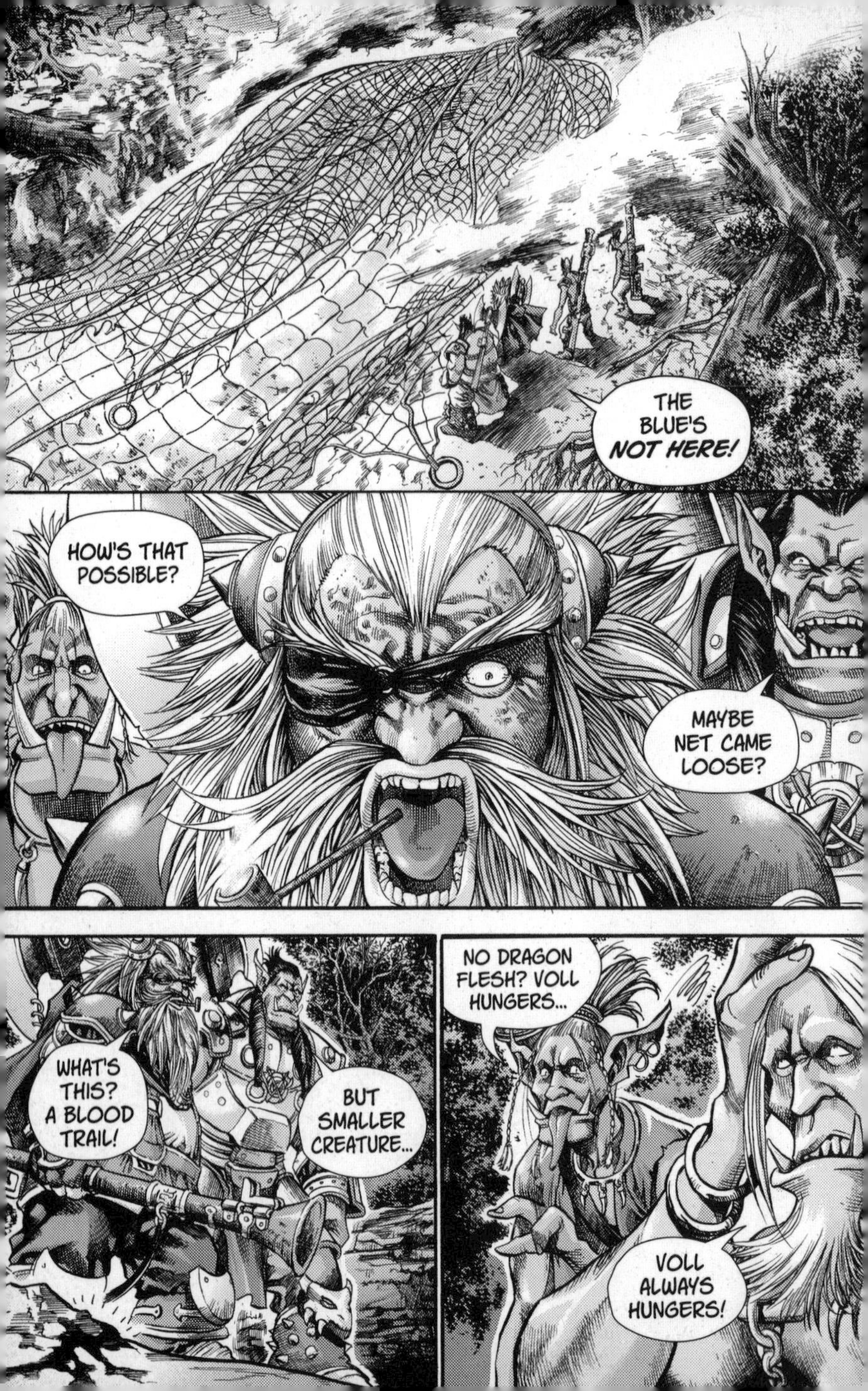
THE BLUE'S *NOT HERE!*
HOW'S THAT POSSIBLE?
MAYBE NET CAME LOOSE?
WHAT'S THIS? A BLOOD TRAIL!
BUT SMALLER CREATURE...
NO DRAGON FLESH? VOLL HUNGERS...
VOLL ALWAYS HUNGERS!

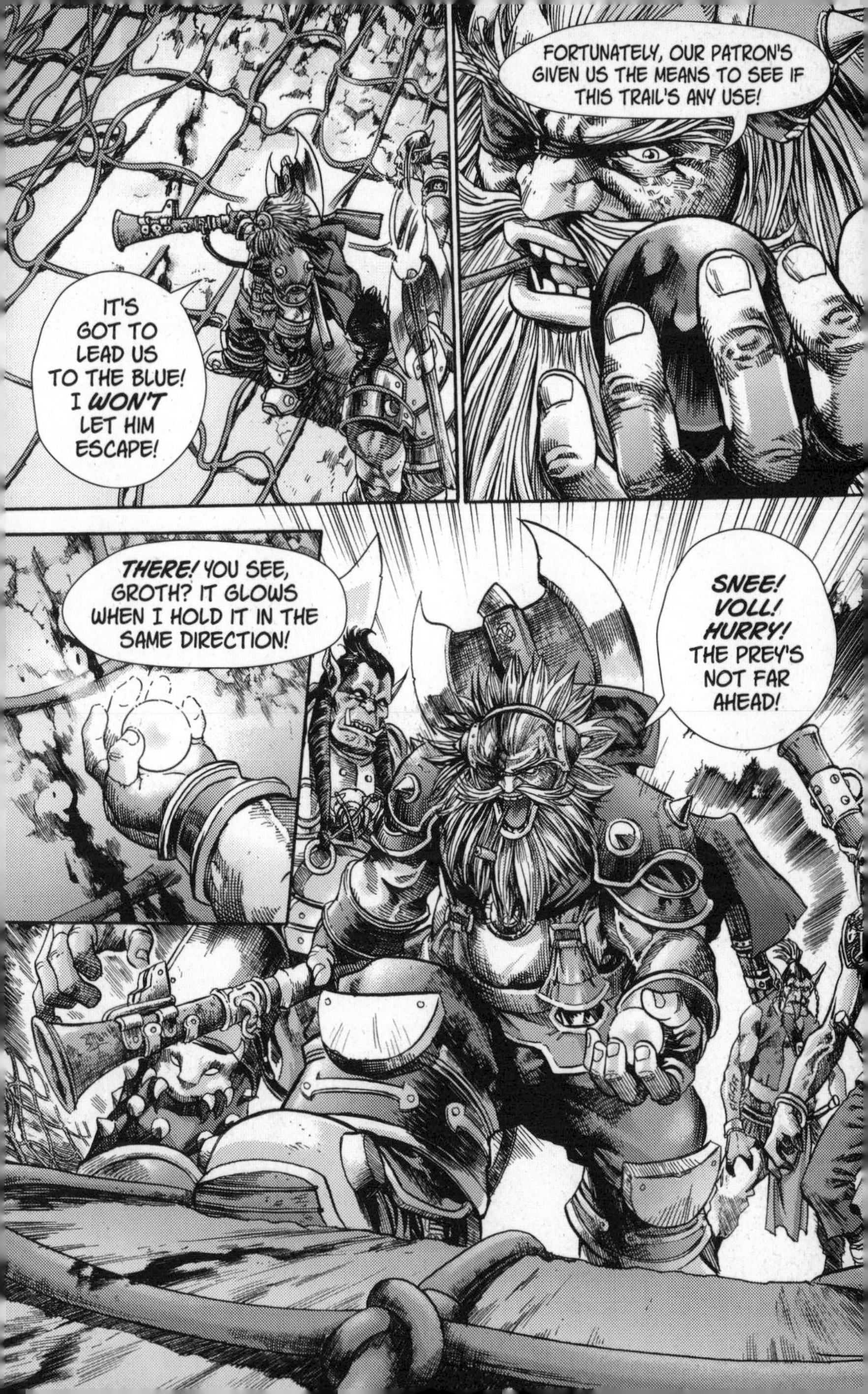
IT'S GOT TO LEAD US TO THE BLUE! I **WON'T** LET HIM ESCAPE!
FORTUNATELY, OUR PATRON'S GIVEN US THE MEANS TO SEE IF THIS TRAIL'S ANY USE!
THERE! YOU SEE, GROTH? IT GLOWS WHEN I HOLD IT IN THE SAME DIRECTION!
SNEE! VOLL! HURRY! THE PREY'S NOT FAR AHEAD!

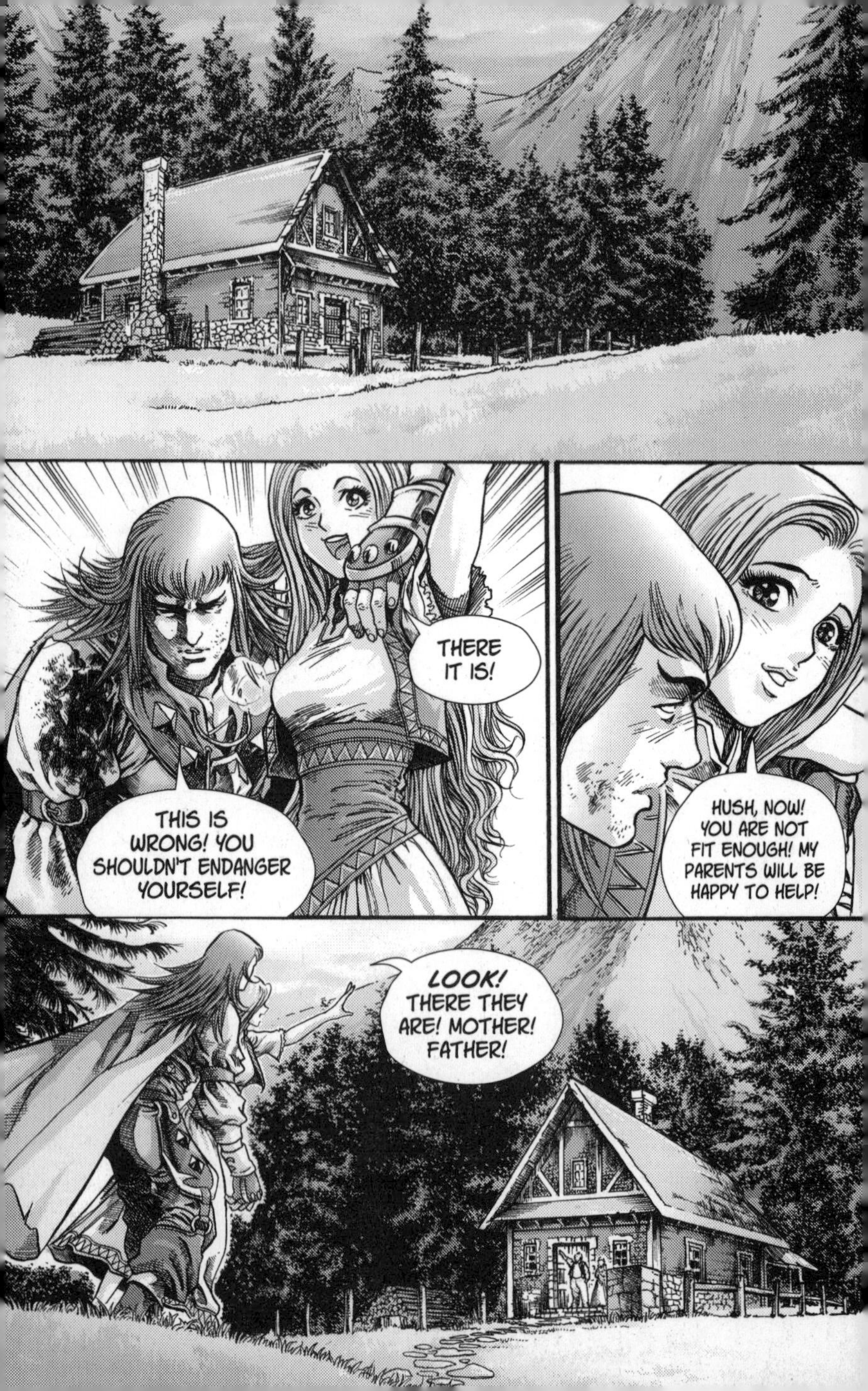
THERE IT IS!
THIS IS WRONG! YOU SHOULDN'T ENDANGER YOURSELF!
HUSH, NOW! YOU ARE NOT FIT ENOUGH! MY PARENTS WILL BE HAPPY TO HELP!
LOOK! THERE THEY ARE! MOTHER! FATHER!

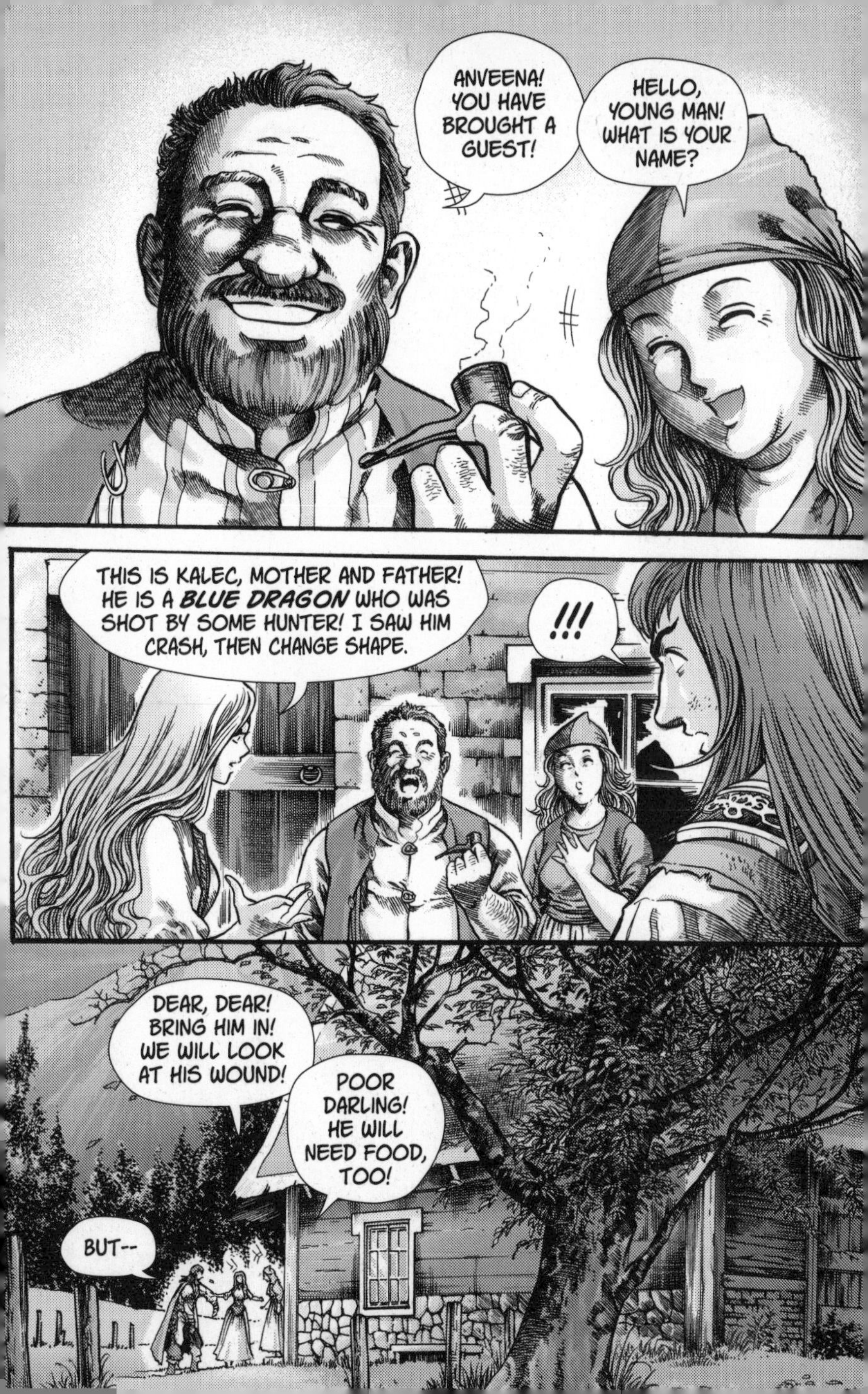
ANVEENA! YOU HAVE BROUGHT A GUEST!
HELLO, YOUNG MAN! WHAT IS YOUR NAME?
THIS IS KALEC, MOTHER AND FATHER! HE IS A *BLUE DRAGON* WHO WAS SHOT BY SOME HUNTER! I SAW HIM CRASH, THEN CHANGE SHAPE.
!!!
DEAR, DEAR! BRING HIM IN! WE WILL LOOK AT HIS WOUND!
POOR DARLING! HE WILL NEED FOOD, TOO!
BUT--

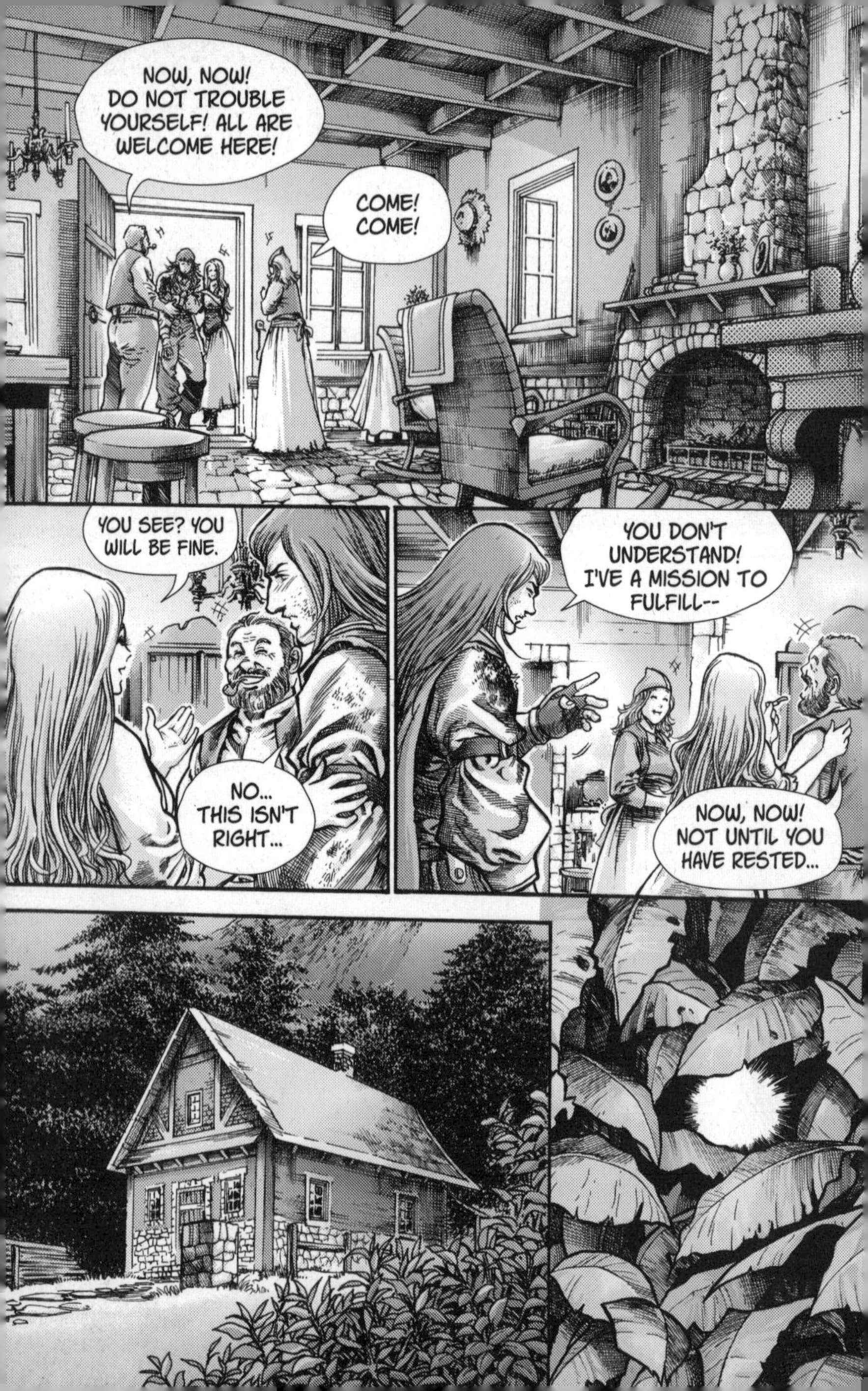
NOW, NOW! DO NOT TROUBLE YOURSELF! ALL ARE WELCOME HERE!
COME! COME!
YOU SEE? YOU WILL BE FINE.
NO... THIS ISN'T RIGHT...
YOU DON'T UNDERSTAND! I'VE A MISSION TO FULFILL--
NOW, NOW! NOT UNTIL YOU HAVE RESTED...

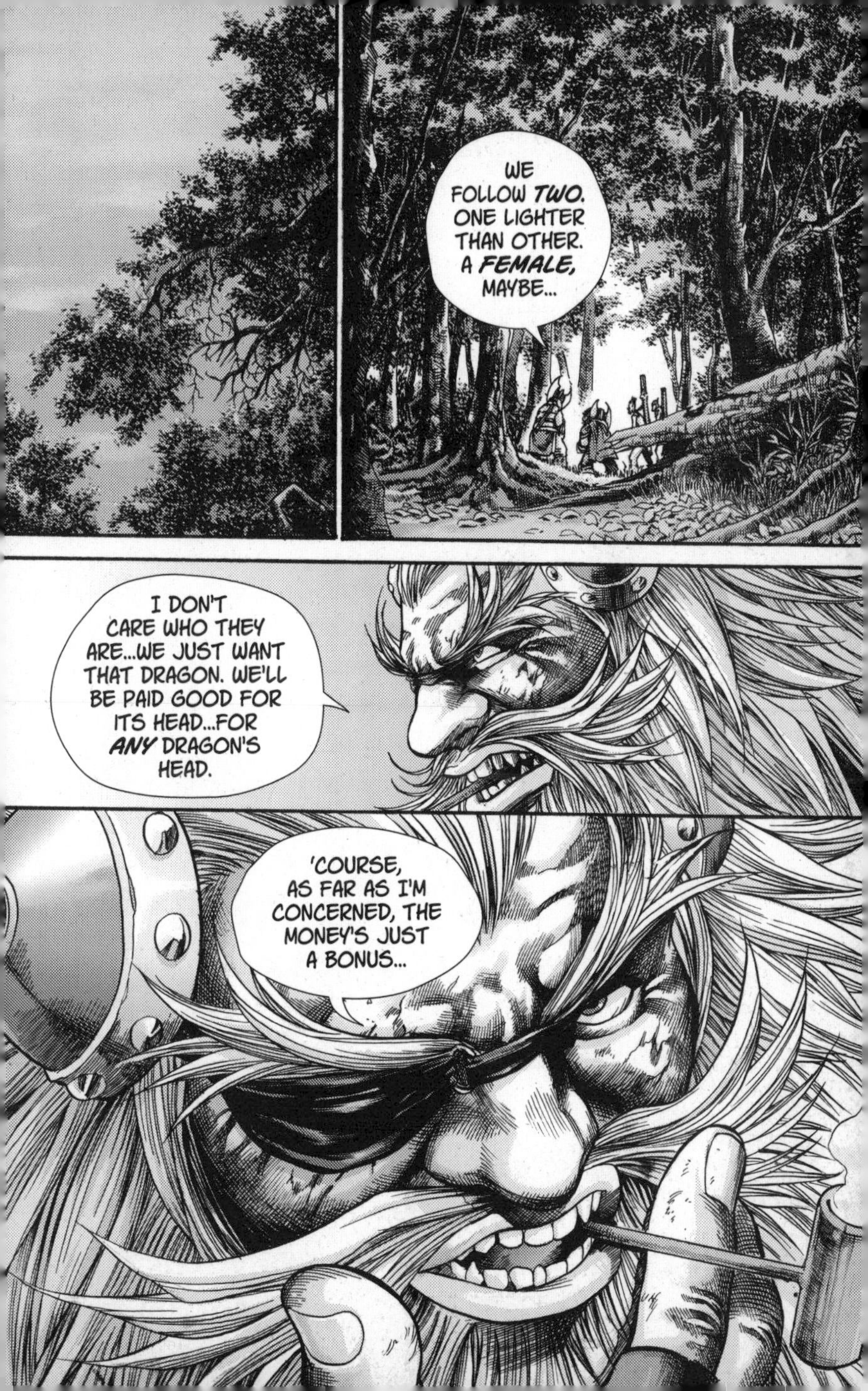
WE FOLLOW TWO. ONE LIGHTER THAN OTHER. A FEMALE, MAYBE...
I DON'T CARE WHO THEY ARE...WE JUST WANT THAT DRAGON. WE'LL BE PAID GOOD FOR ITS HEAD...FOR ANY DRAGON'S HEAD.
'COURSE, AS FAR AS I'M CONCERNED, THE MONEY'S JUST A BONUS...

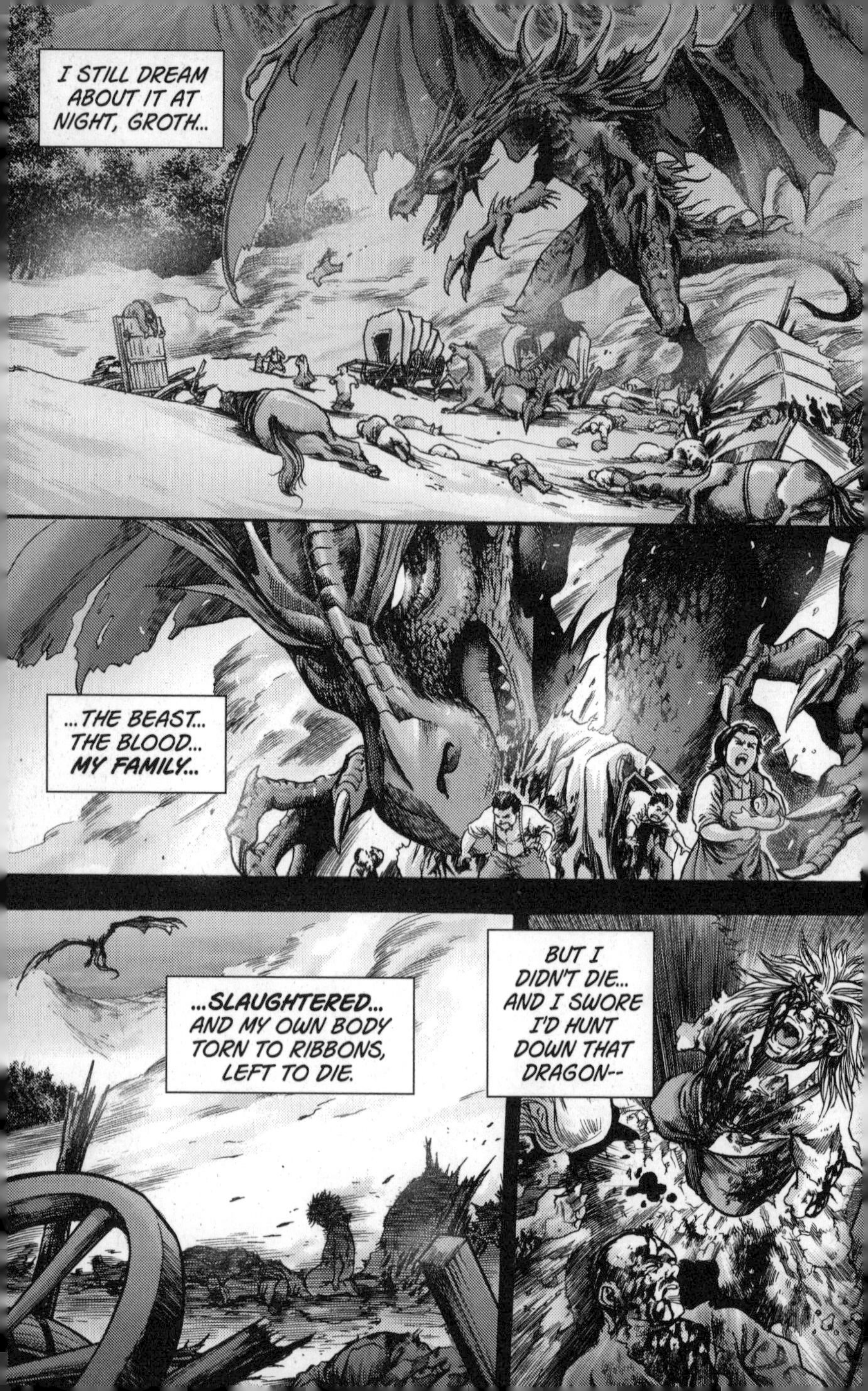
I STILL DREAM ABOUT IT AT NIGHT, GROTH...
...THE BEAST... THE BLOOD... MY FAMILY...
...SLAUGHTERED... AND MY OWN BODY TORN TO RIBBONS, LEFT TO DIE.
BUT I DIDN'T DIE... AND I SWORE I'D HUNT DOWN THAT DRAGON--

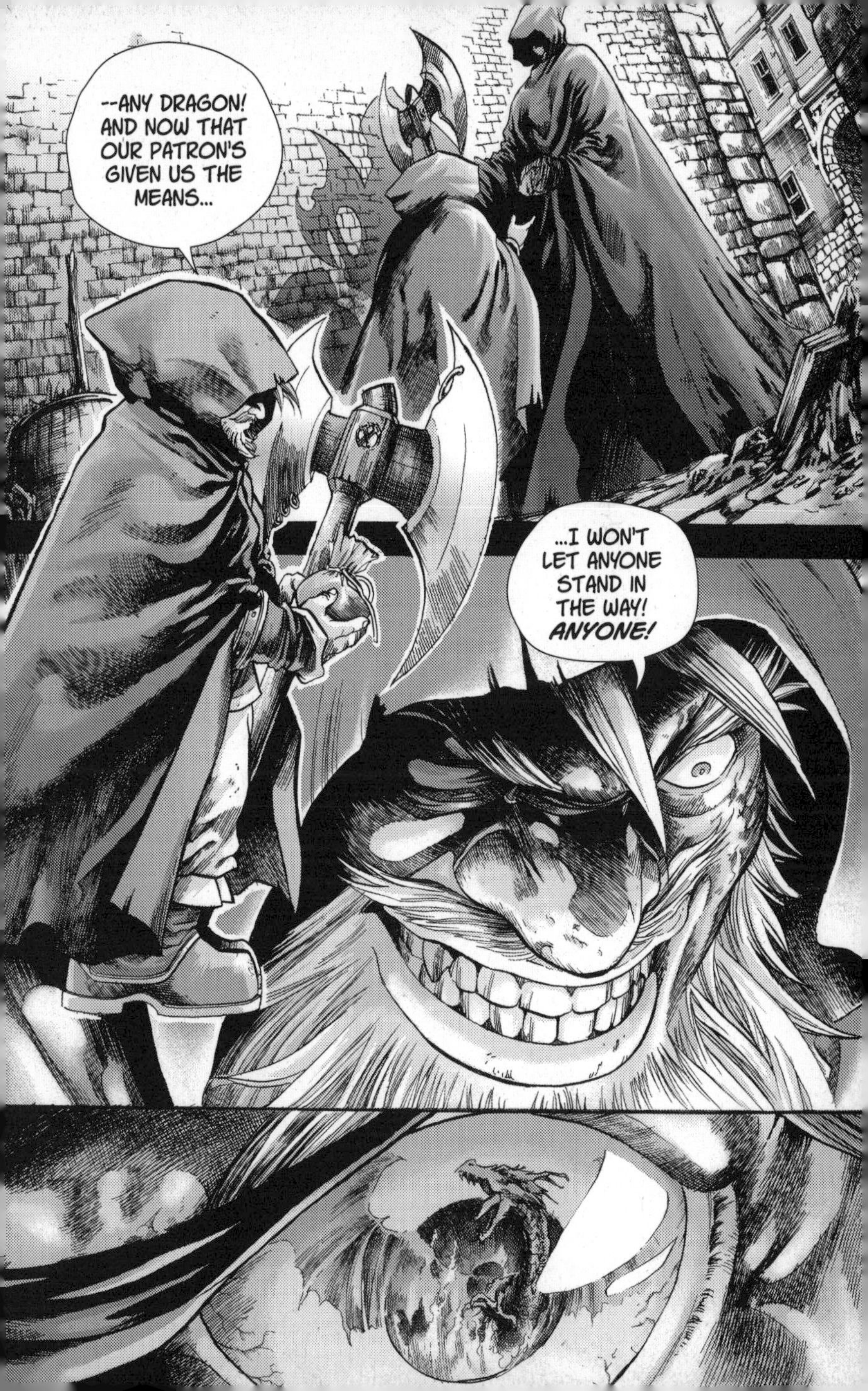
--ANY DRAGON! AND NOW THAT OUR PATRON'S GIVEN US THE MEANS...
...I WON'T LET ANYONE STAND IN THE WAY! *ANYONE!*

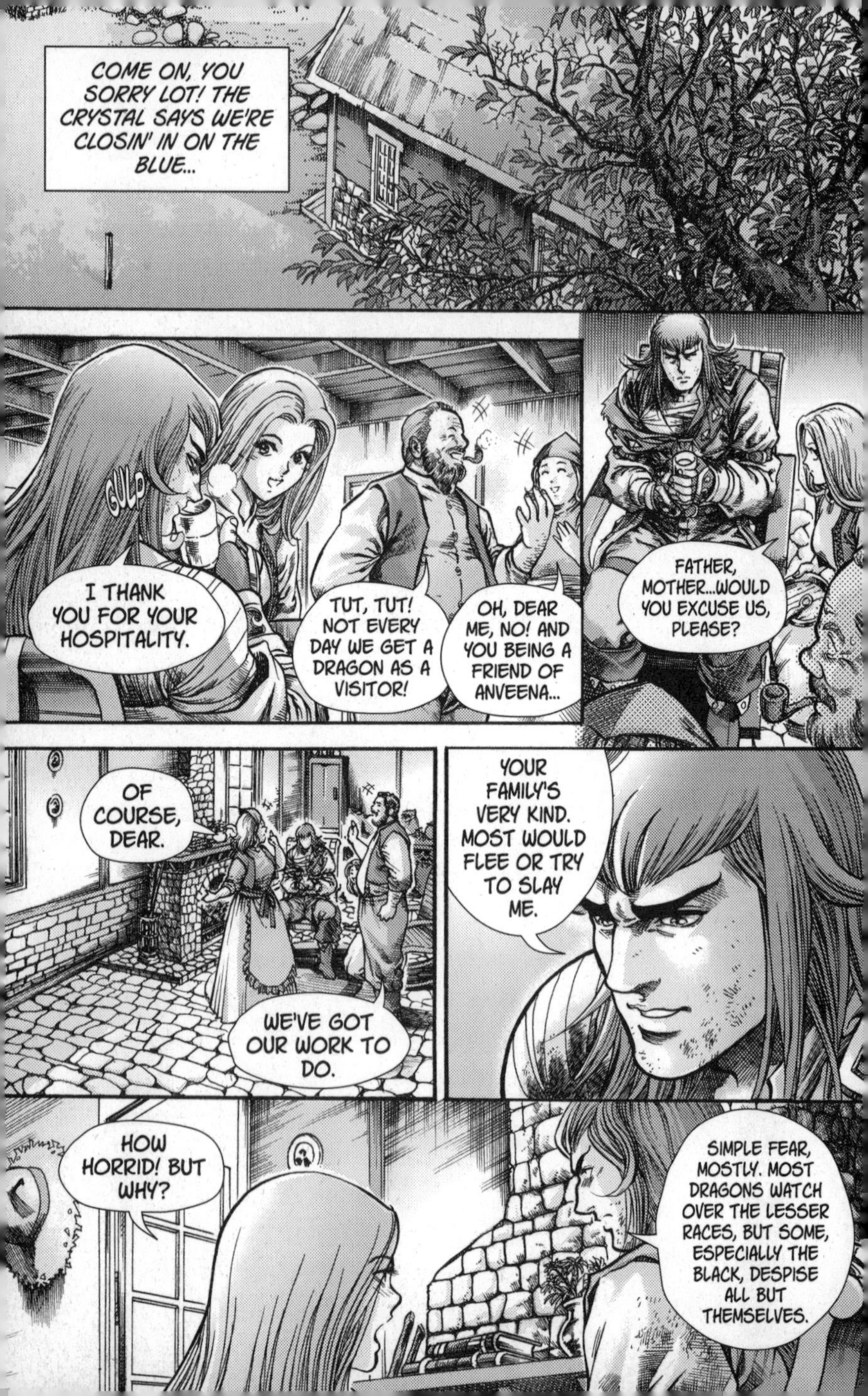
COME ON, YOU SORRY LOT! THE CRYSTAL SAYS WE'RE CLOSIN' IN ON THE BLUE...
GULP
I THANK YOU FOR YOUR HOSPITALITY.
TUT, TUT! NOT EVERY DAY WE GET A DRAGON AS A VISITOR!
OH, DEAR ME, NO! AND YOU BEING A FRIEND OF ANVEENA...
FATHER, MOTHER...WOULD YOU EXCUSE US, PLEASE?
OF COURSE, DEAR.
WE'VE GOT OUR WORK TO DO.
YOUR FAMILY'S VERY KIND. MOST WOULD FLEE OR TRY TO SLAY ME.
HOW HORRID! BUT WHY?
SIMPLE FEAR, MOSTLY. MOST DRAGONS WATCH OVER THE LESSER RACES, BUT SOME, ESPECIALLY THE BLACK, DESPISE ALL BUT THEMSELVES.

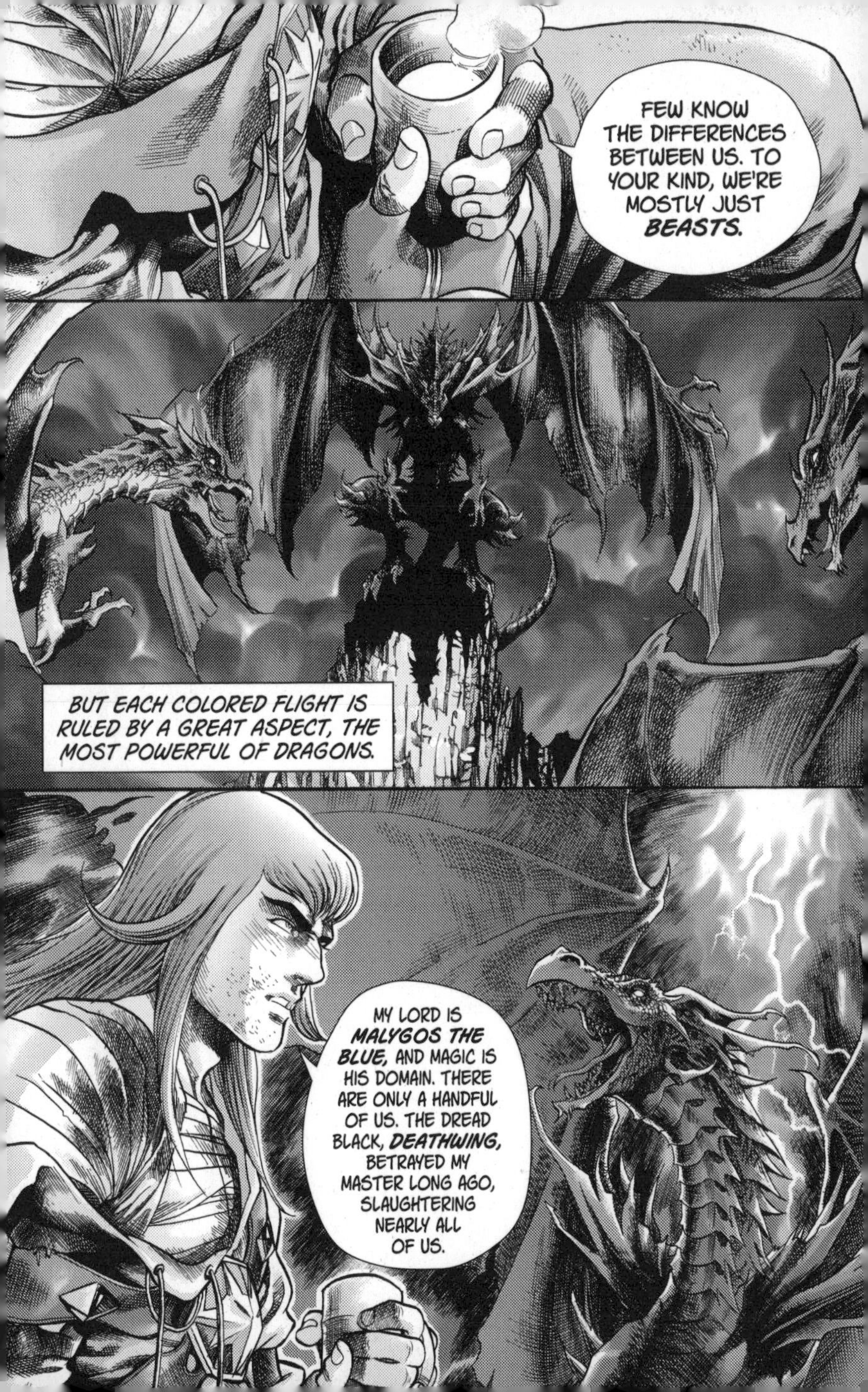
FEW KNOW THE DIFFERENCES BETWEEN US. TO YOUR KIND, WE'RE MOSTLY JUST BEASTS.
BUT EACH COLORED FLIGHT IS RULED BY A GREAT ASPECT, THE MOST POWERFUL OF DRAGONS.
MY LORD IS MALYGOS THE BLUE, AND MAGIC IS HIS DOMAIN. THERE ARE ONLY A HANDFUL OF US. THE DREAD BLACK, DEATHWING, BETRAYED MY MASTER LONG AGO, SLAUGHTERING NEARLY ALL OF US.

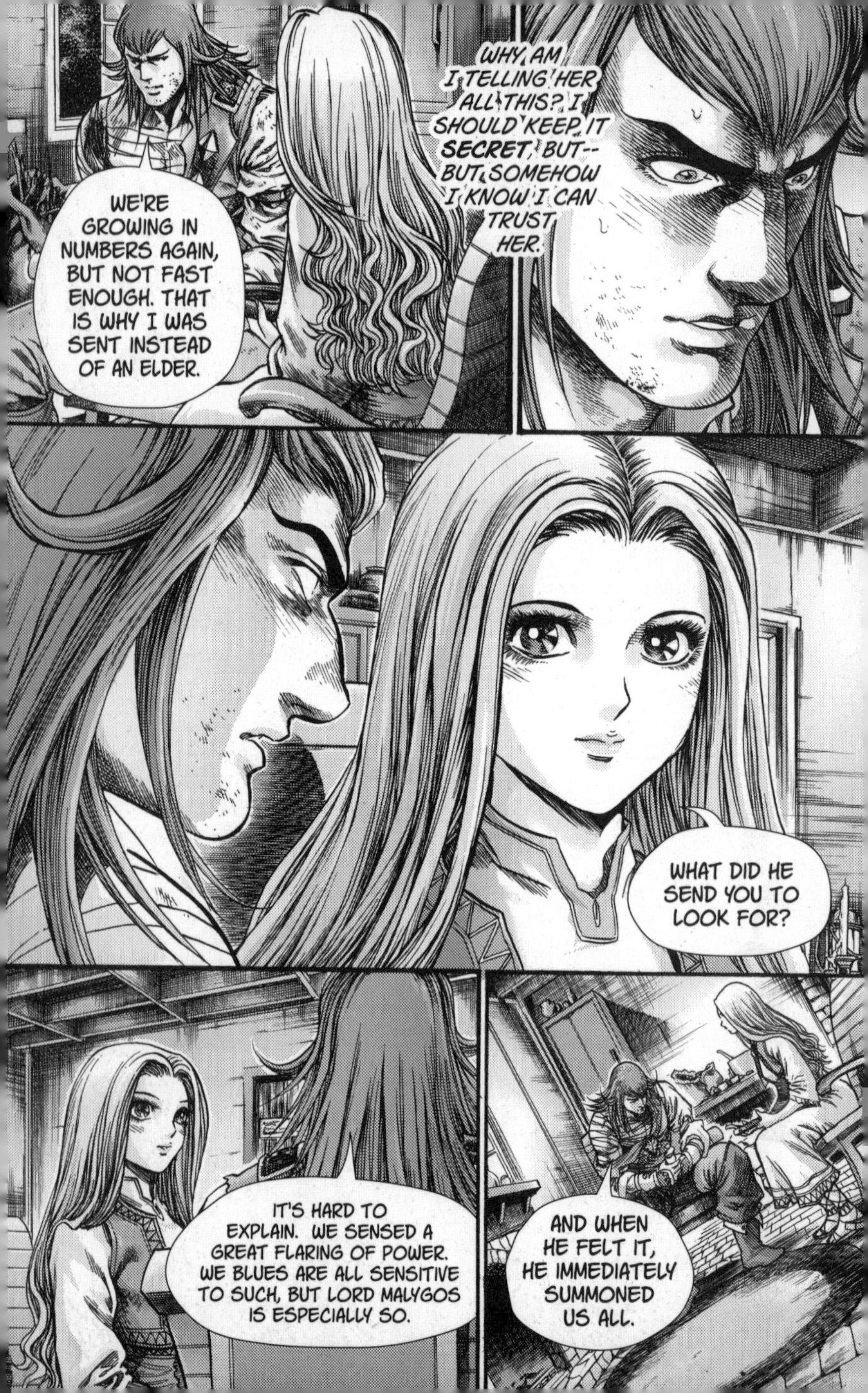
WE'RE GROWING IN NUMBERS AGAIN, BUT NOT FAST ENOUGH. THAT IS WHY I WAS SENT INSTEAD OF AN ELDER.
WHY AM I TELLING HER ALL THIS? I SHOULD KEEP IT **SECRET**, BUT-- BUT SOMEHOW I KNOW I CAN TRUST HER.
WHAT DID HE SEND YOU TO LOOK FOR?
IT'S HARD TO EXPLAIN. WE SENSED A GREAT FLARING OF POWER. WE BLUES ARE ALL SENSITIVE TO SUCH, BUT LORD MALYGOS IS ESPECIALLY SO.
AND WHEN HE FELT IT, HE IMMEDIATELY SUMMONED US ALL.

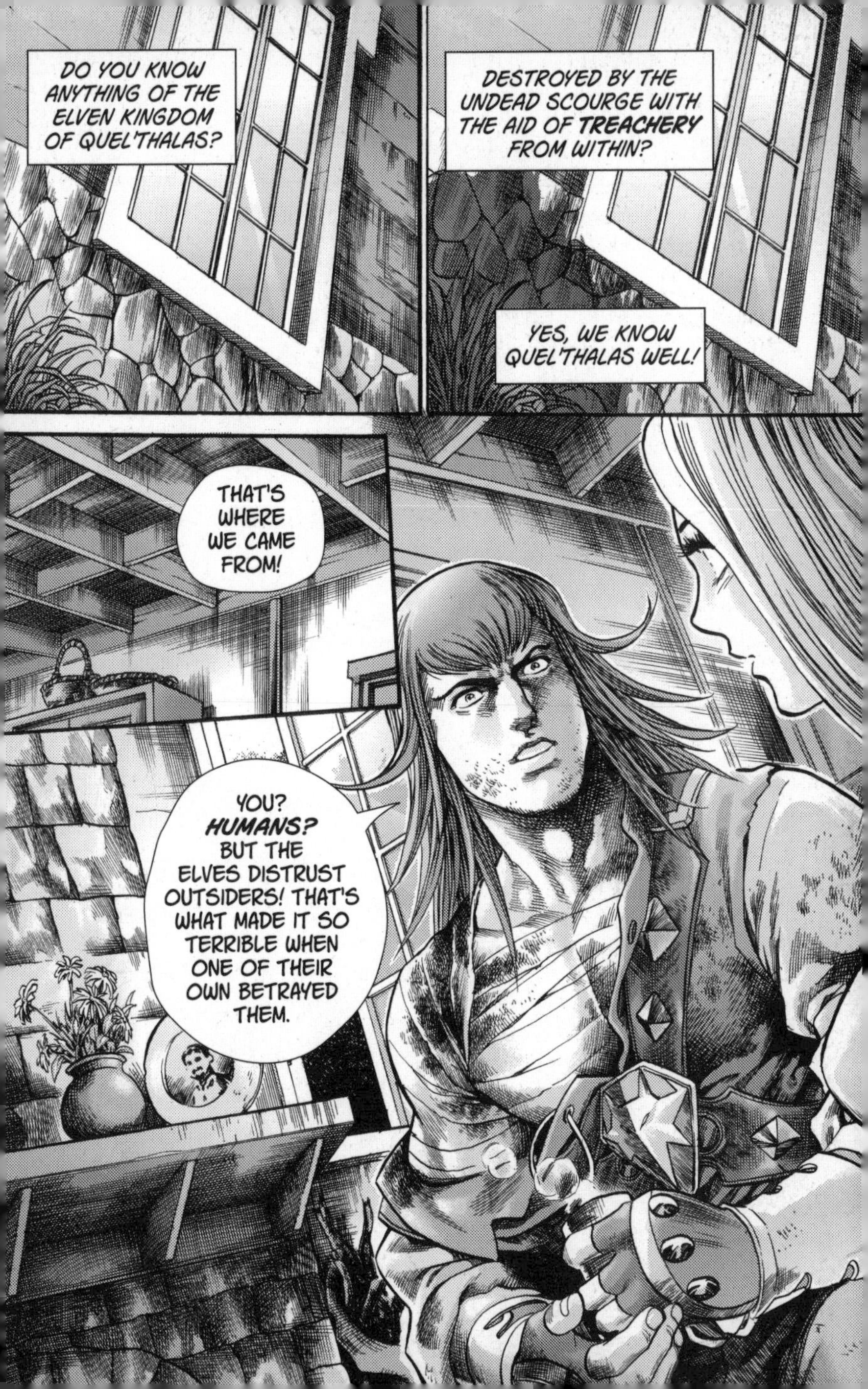
DO YOU KNOW ANYTHING OF THE ELVEN KINGDOM OF QUEL'THALAS?
DESTROYED BY THE UNDEAD SCOURGE WITH THE AID OF **TREACHERY** FROM WITHIN?
YES, WE KNOW QUEL'THALAS WELL!
THAT'S WHERE WE CAME FROM!
YOU? ***HUMANS?*** BUT THE ELVES DISTRUST OUTSIDERS! THAT'S WHAT MADE IT SO TERRIBLE WHEN ONE OF THEIR OWN BETRAYED THEM.

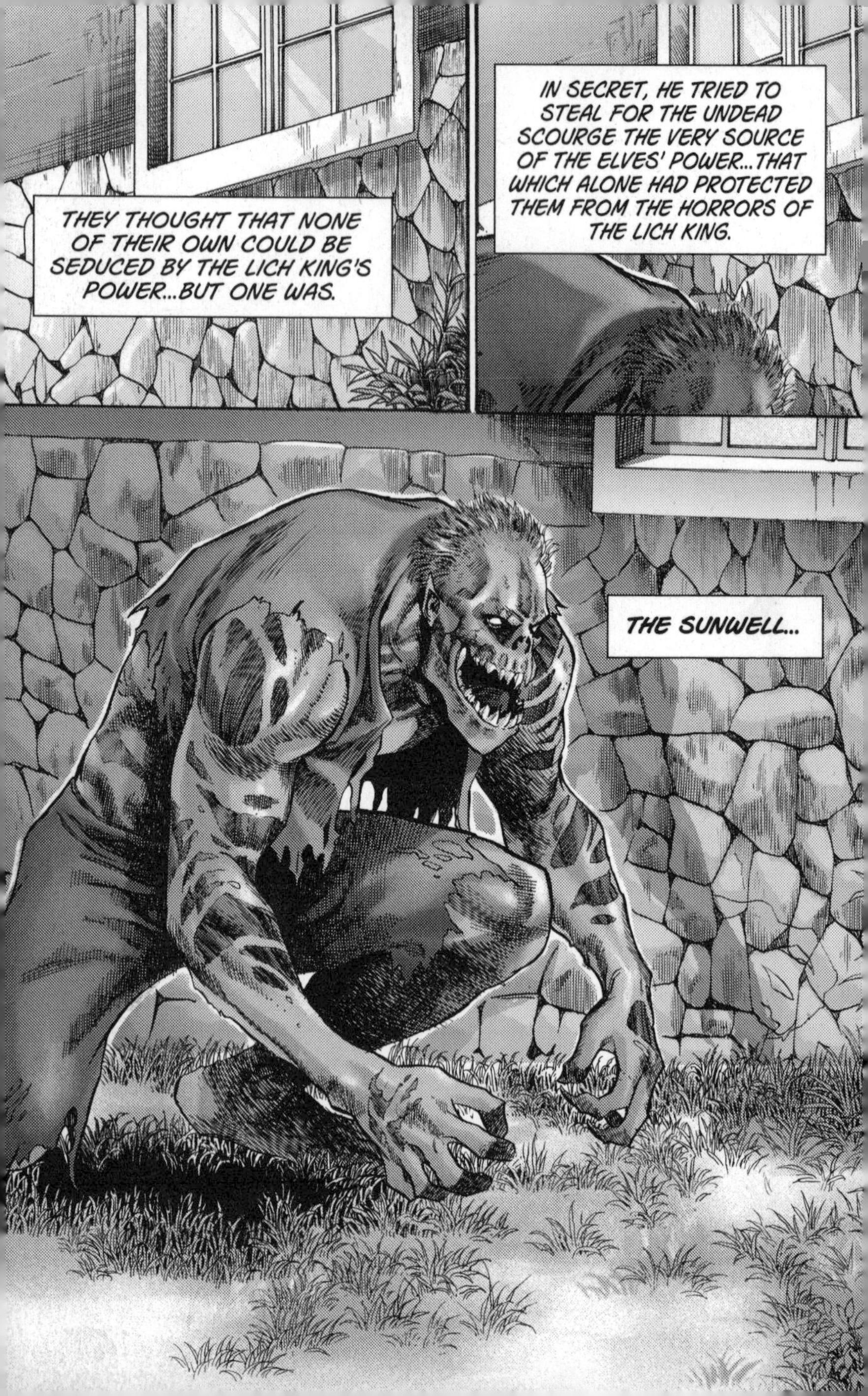
THEY THOUGHT THAT NONE OF THEIR OWN COULD BE SEDUCED BY THE LICH KING'S POWER...BUT ONE WAS.
IN SECRET, HE TRIED TO STEAL FOR THE UNDEAD SCOURGE THE VERY SOURCE OF THE ELVES' POWER...THAT WHICH ALONE HAD PROTECTED THEM FROM THE HORRORS OF THE LICH KING.
THE SUNWELL...

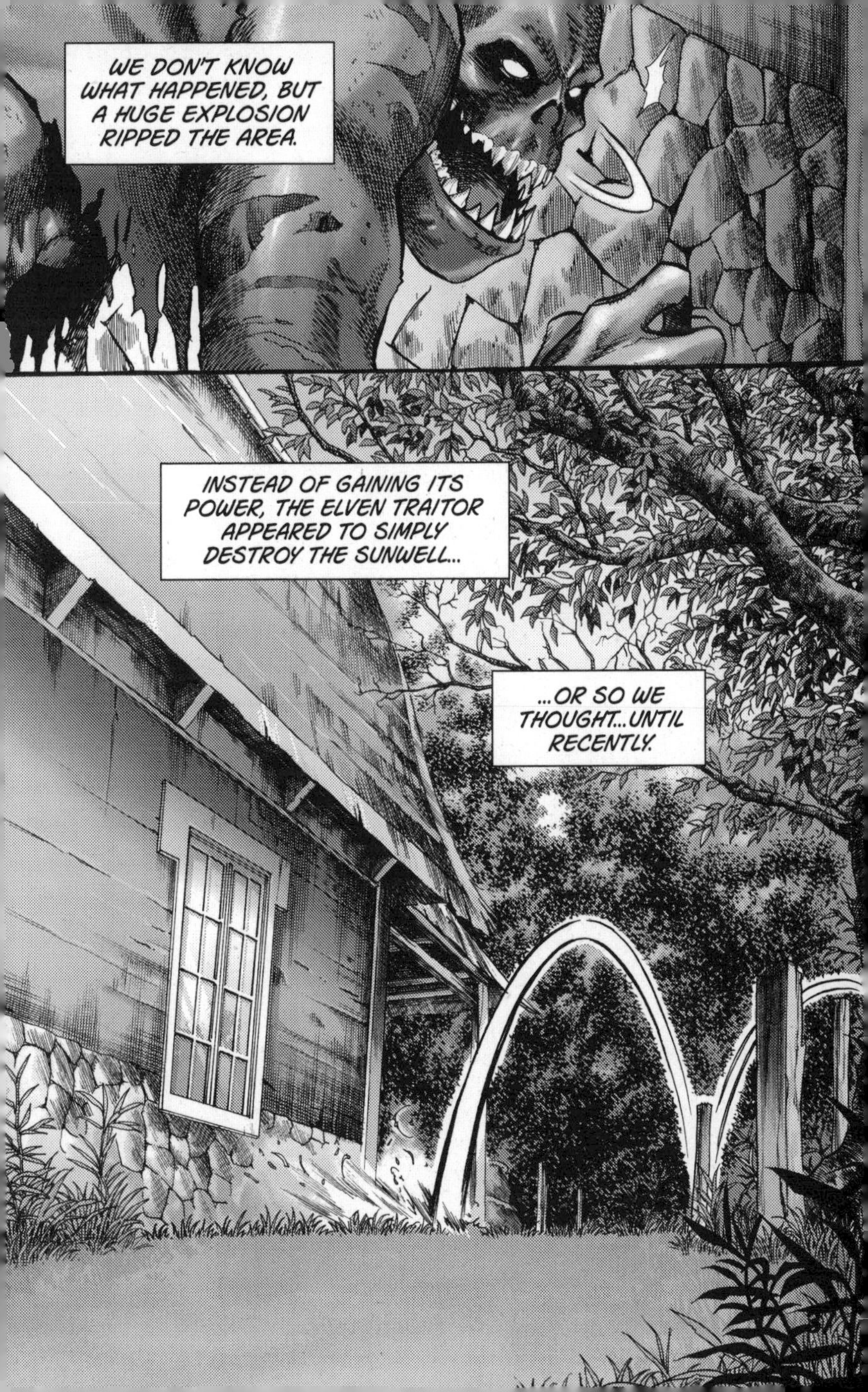
WE DON'T KNOW WHAT HAPPENED, BUT A HUGE EXPLOSION RIPPED THE AREA.
INSTEAD OF GAINING ITS POWER, THE ELVEN TRAITOR APPEARED TO SIMPLY DESTROY THE SUNWELL...
...OR SO WE THOUGHT...UNTIL RECENTLY.

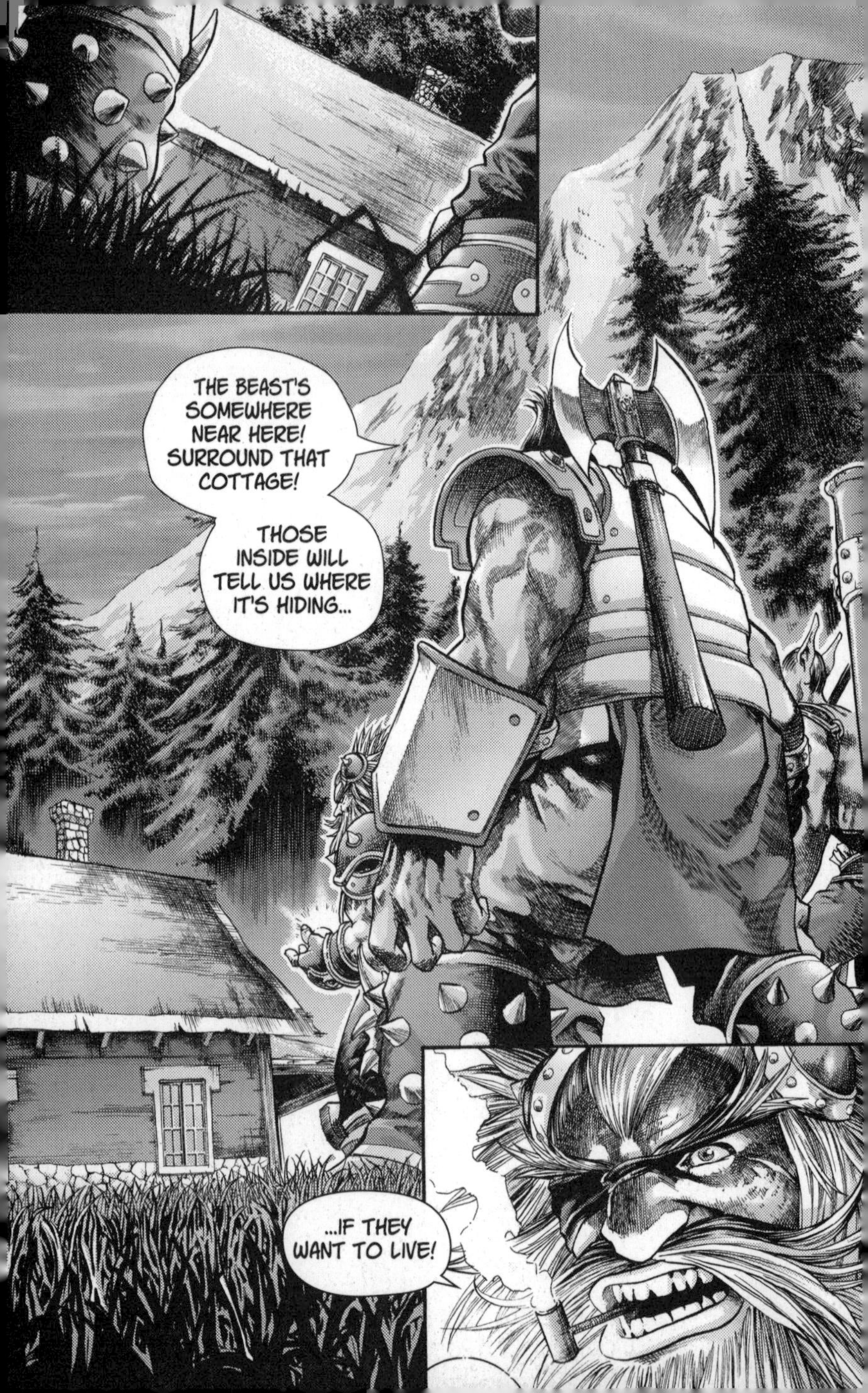
THE BEAST'S SOMEWHERE NEAR HERE! SURROUND THAT COTTAGE!
THOSE INSIDE WILL TELL US WHERE IT'S HIDING...
...IF THEY WANT TO LIVE!

CHAPTER TWO PURSUED

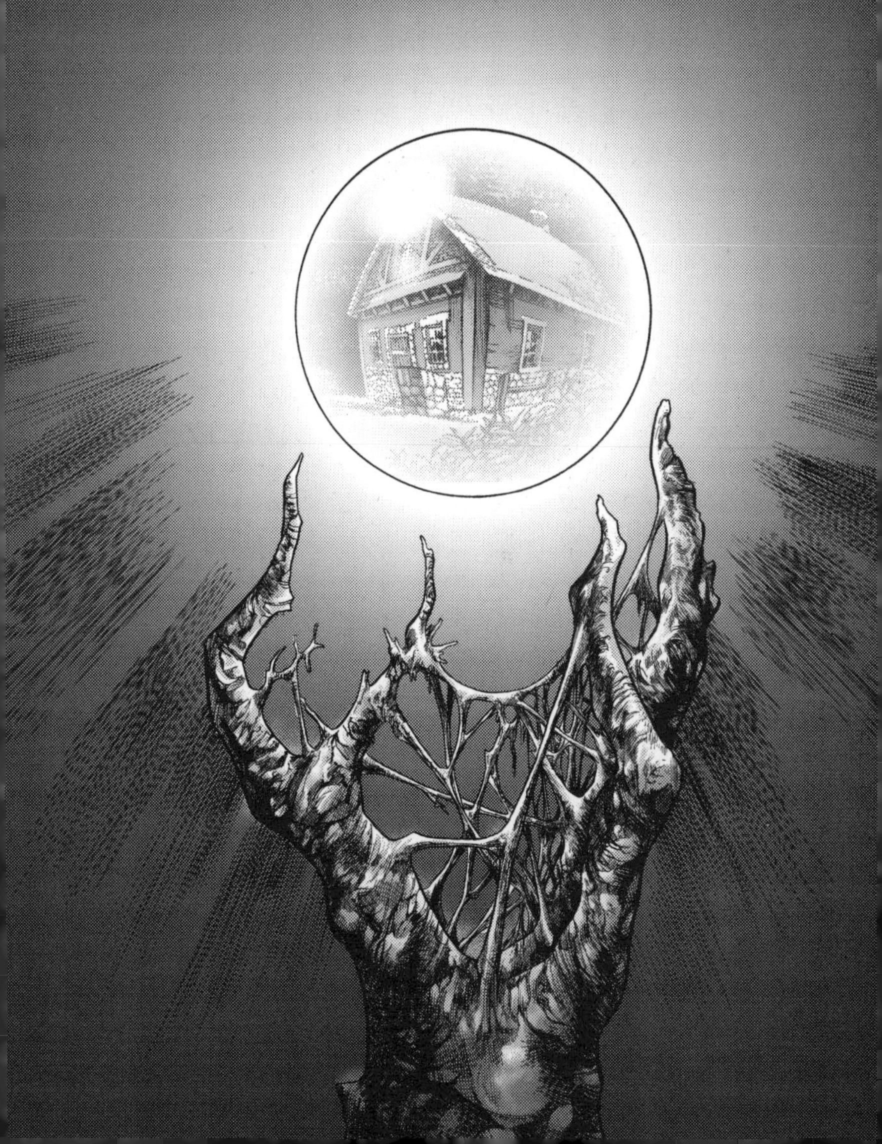

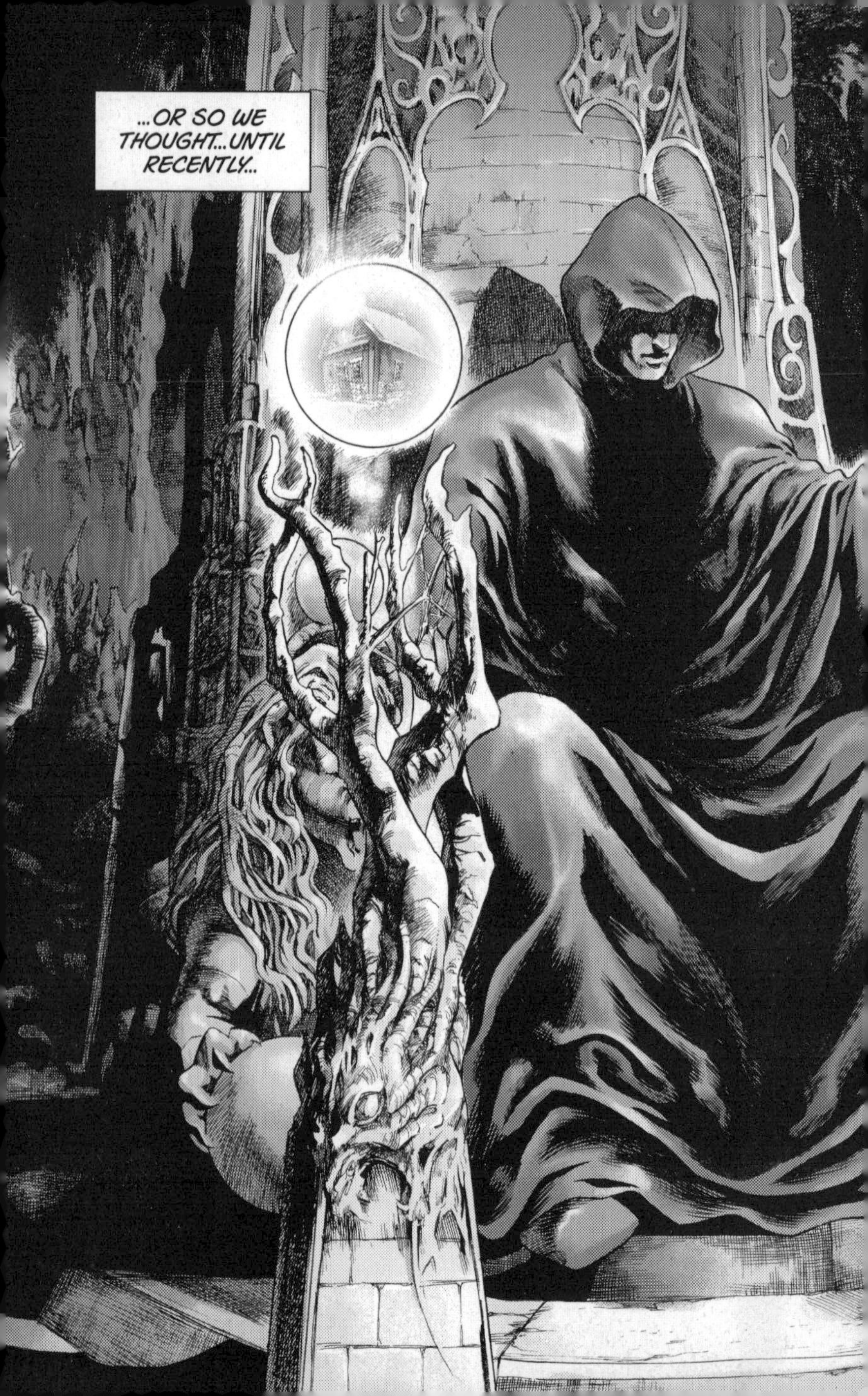
...OR SO WE THOUGHT...UNTIL RECENTLY...

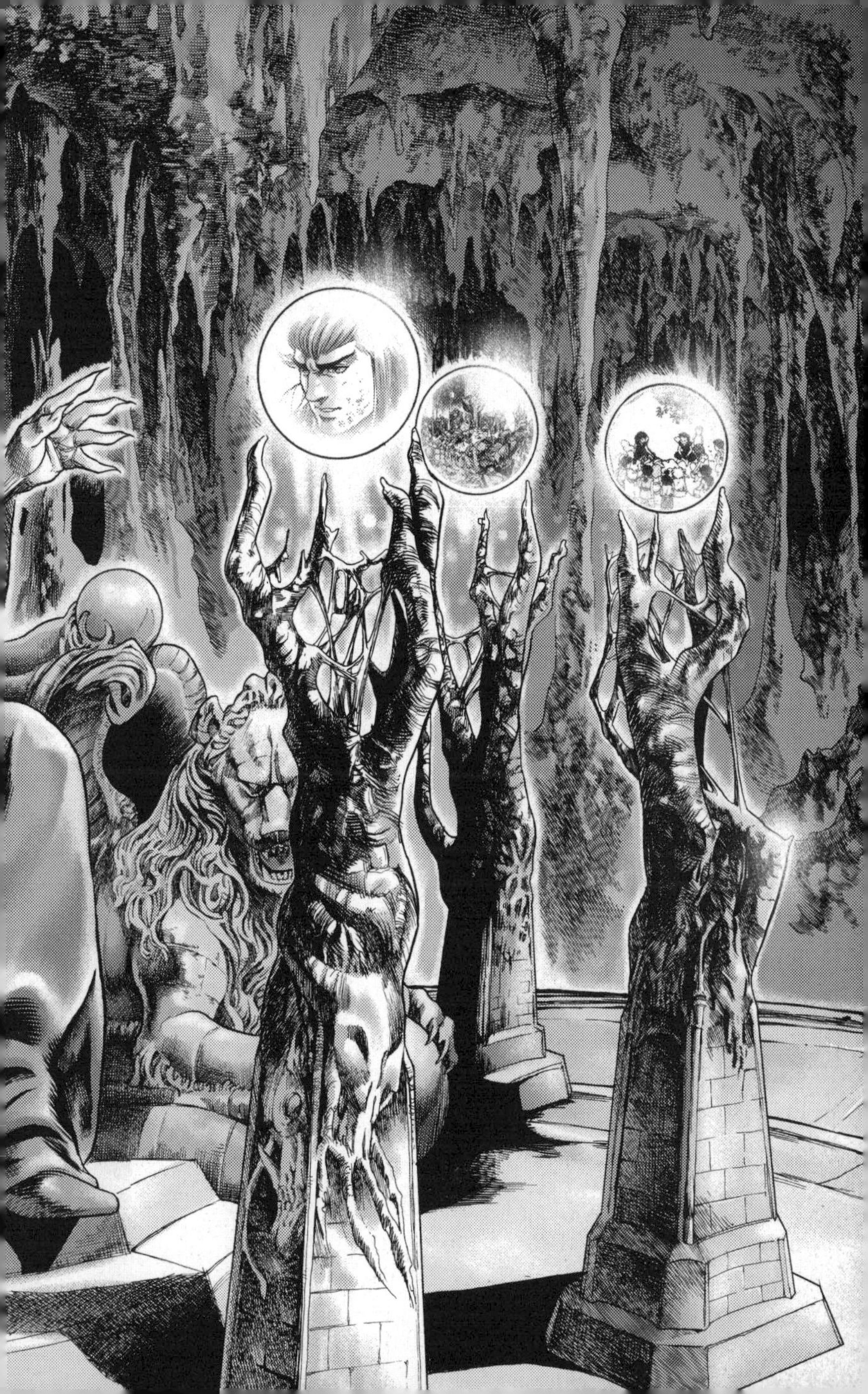

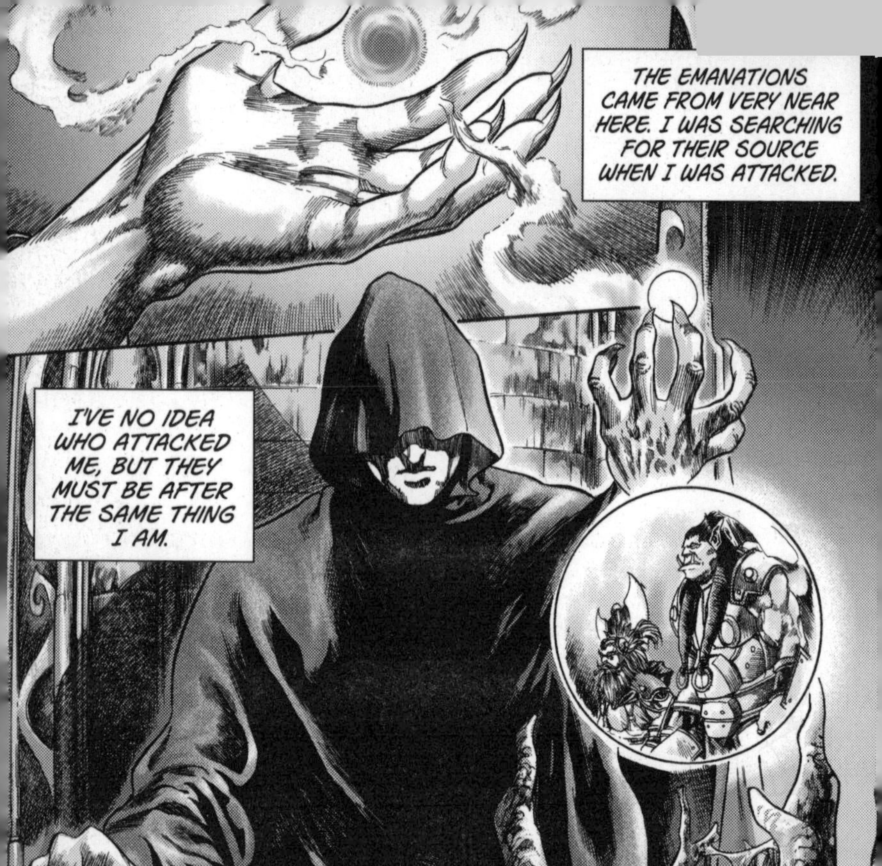
THE EMANATIONS CAME FROM VERY NEAR HERE. I WAS SEARCHING FOR THEIR SOURCE WHEN I WAS ATTACKED.
I'VE NO IDEA WHO ATTACKED ME, BUT THEY MUST BE AFTER THE SAME THING I AM.
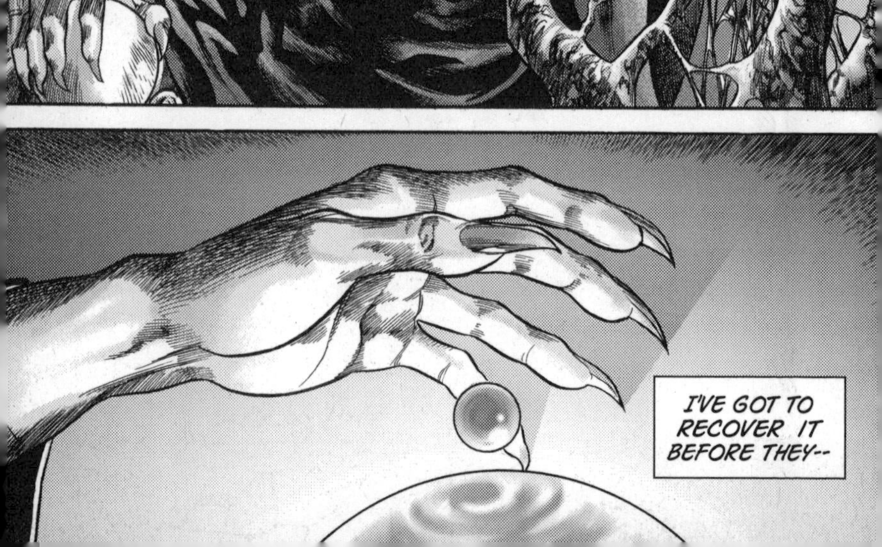
I'VE GOT TO RECOVER IT BEFORE THEY--

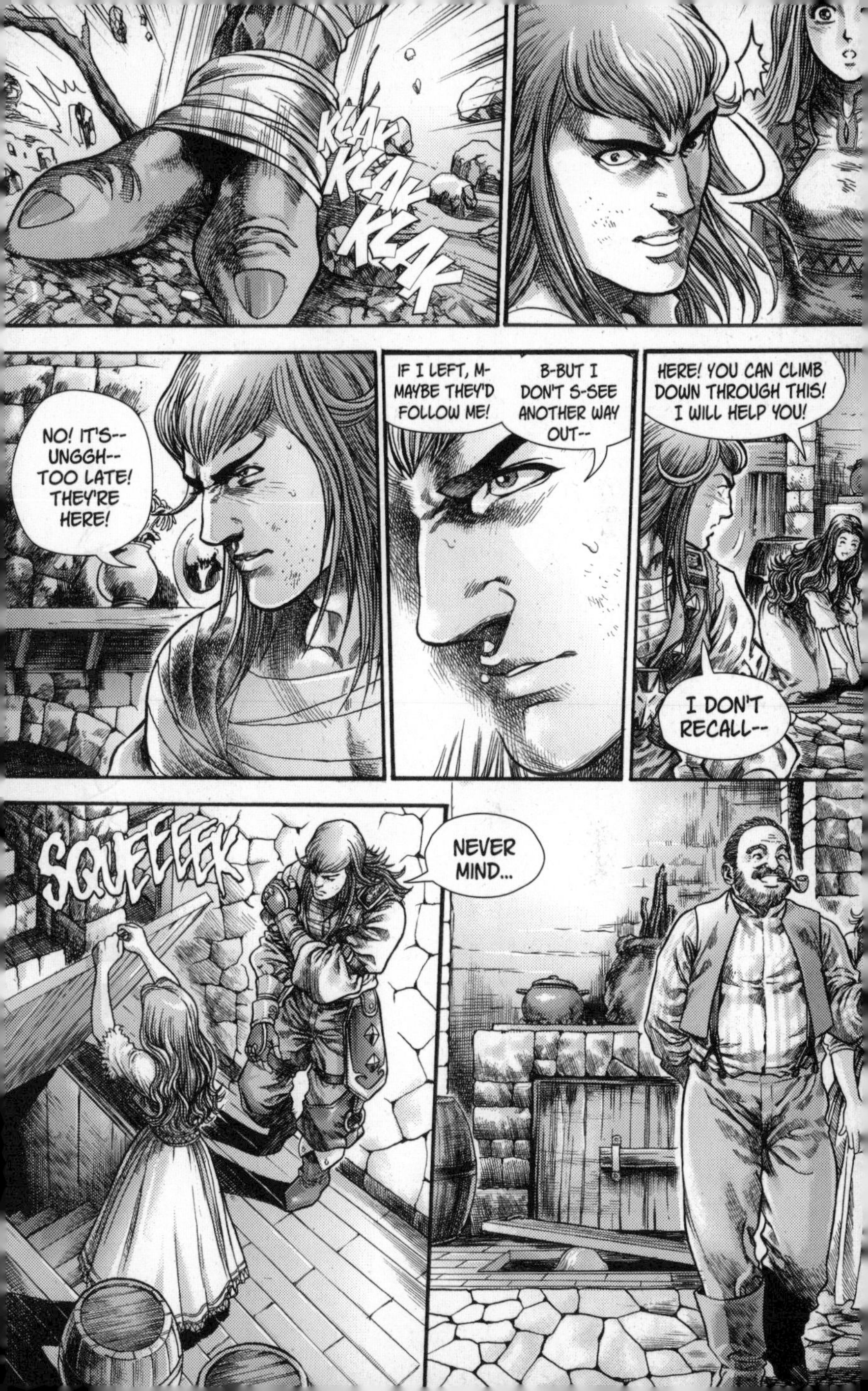
KLAK
KLAK
KLAK
KLAK
NO! IT'S-- UNGGH-- TOO LATE! THEY'RE HERE!
IF I LEFT, M-MAYBE THEY'D FOLLOW ME!
B-BUT I DON'T S-SEE ANOTHER WAY OUT--
HERE! YOU CAN CLIMB DOWN THROUGH THIS! I WILL HELP YOU!
I DON'T RECALL--
SQUEEEEK
NEVER MIND...

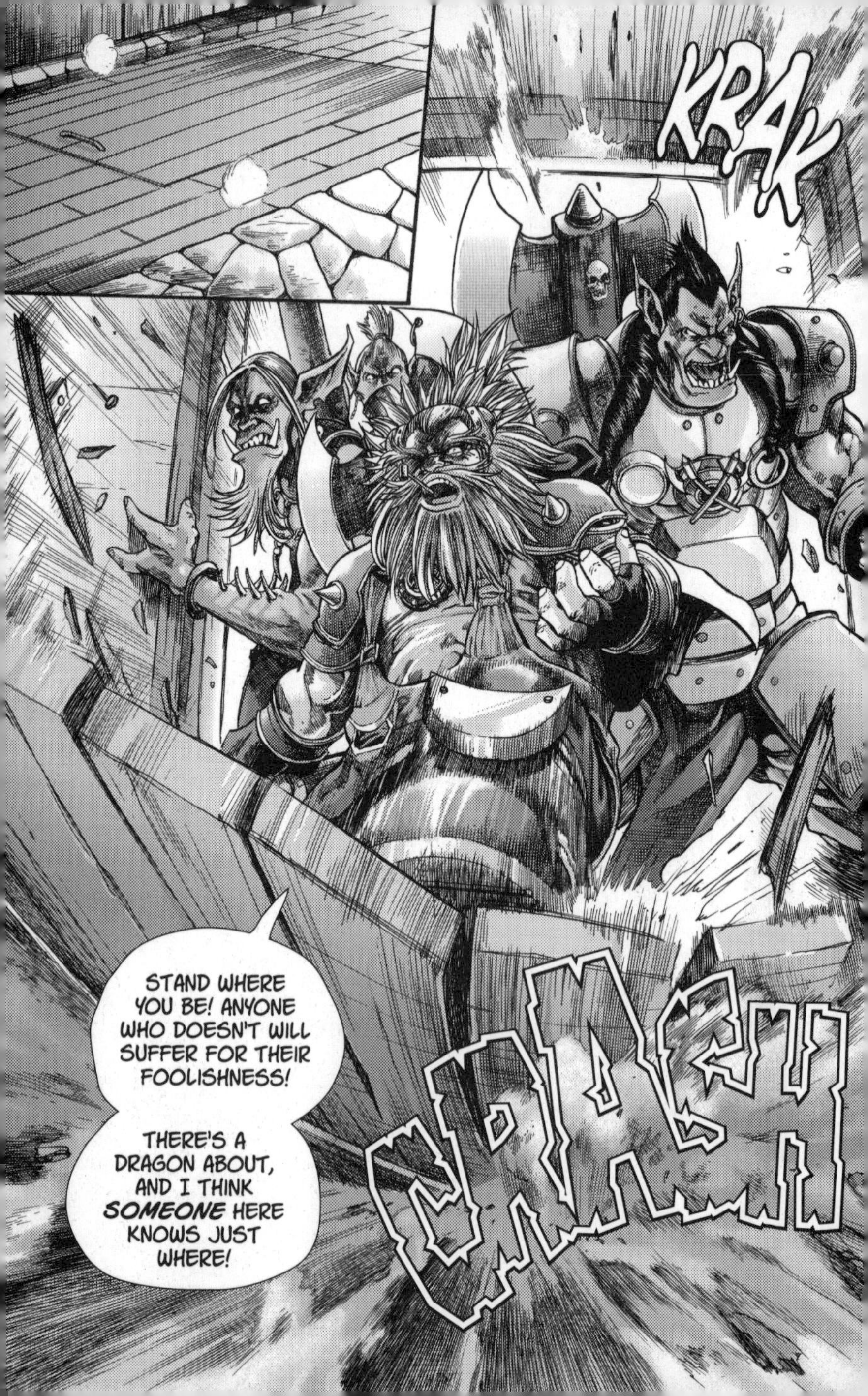
KRAK
STAND WHERE YOU BE! ANYONE WHO DOESN'T WILL SUFFER FOR THEIR FOOLISHNESS!
THERE'S A DRAGON ABOUT, AND I THINK ***SOMEONE*** HERE KNOWS JUST WHERE!
CRASH

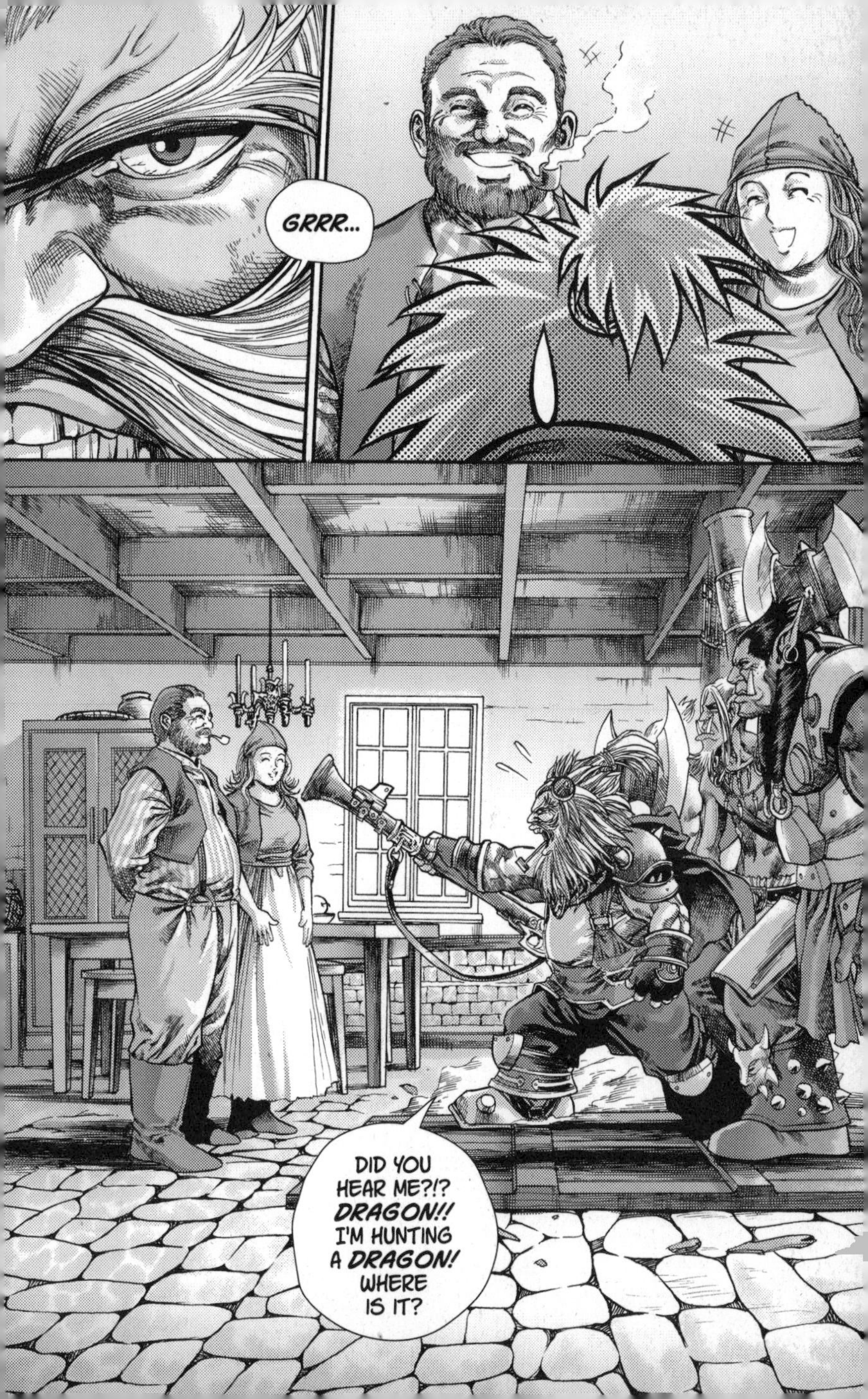
GRRR...
DID YOU HEAR ME?!? DRAGON!! I'M HUNTING A DRAGON! WHERE IS IT?

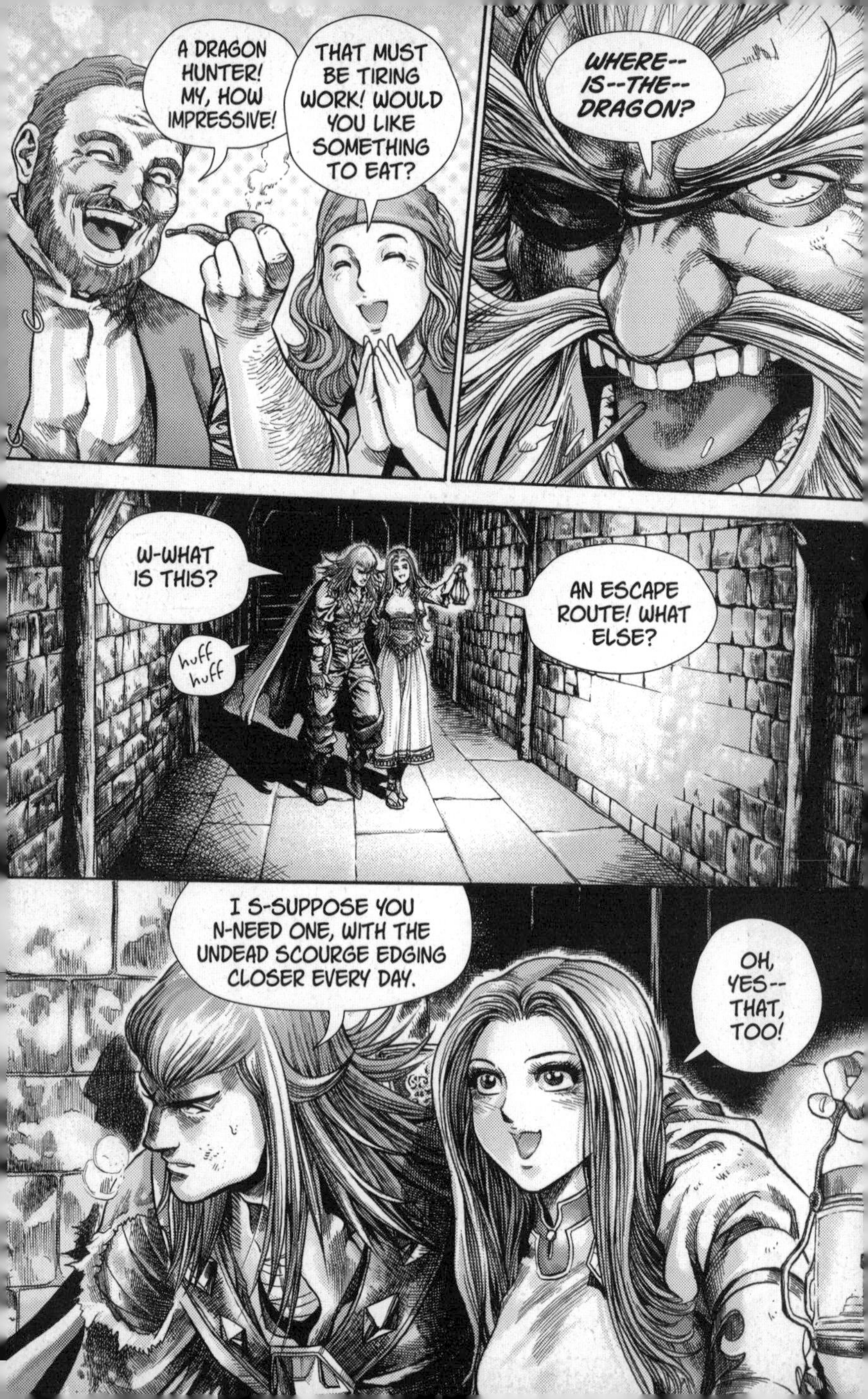
A DRAGON HUNTER! MY, HOW IMPRESSIVE!
THAT MUST BE TIRING WORK! WOULD YOU LIKE SOMETHING TO EAT?
WHERE-- IS--THE-- DRAGON?
W-WHAT IS THIS?
huff huff
AN ESCAPE ROUTE! WHAT ELSE?
I S-SUPPOSE YOU N-NEED ONE, WITH THE UNDEAD SCOURGE EDGING CLOSER EVERY DAY.
OH, YES-- THAT, TOO!

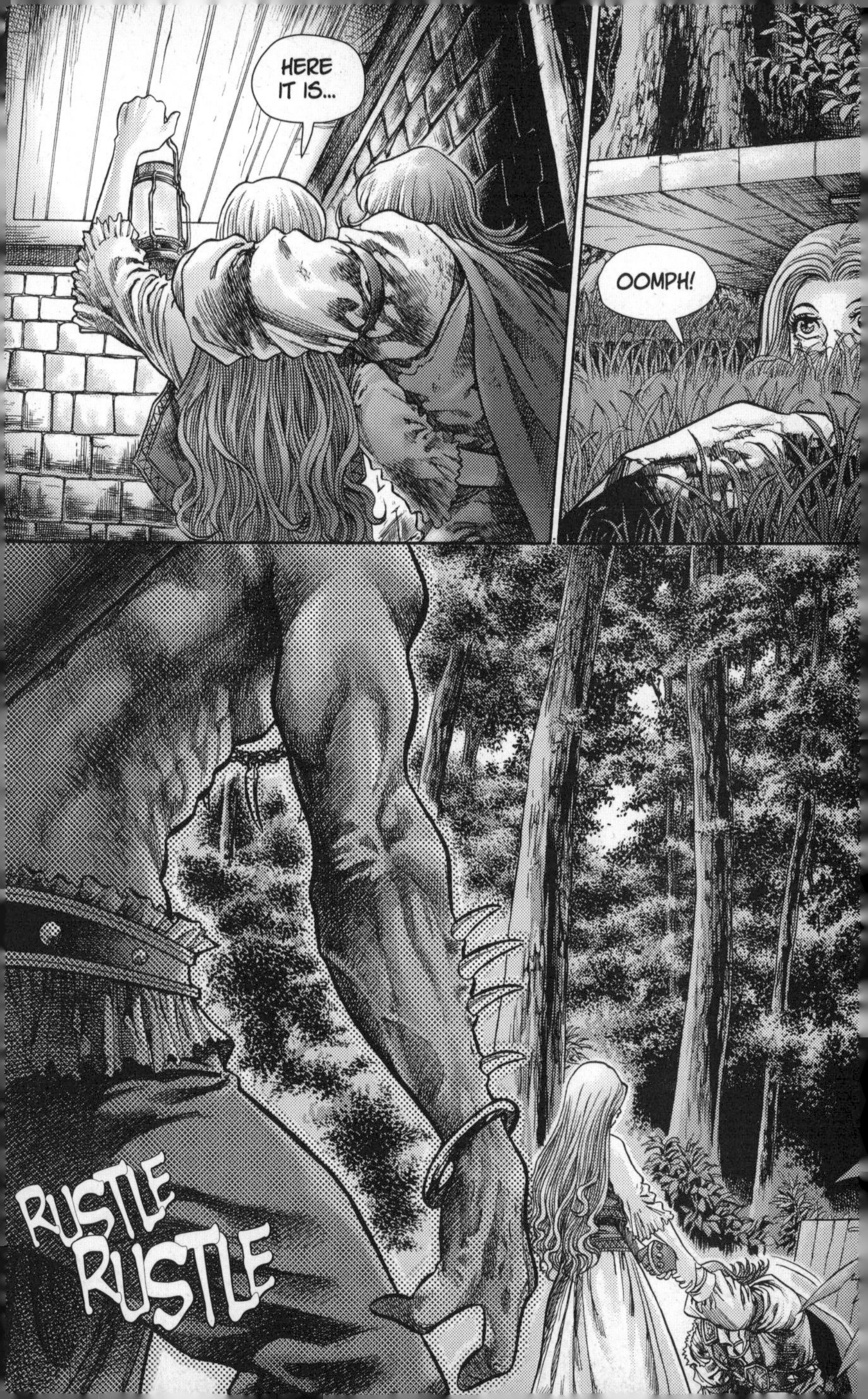
HERE IT IS...
OOMPH!
RUSTLE RUSTLE

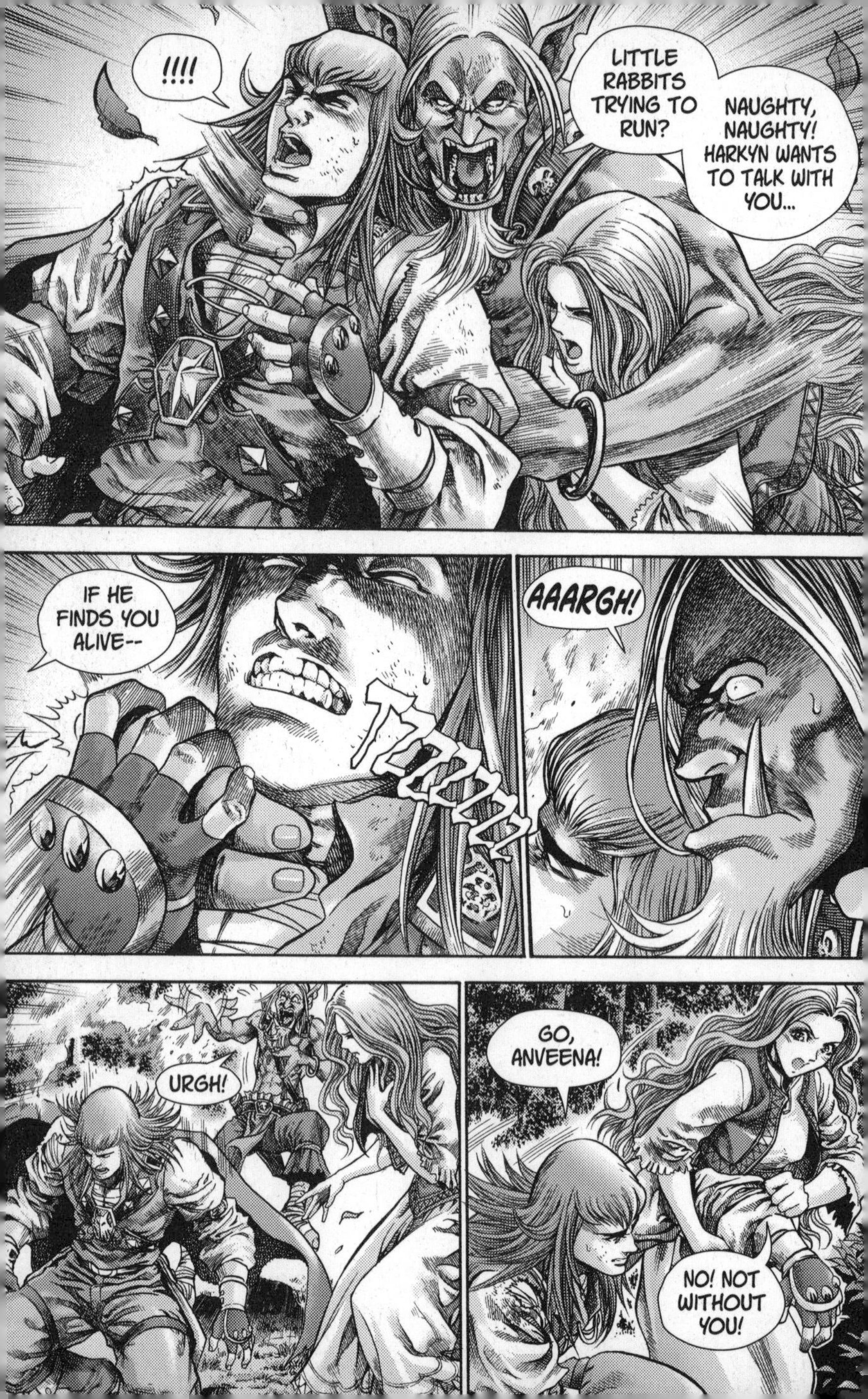
!!!!
LITTLE RABBITS TRYING TO RUN?
NAUGHTY, NAUGHTY! HARKYN WANTS TO TALK WITH YOU...
IF HE FINDS YOU ALIVE--
AAARGH!
URGH!
GO, ANVEENA!
NO! NOT WITHOUT YOU!

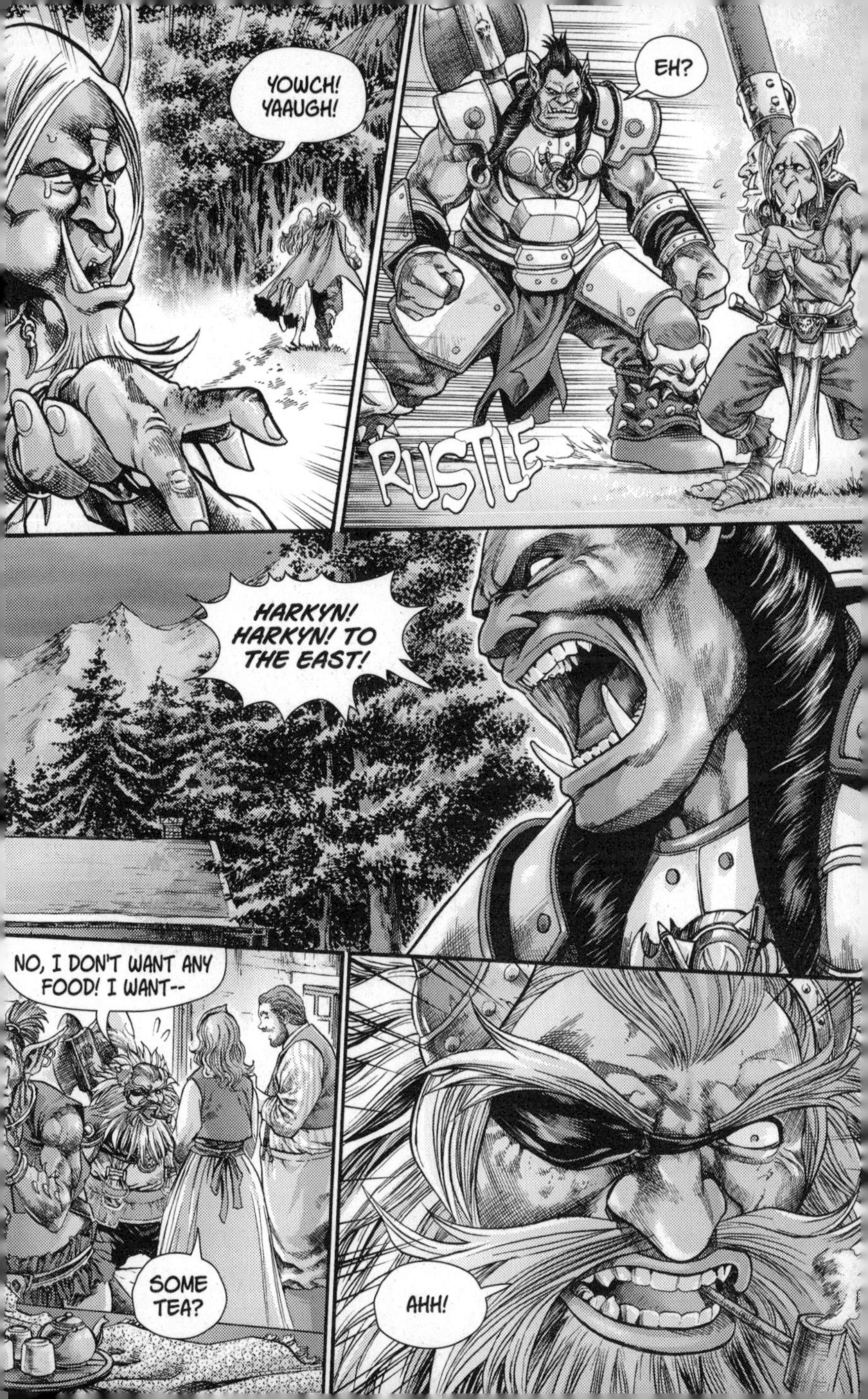
YOWCH! YAAUGH!
EH?
RUSTLE
HARKYN! HARKYN! TO THE EAST!
NO, I DON'T WANT ANY FOOD! I WANT--
SOME TEA?
AHH!

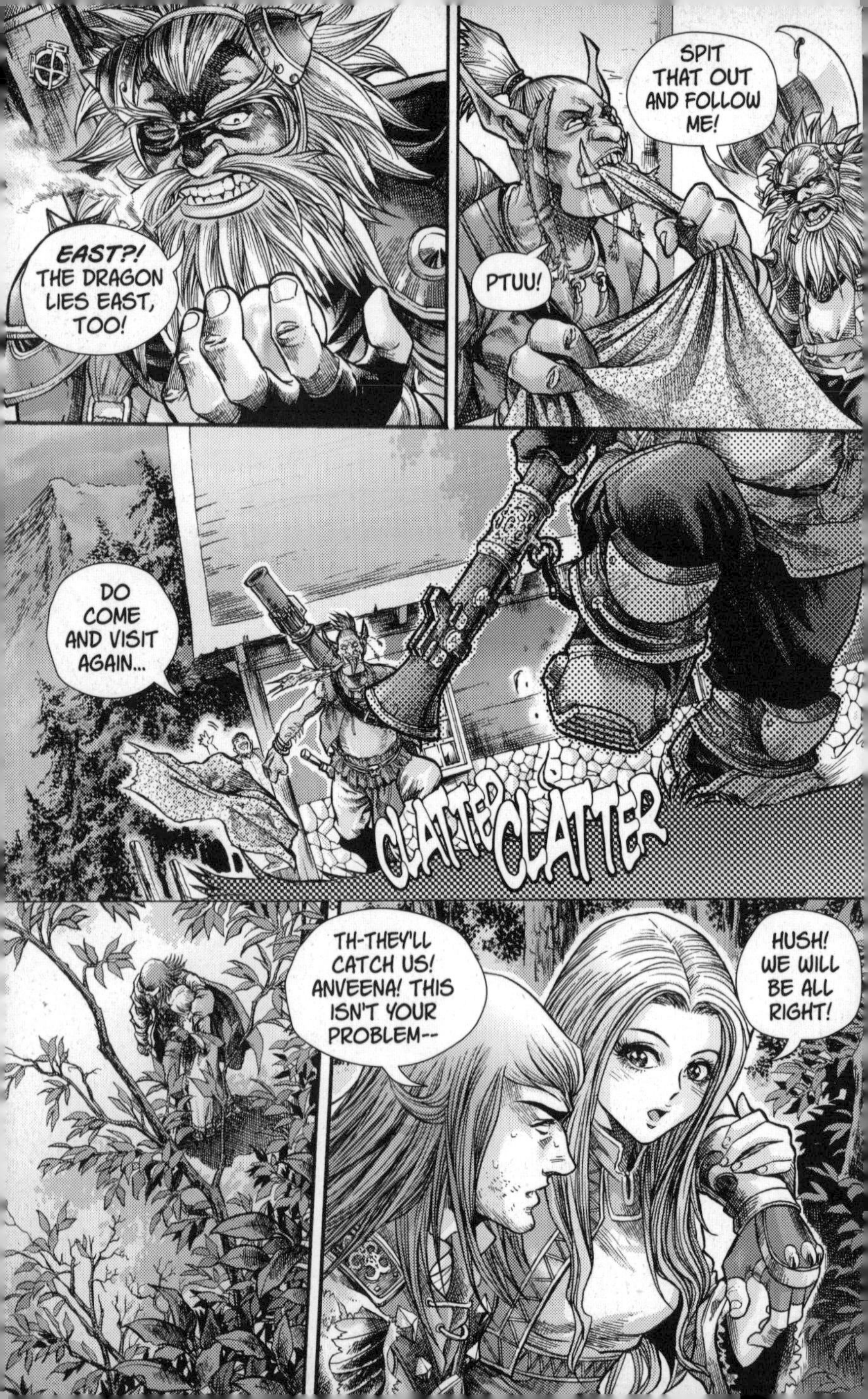
EAST?! THE DRAGON LIES EAST, TOO!
SPIT THAT OUT AND FOLLOW ME!
PTUU!
DO COME AND VISIT AGAIN...
CLATTER CLATTER
TH-THEY'LL CATCH US! ANVEENA! THIS ISN'T YOUR PROBLEM--
HUSH! WE WILL BE ALL RIGHT!

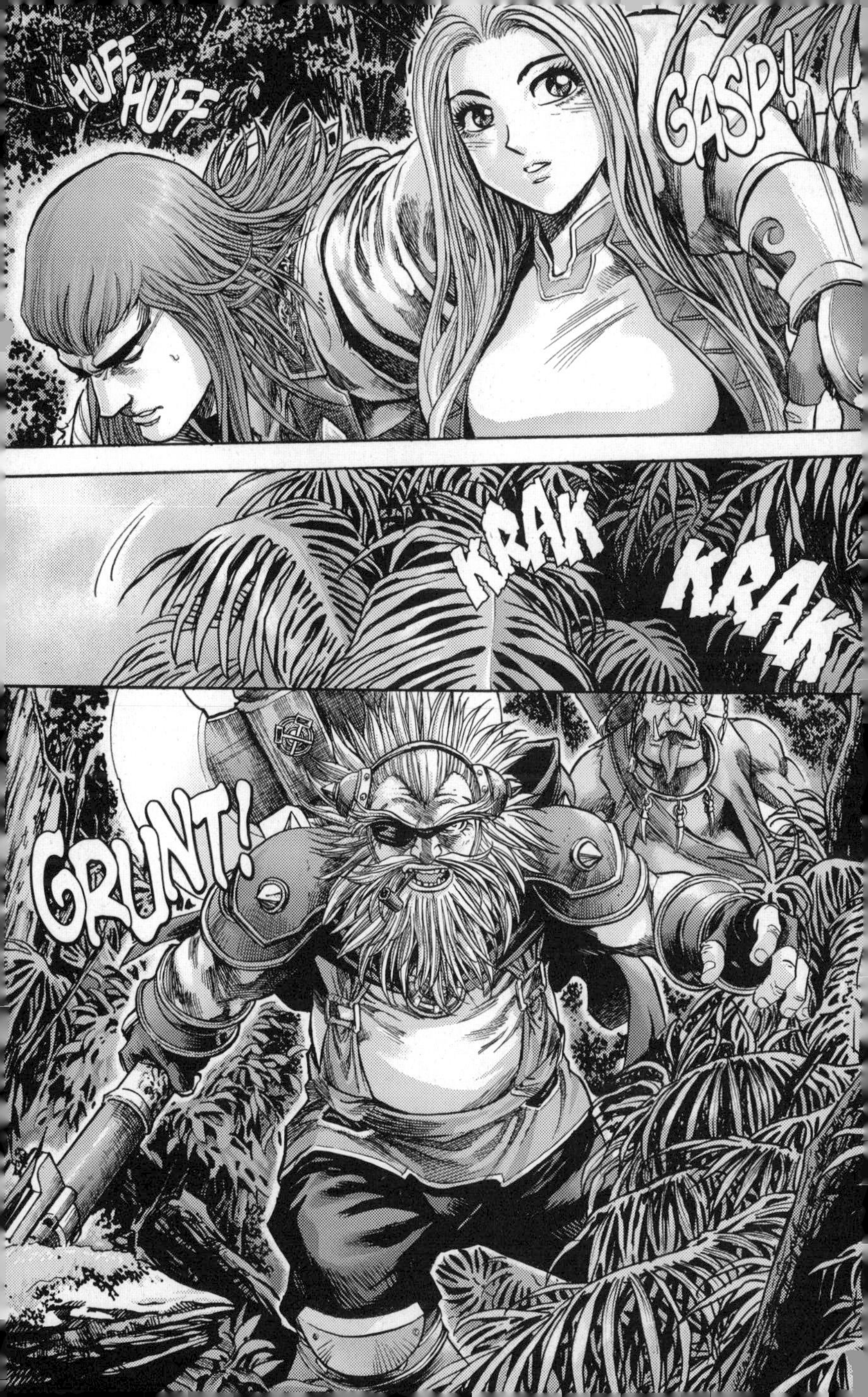
HUFF HUFF
GASP!
KRAK
KRAK
GRUNT!

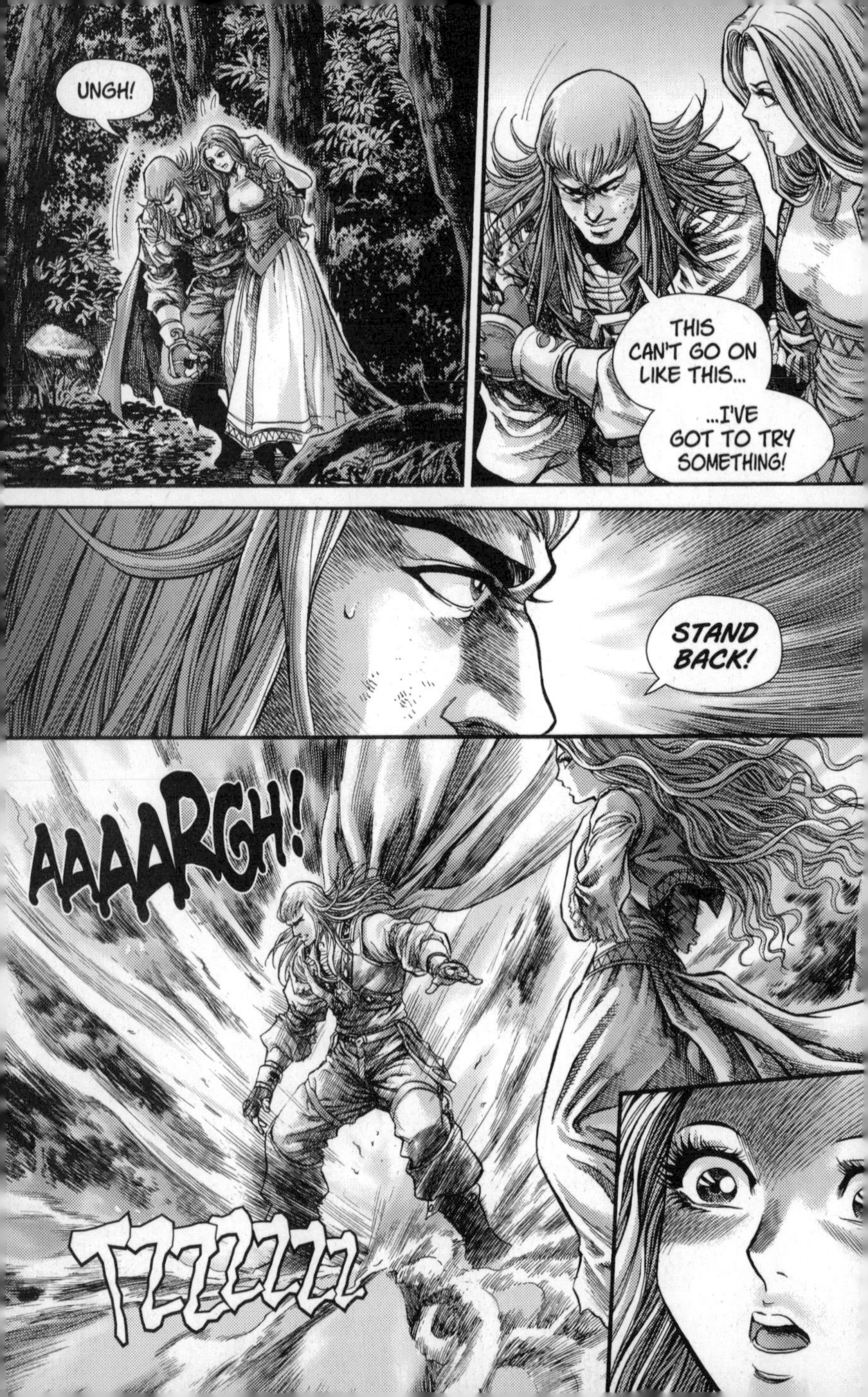
UNGH!
THIS CAN'T GO ON LIKE THIS...
...I'VE GOT TO TRY SOMETHING!
STAND BACK!
AAAARGH!
TZZZZZZZ

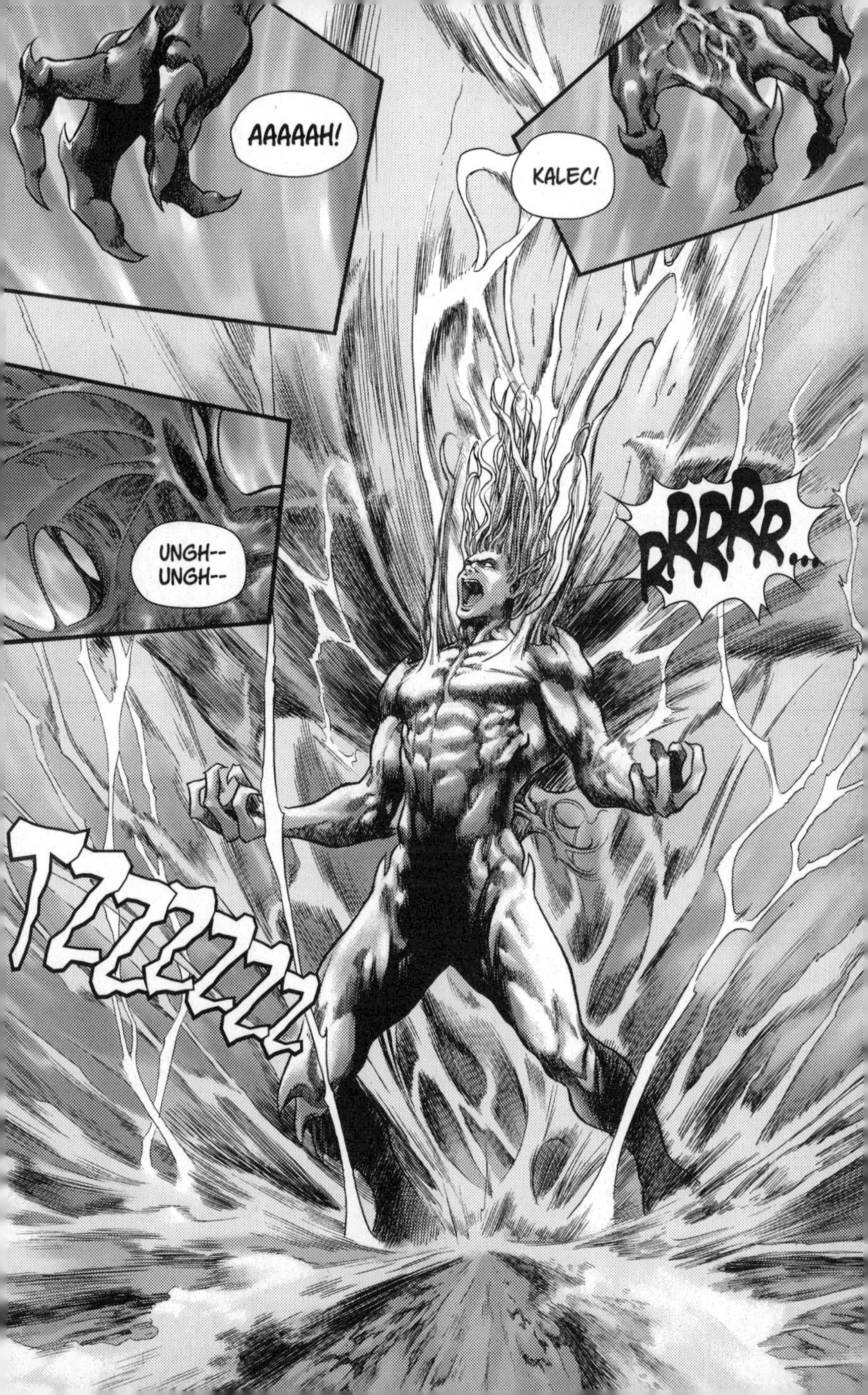
AAAAAH!
KALEC!
UNGH--
UNGH--
RRRRR...
TZZZZZZ

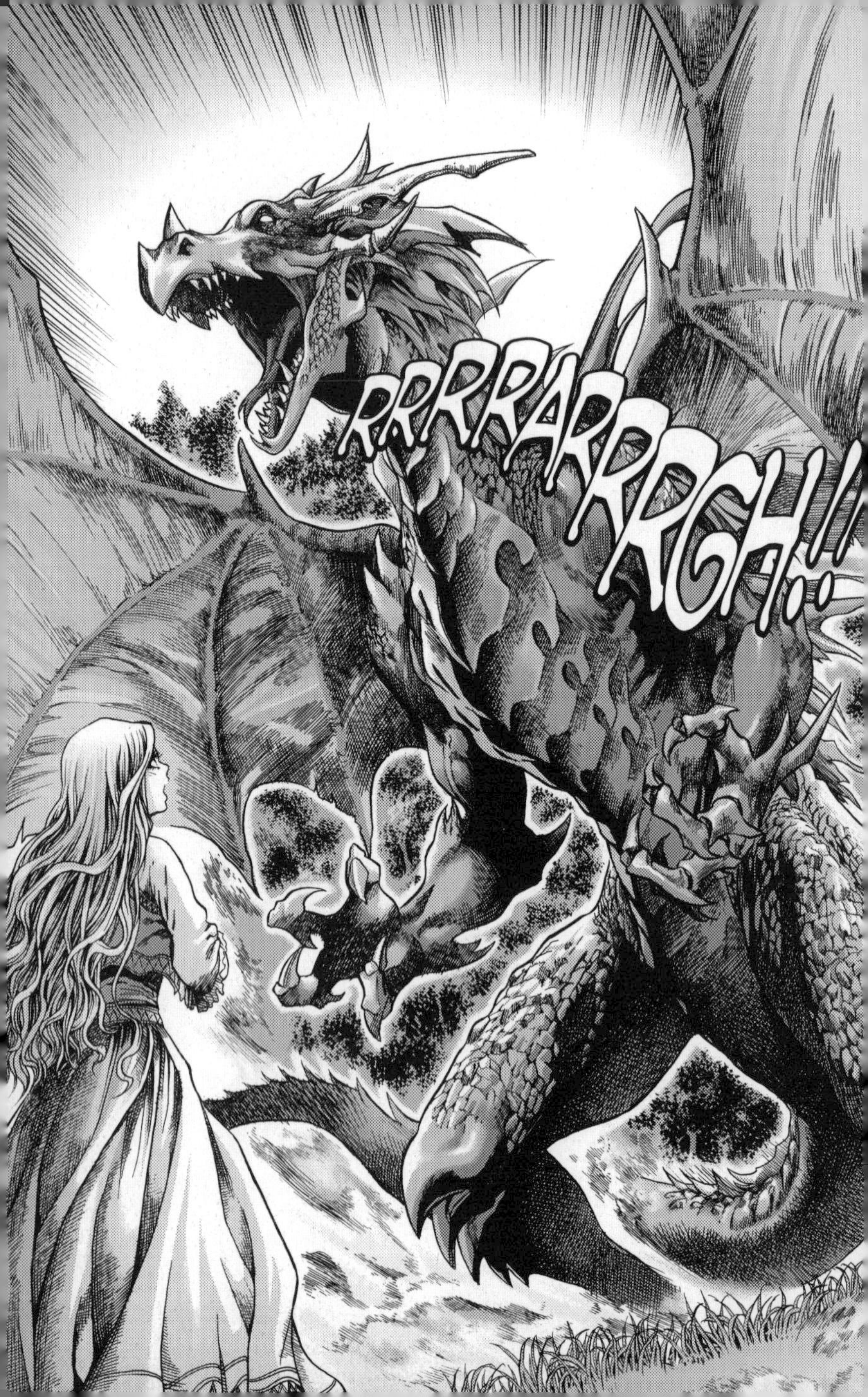
RRRRRARRRRGH!!

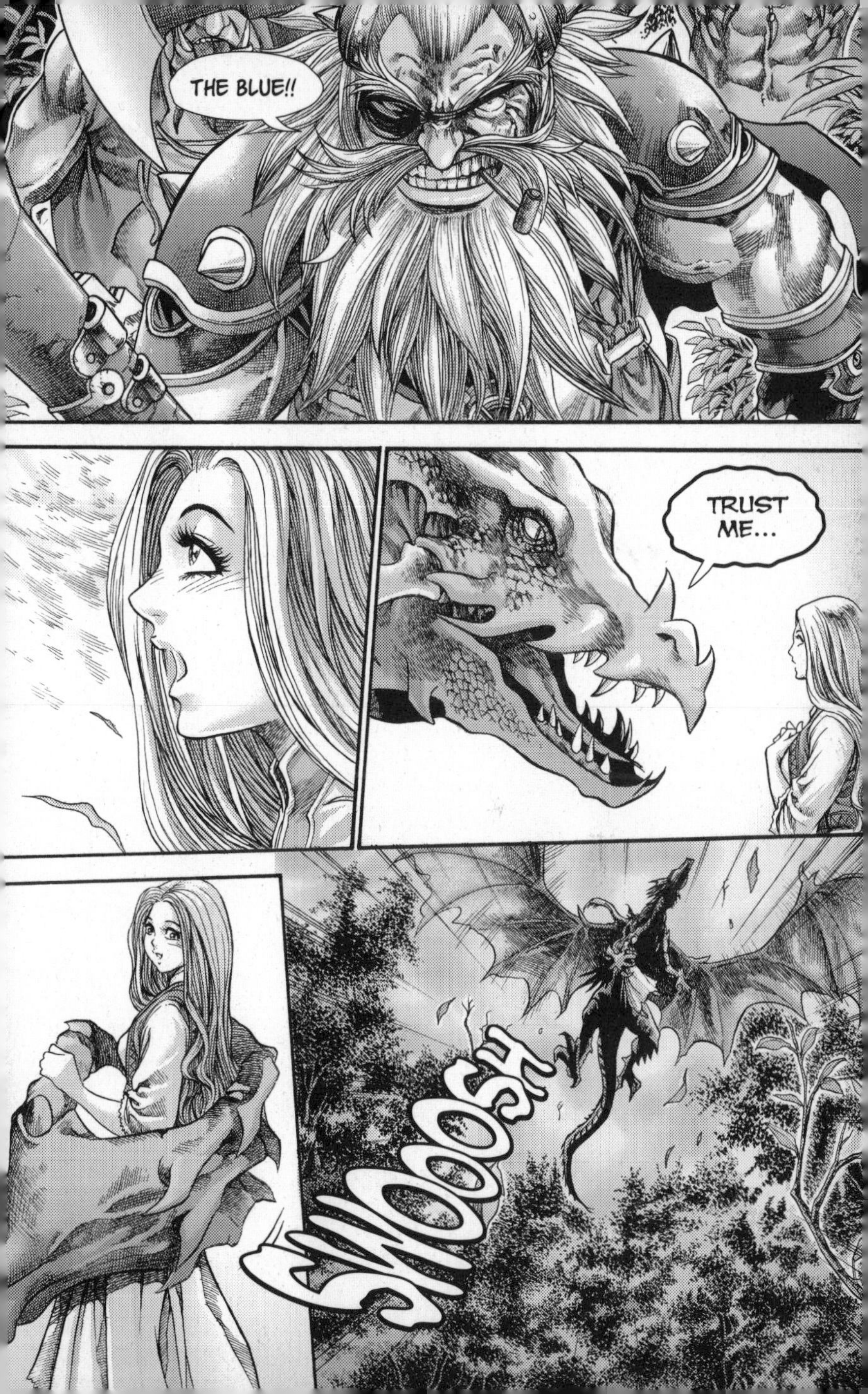
THE BLUE!!
TRUST ME...
SWOOSH

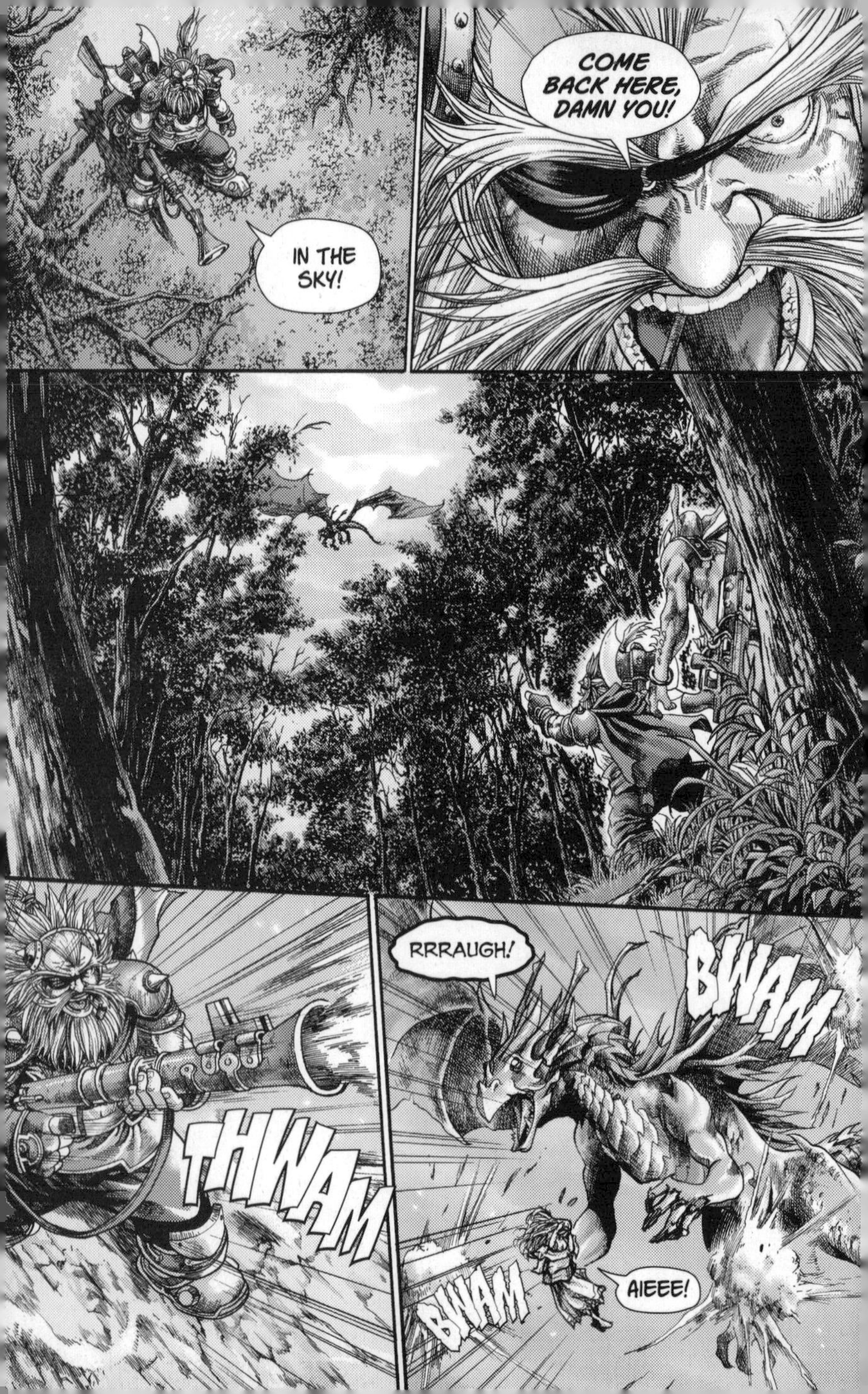
IN THE SKY!
COME BACK HERE, DAMN YOU!
THWAM
RRRAUGH!
BWAM
BWAM
AIEEE!

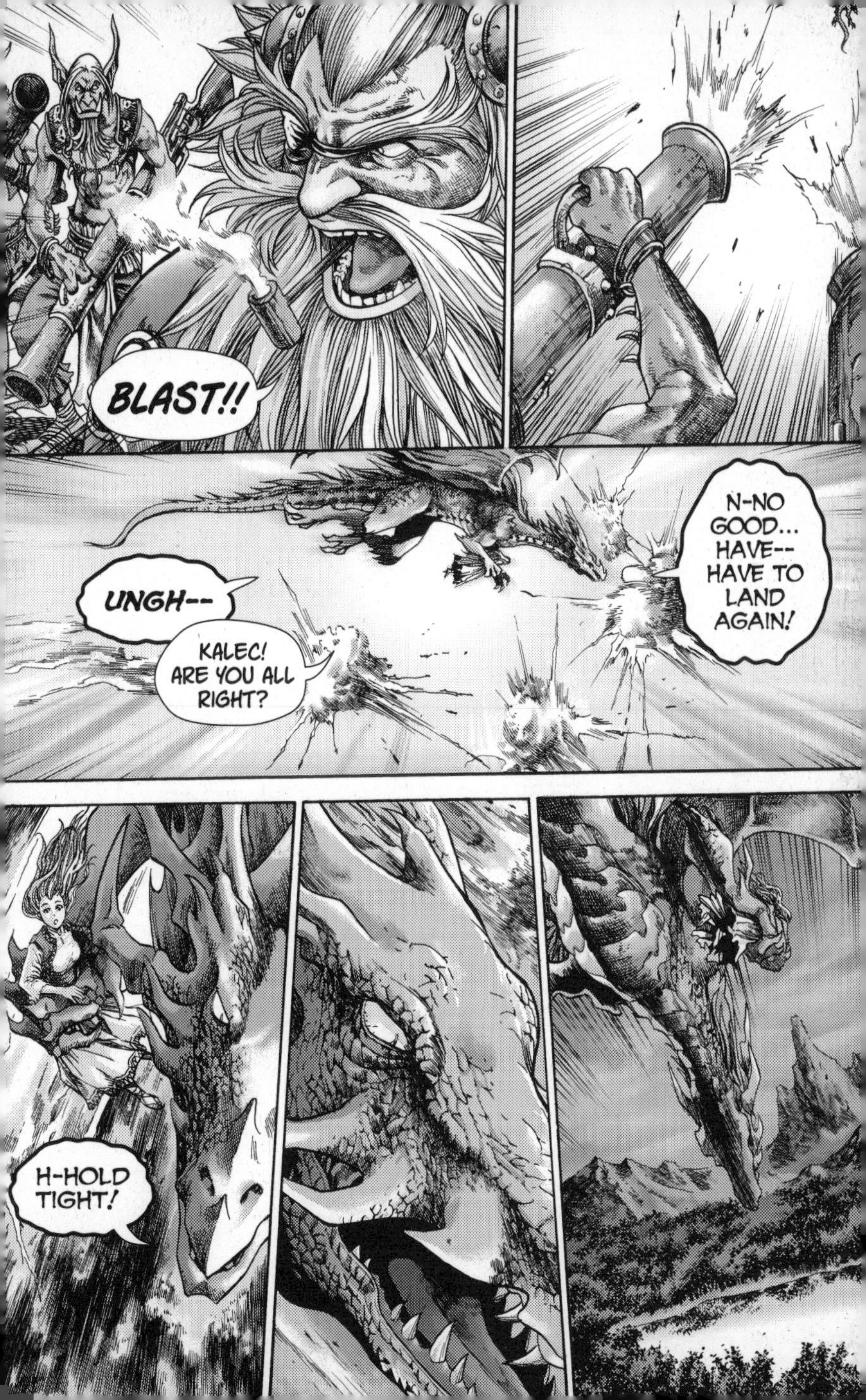
BLAST!!
UNGH--
KALEC! ARE YOU ALL RIGHT?
N-NO GOOD... HAVE-- HAVE TO LAND AGAIN!
H-HOLD TIGHT!

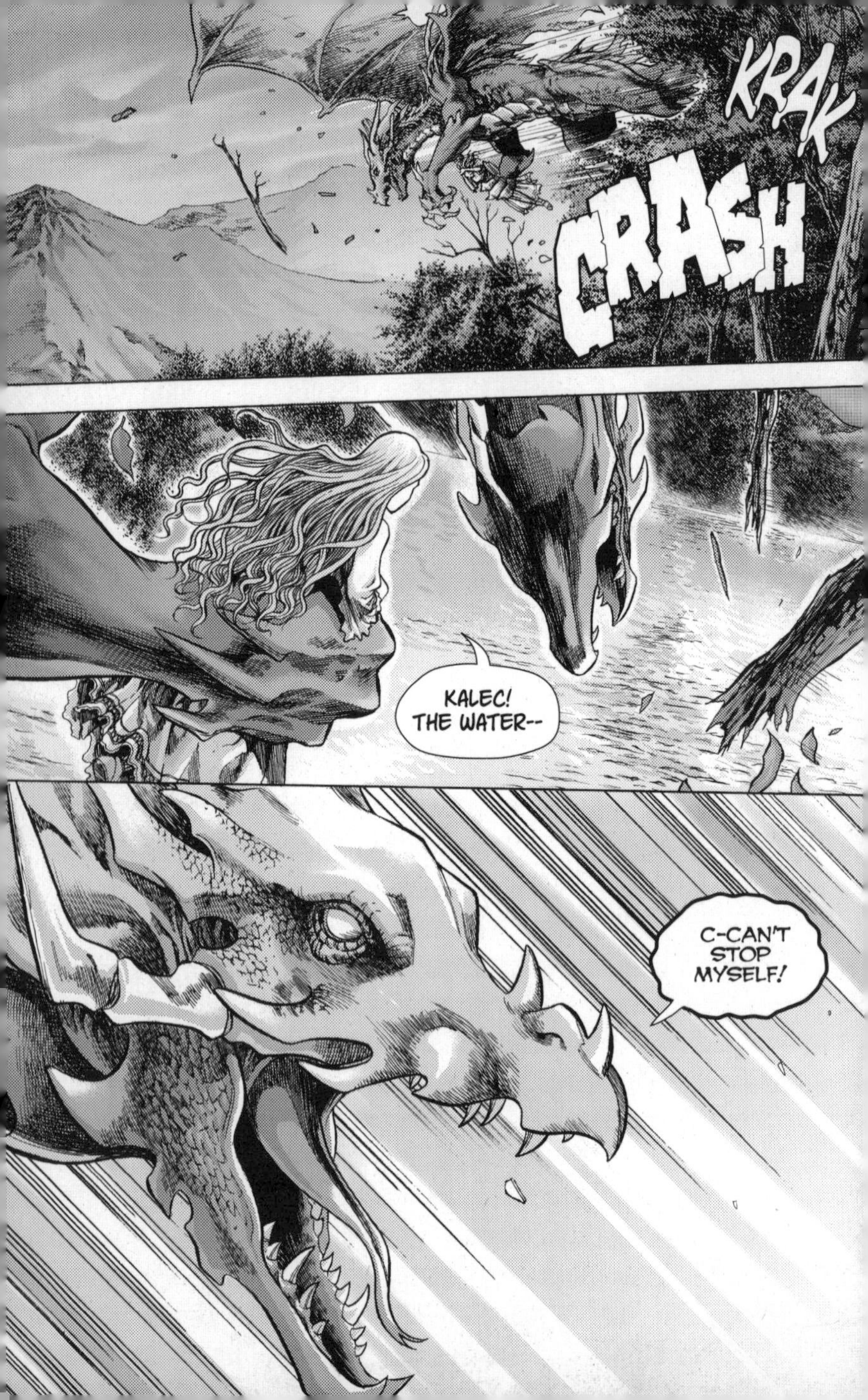
KRAK
CRASH
KALEC! THE WATER--
C-CAN'T STOP MYSELF!

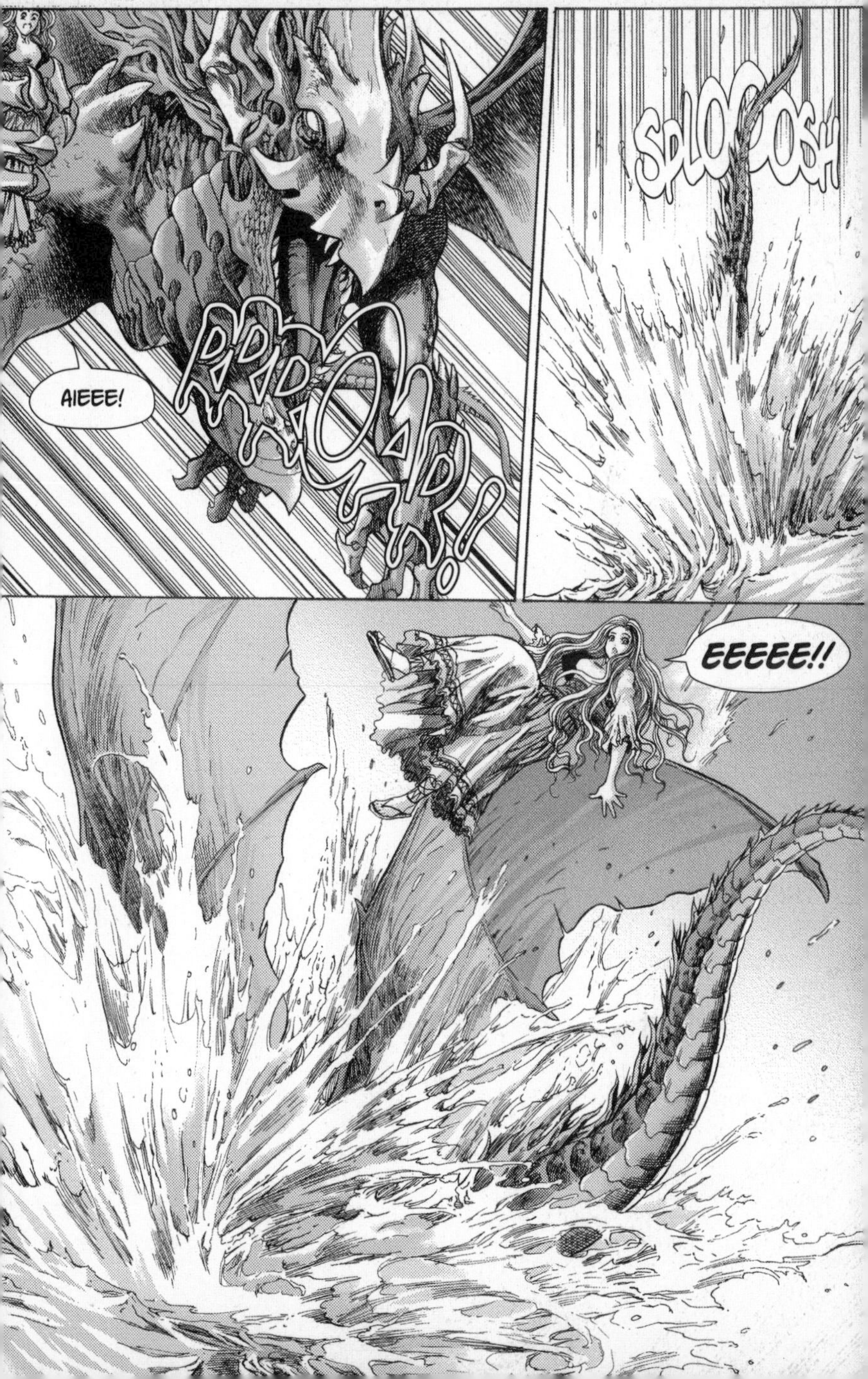
AIEEE!
RRROAR!!
SPLOOOSH
EEEEE!!

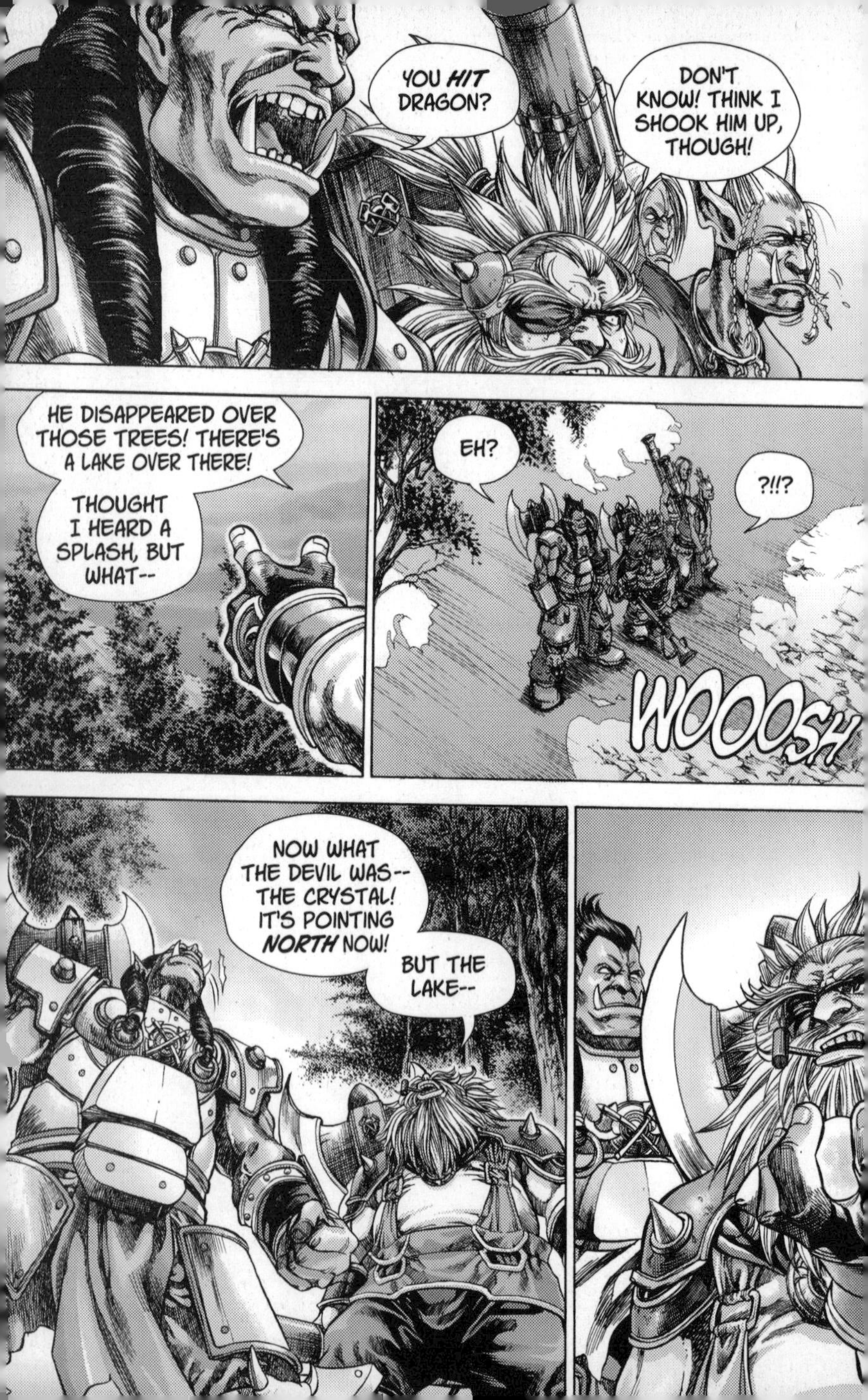

YOU *HIT* DRAGON?
DON'T KNOW! THINK I SHOOK HIM UP, THOUGH!
HE DISAPPEARED OVER THOSE TREES! THERE'S A LAKE OVER THERE!
THOUGHT I HEARD A SPLASH, BUT WHAT--
EH?
?!!?
WOOOSH
NOW WHAT THE DEVIL WAS-- THE CRYSTAL! IT'S POINTING *NORTH* NOW!
BUT THE LAKE--

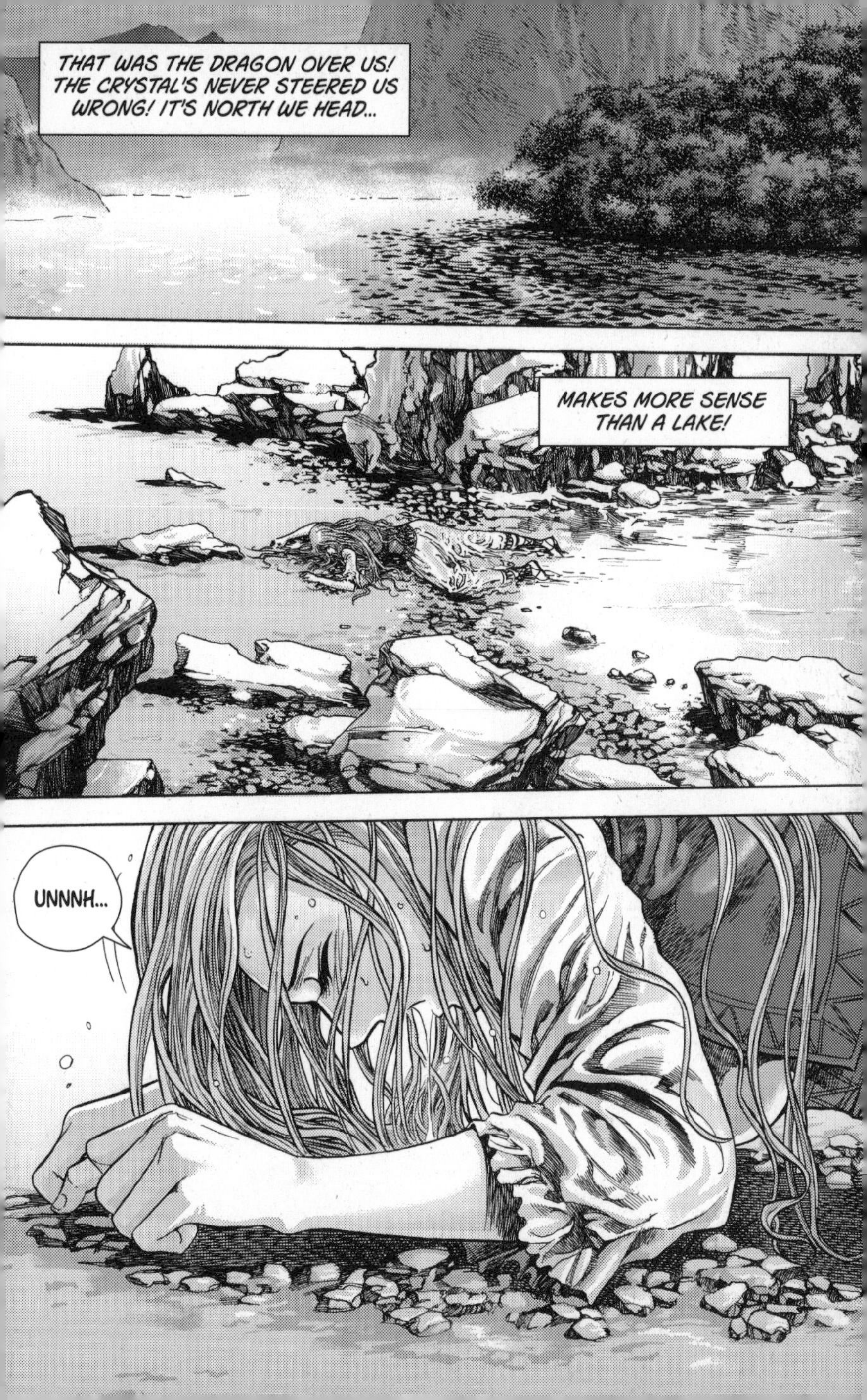
THAT WAS THE DRAGON OVER US! THE CRYSTAL'S NEVER STEERED US WRONG! IT'S NORTH WE HEAD...
MAKES MORE SENSE THAN A LAKE!
UNNNH...

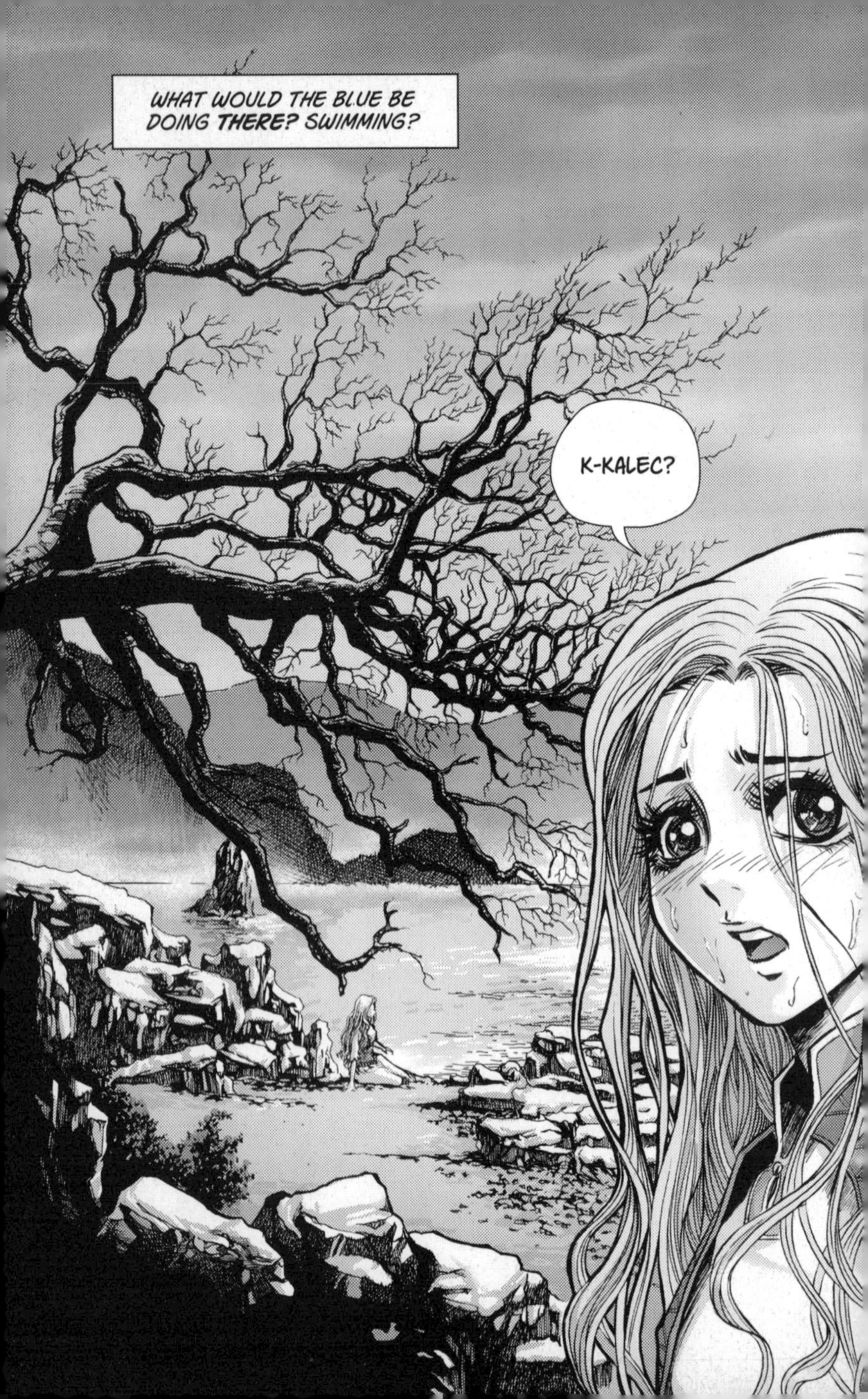
WHAT WOULD THE BLUE BE DOING THERE? SWIMMING?
K-KALEC?

CHAPTER THREE
DAR'KHAN

UNNGH!

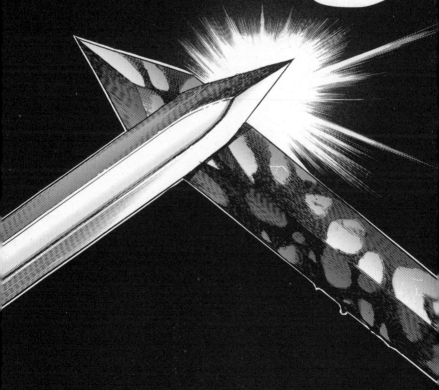

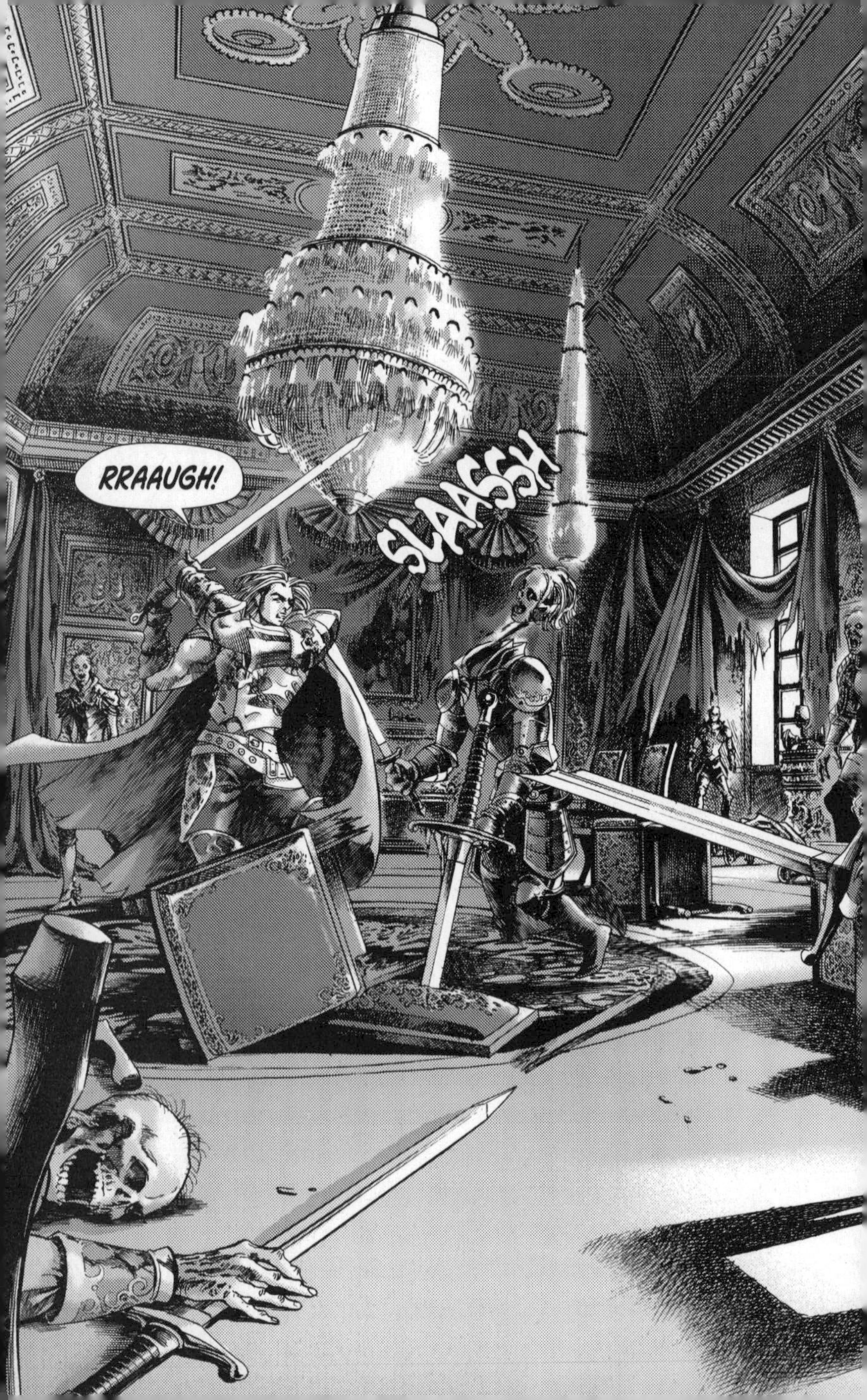
RRAAUGH!
SLASSH

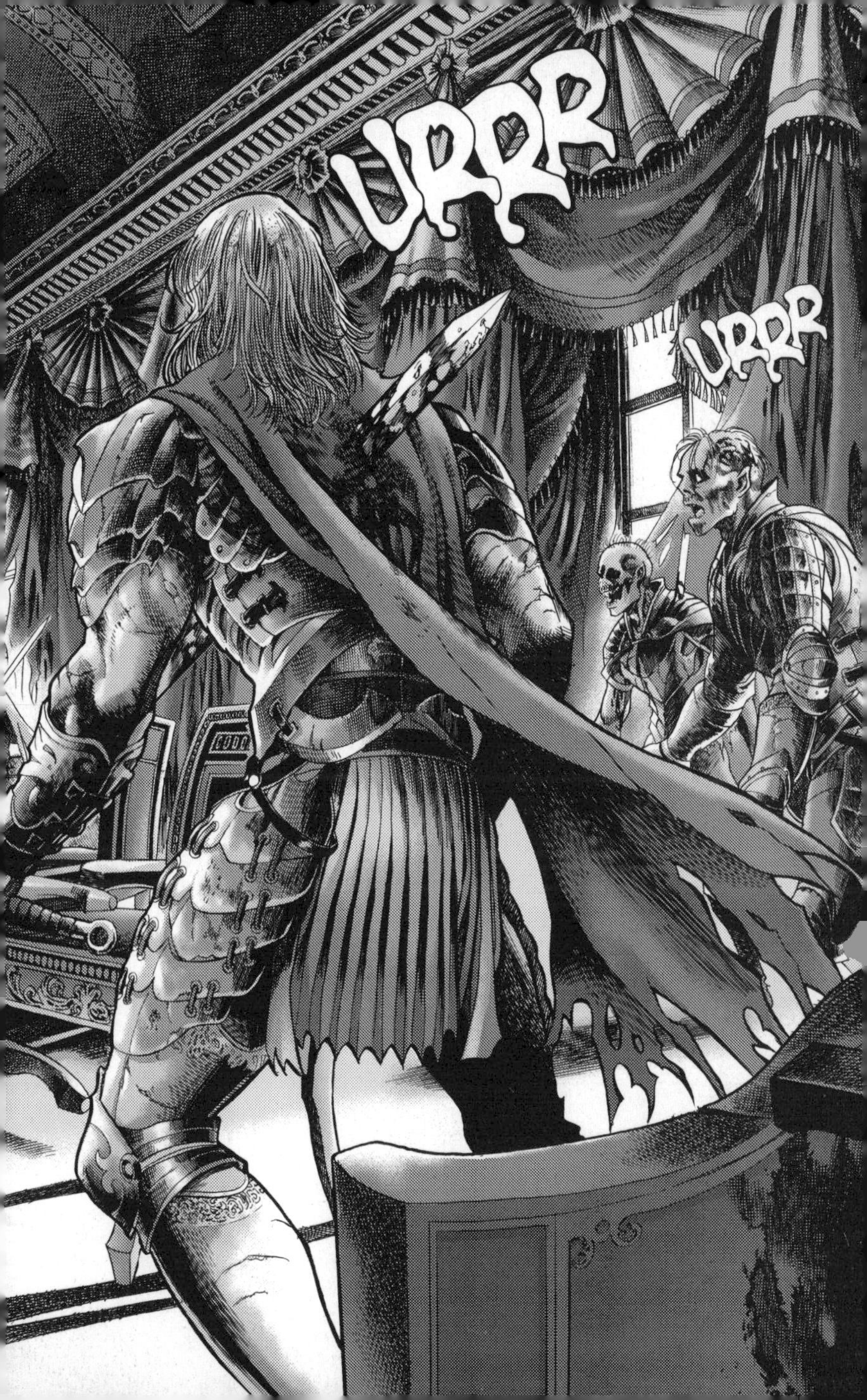
URRR
URRR

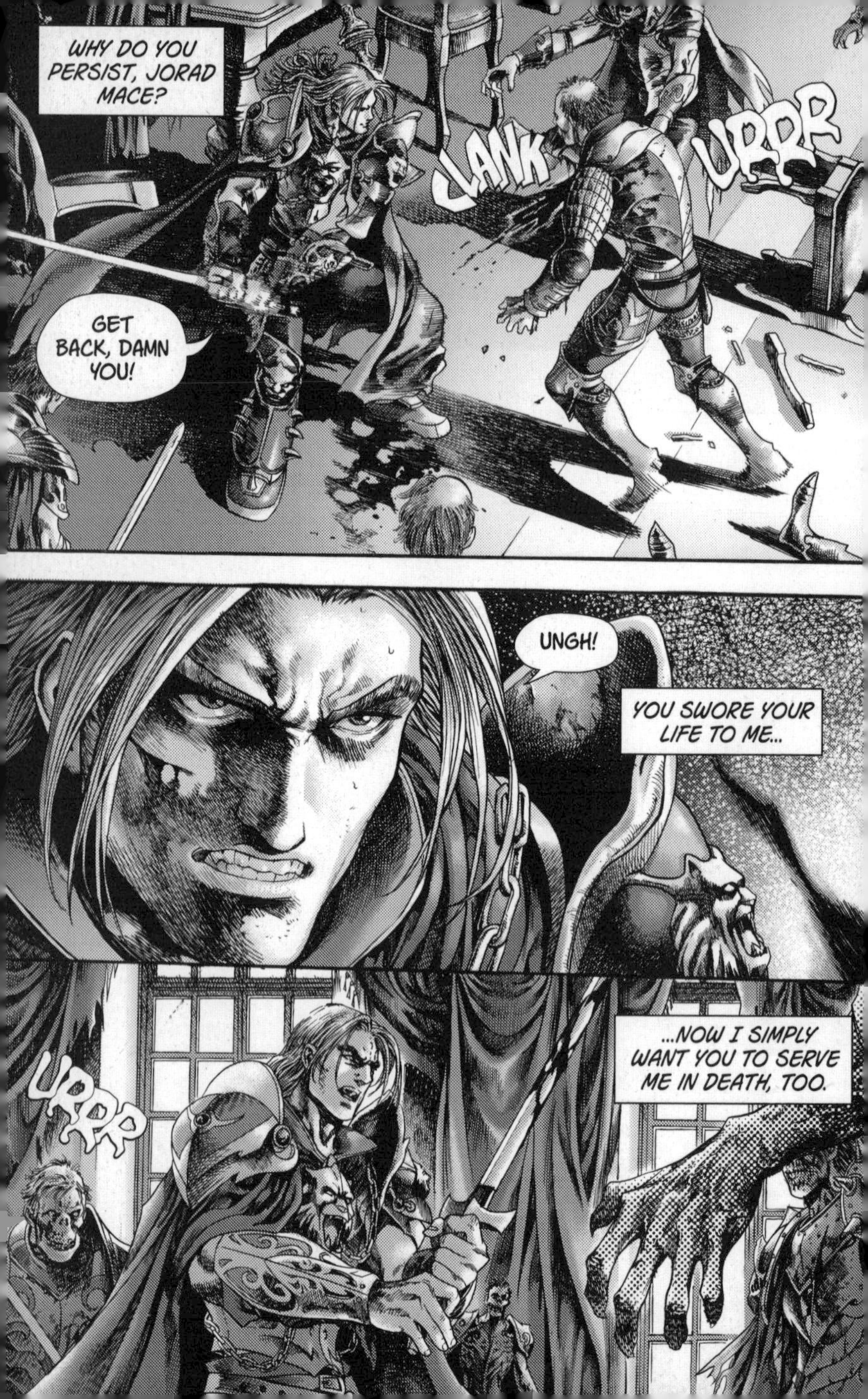
WHY DO YOU PERSIST, JORAD MACE?
CLANK
URRR
GET BACK, DAMN YOU!
UNGH!
YOU SWORE YOUR LIFE TO ME...
URRR
...NOW I SIMPLY WANT YOU TO SERVE ME IN DEATH, TOO.

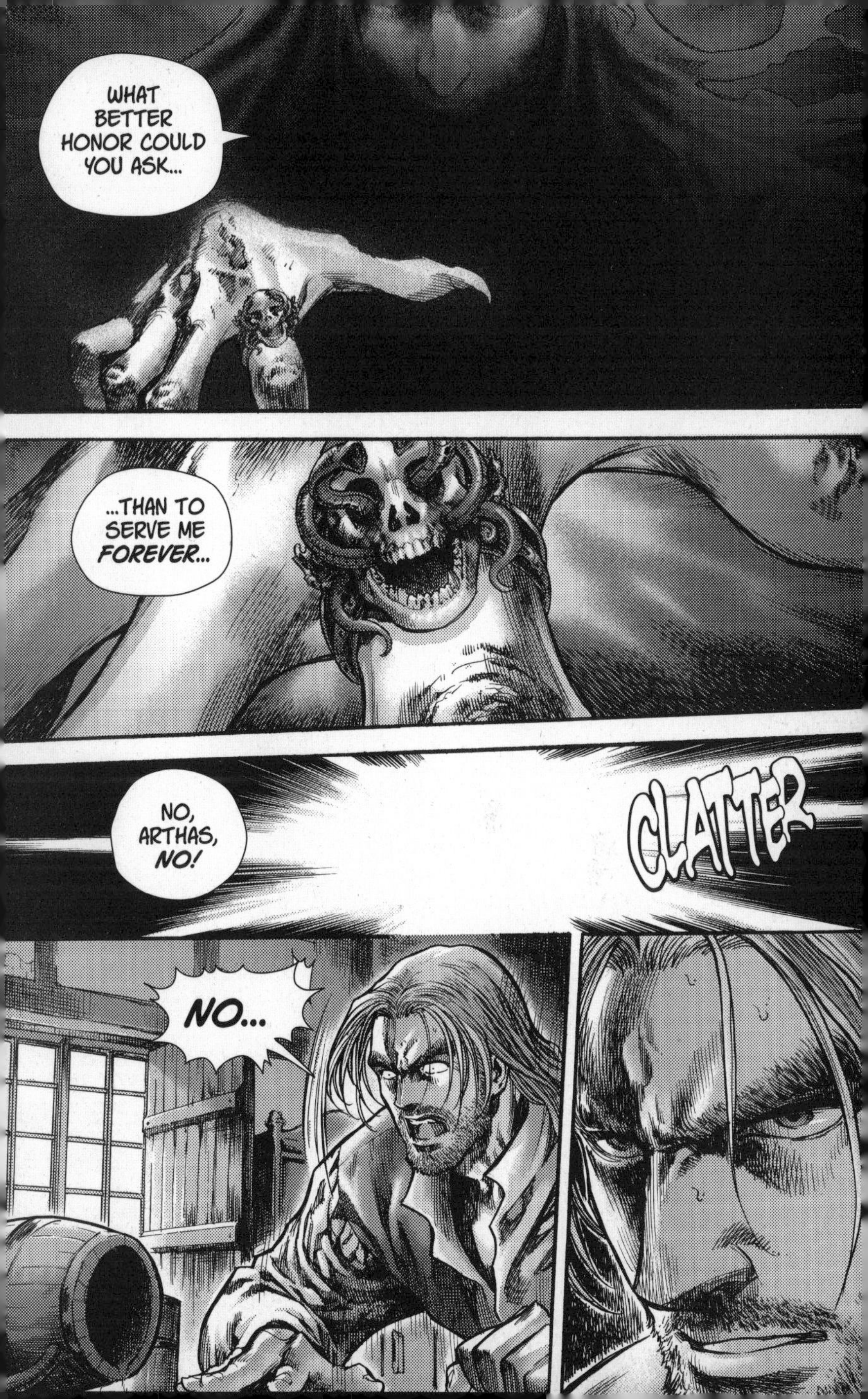
WHAT BETTER HONOR COULD YOU ASK...
...THAN TO SERVE ME *FOREVER*...
NO, ARTHAS, *NO!*
CLATTER
NO...

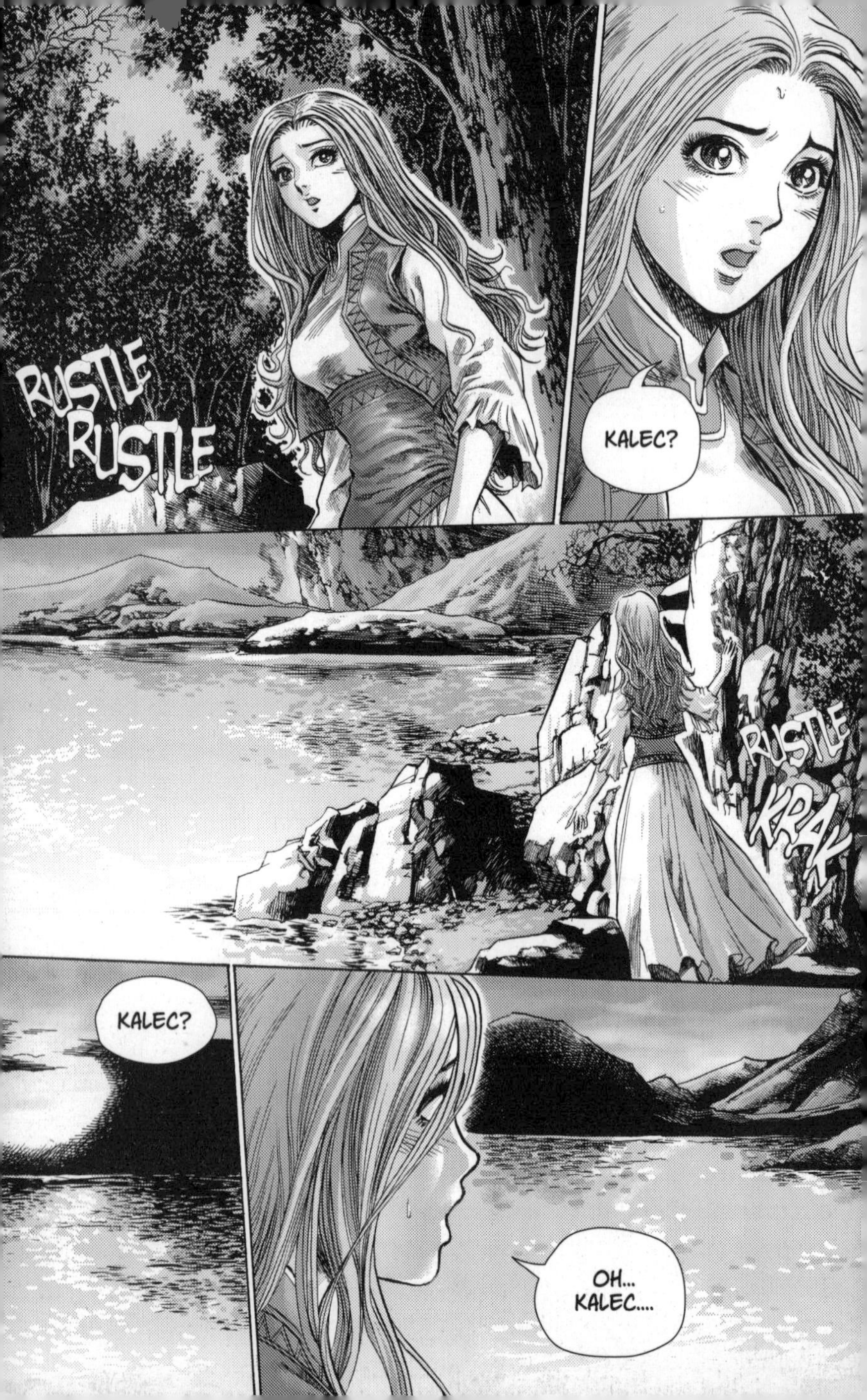
RUSTLE
RUSTLE
KALEC?
RUSTLE
KRAK
KALEC?
OH... KALEC....

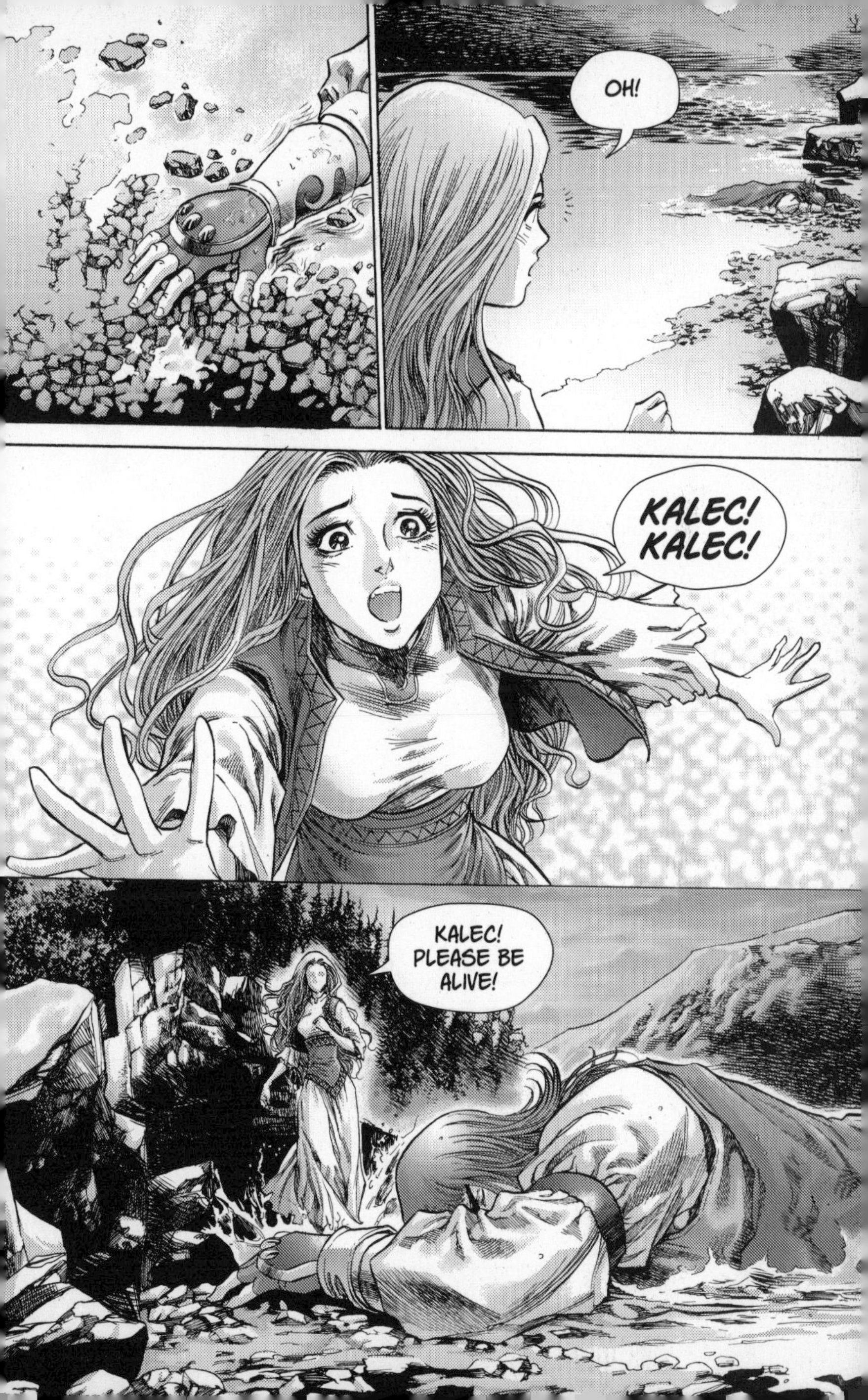
OH!
KALEC! KALEC!
KALEC! PLEASE BE ALIVE!

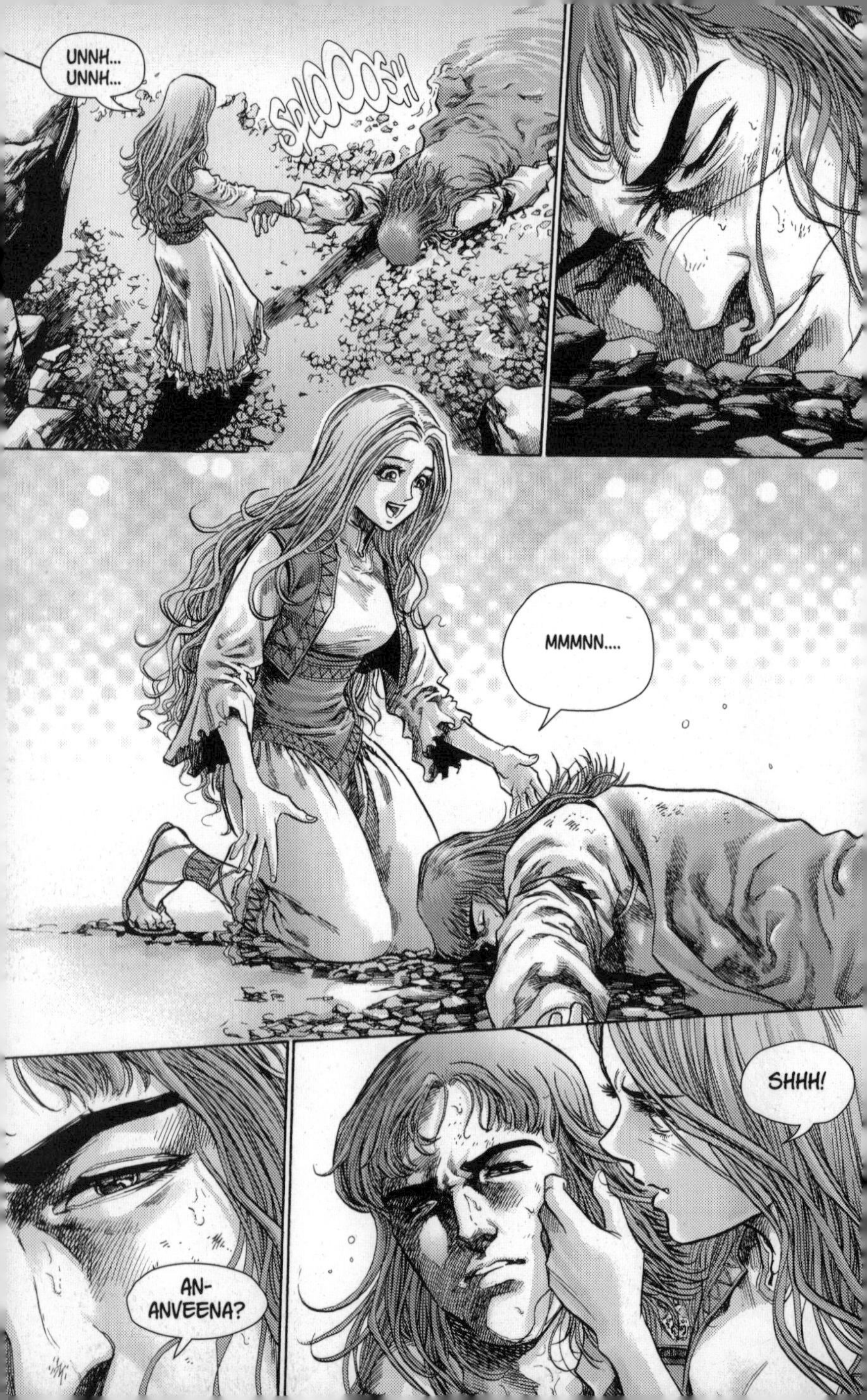
UNNH... UNNH...
SPLOOOSH!
MMMNN....
AN-ANVEENA?
SHHH!

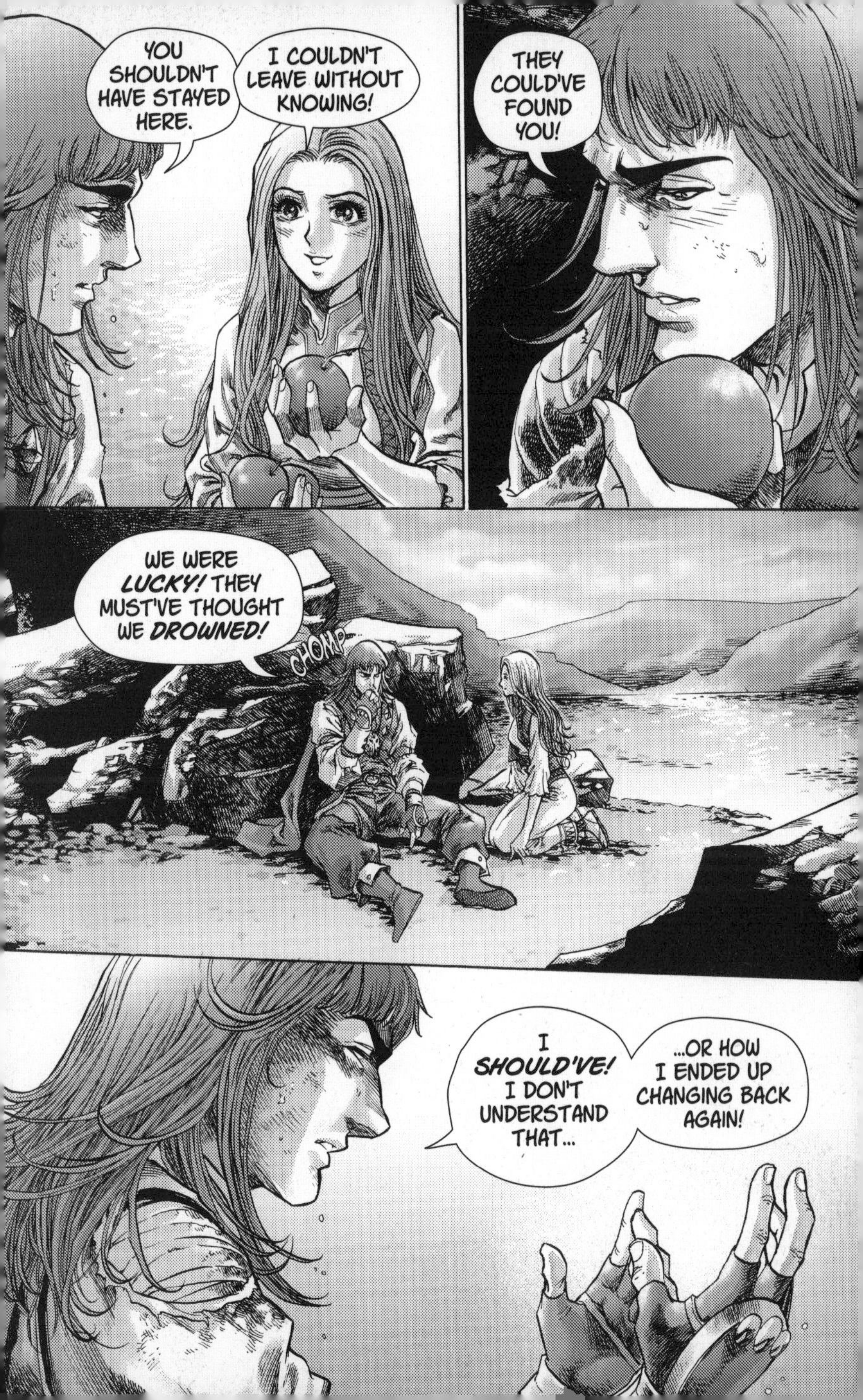
YOU SHOULDN'T HAVE STAYED HERE.
I COULDN'T LEAVE WITHOUT KNOWING!
THEY COULD'VE FOUND YOU!
WE WERE *LUCKY!* THEY MUST'VE THOUGHT WE *DROWNED!*
CHOMP
I *SHOULD'VE!* I DON'T UNDERSTAND THAT...
...OR HOW I ENDED UP CHANGING BACK AGAIN!

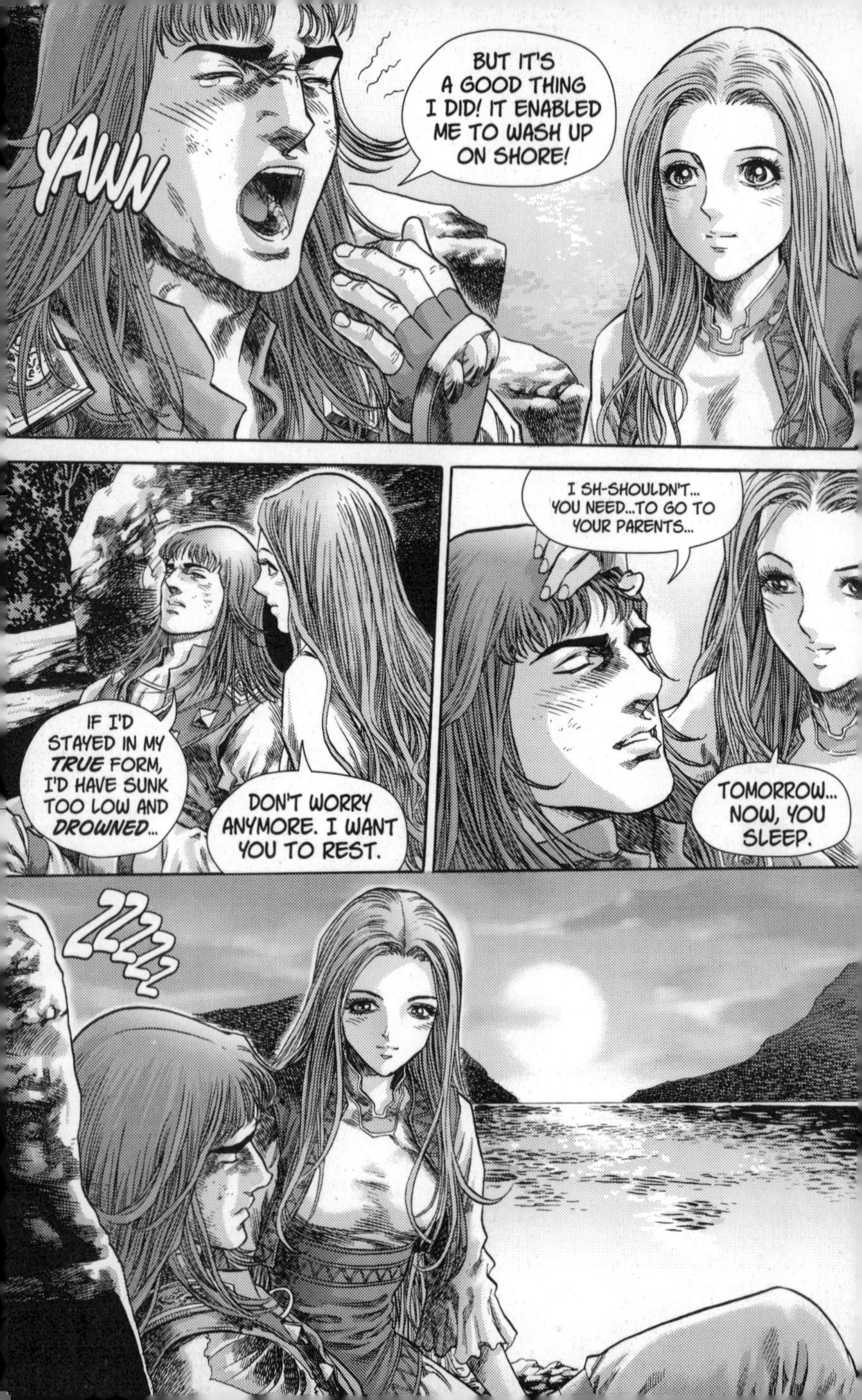
YAWN
BUT IT'S A GOOD THING I DID! IT ENABLED ME TO WASH UP ON SHORE!
IF I'D STAYED IN MY TRUE FORM, I'D HAVE SUNK TOO LOW AND DROWNED...
DON'T WORRY ANYMORE. I WANT YOU TO REST.
I SH-SHOULDN'T... YOU NEED...TO GO TO YOUR PARENTS...
TOMORROW... NOW, YOU SLEEP.
ZZZZZ

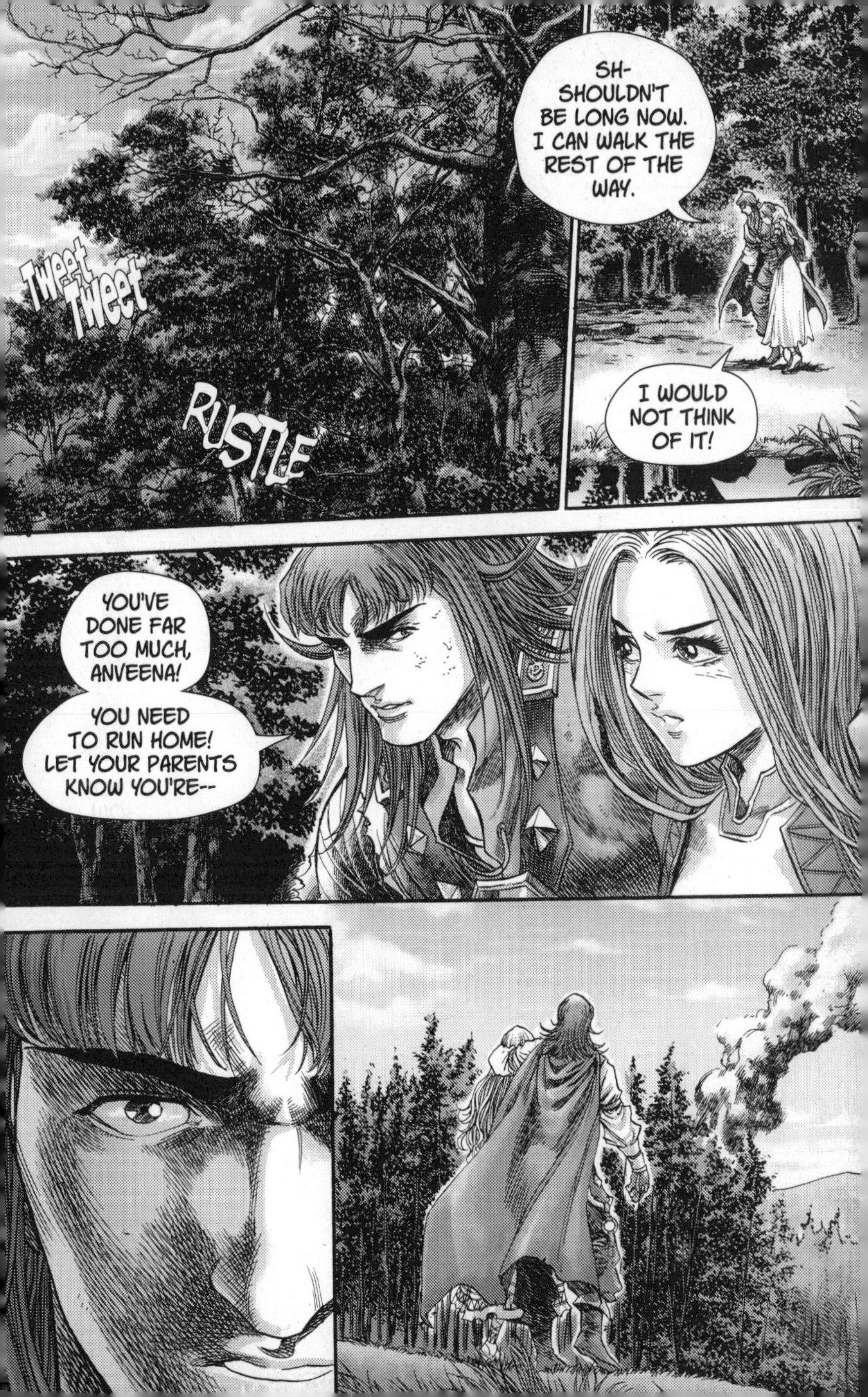

TWEET TWEET
RUSTLE
SH- SHOULDN'T BE LONG NOW. I CAN WALK THE REST OF THE WAY.
I WOULD NOT THINK OF IT!
YOU'VE DONE FAR TOO MUCH, ANVEENA!
YOU NEED TO RUN HOME! LET YOUR PARENTS KNOW YOU'RE--

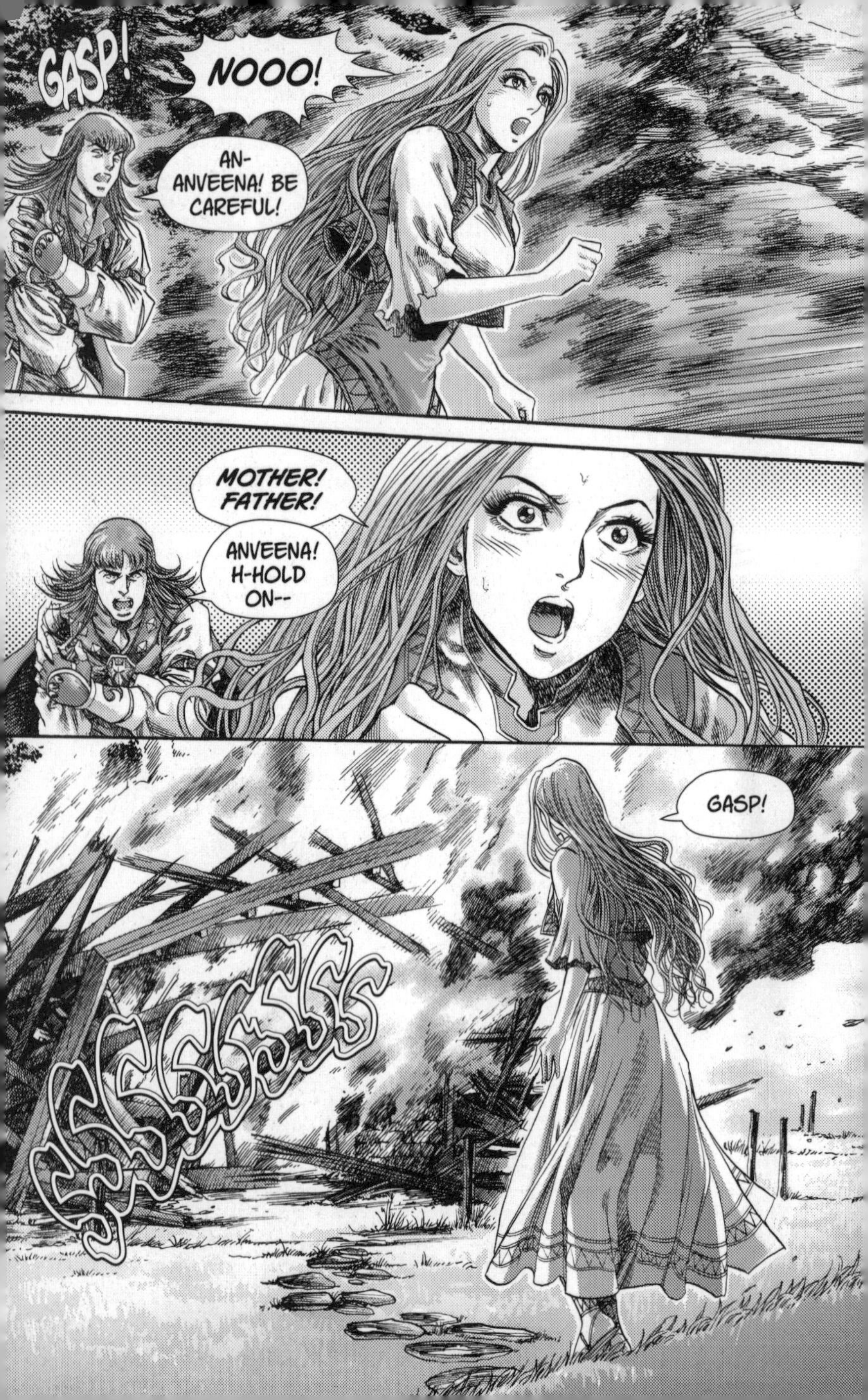
GASP!
NOOO!
AN- ANVEENA! BE CAREFUL!
MOTHER! FATHER!
ANVEENA! H-HOLD ON--
GASP!

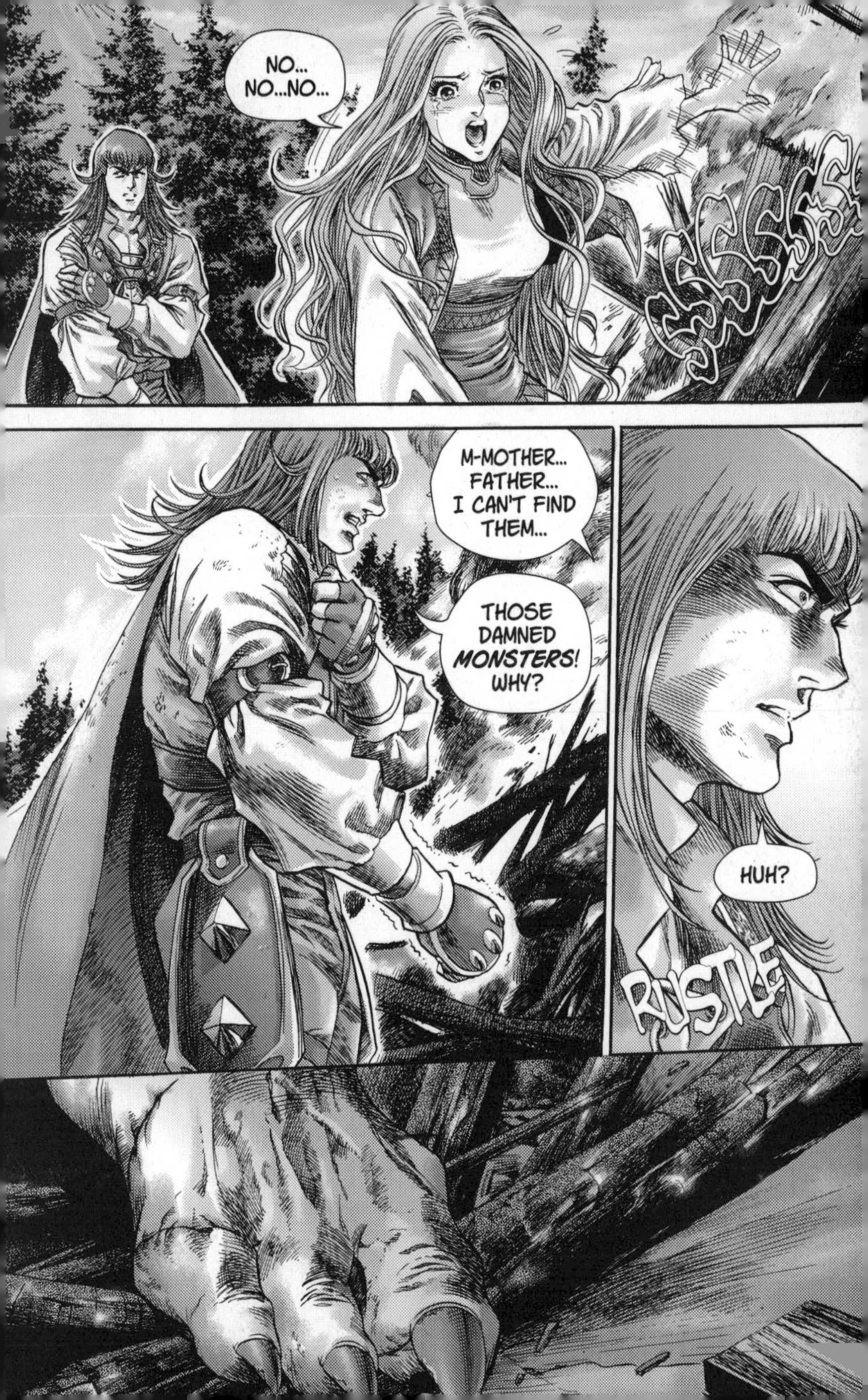
NO... NO...NO...
M-MOTHER... FATHER... I CAN'T FIND THEM...
THOSE DAMNED *MONSTERS!* WHY?
HUH?
RUSTLE

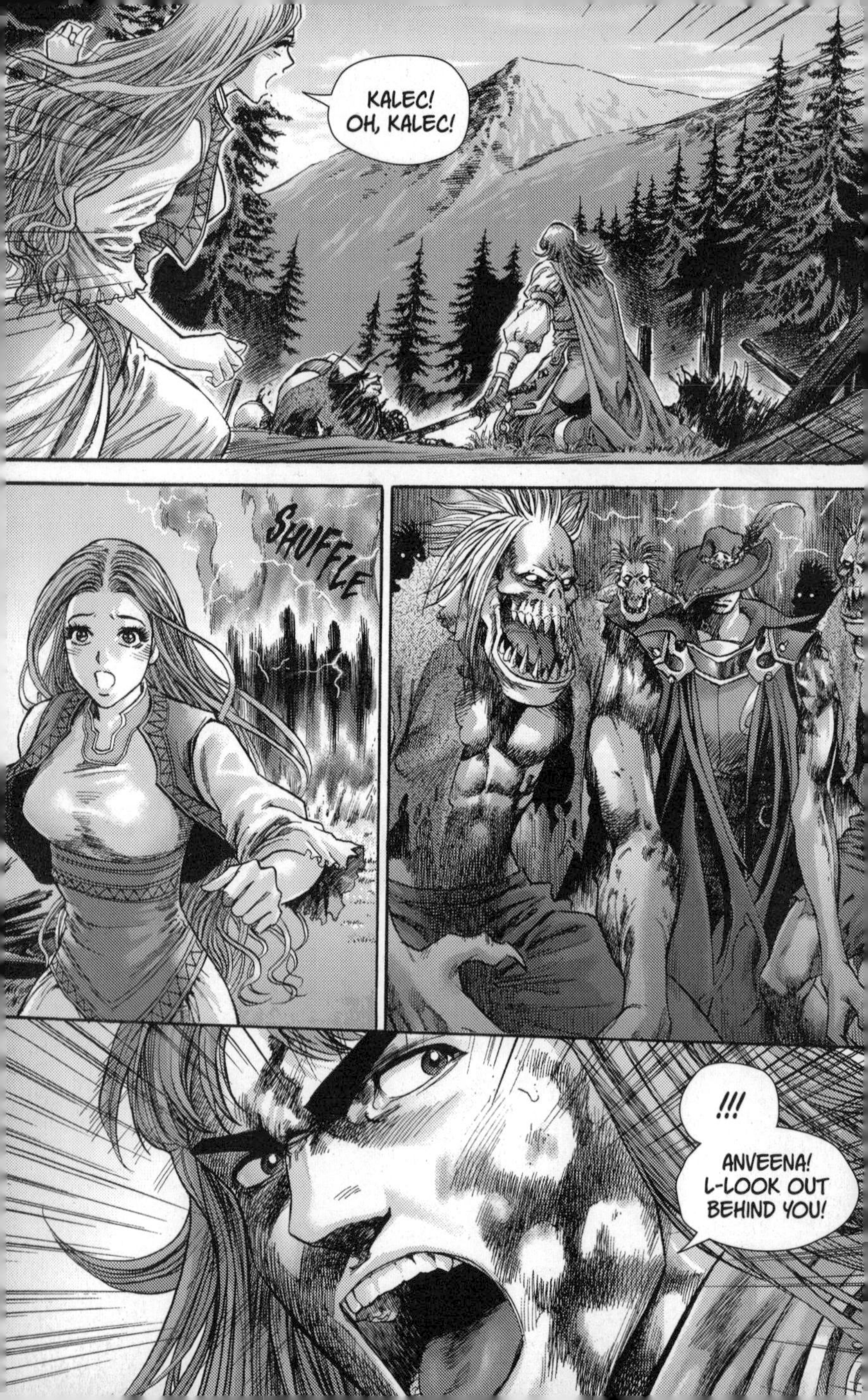
KALEC! OH, KALEC!
SHUFFLE
!!!
ANVEENA! L-LOOK OUT BEHIND YOU!

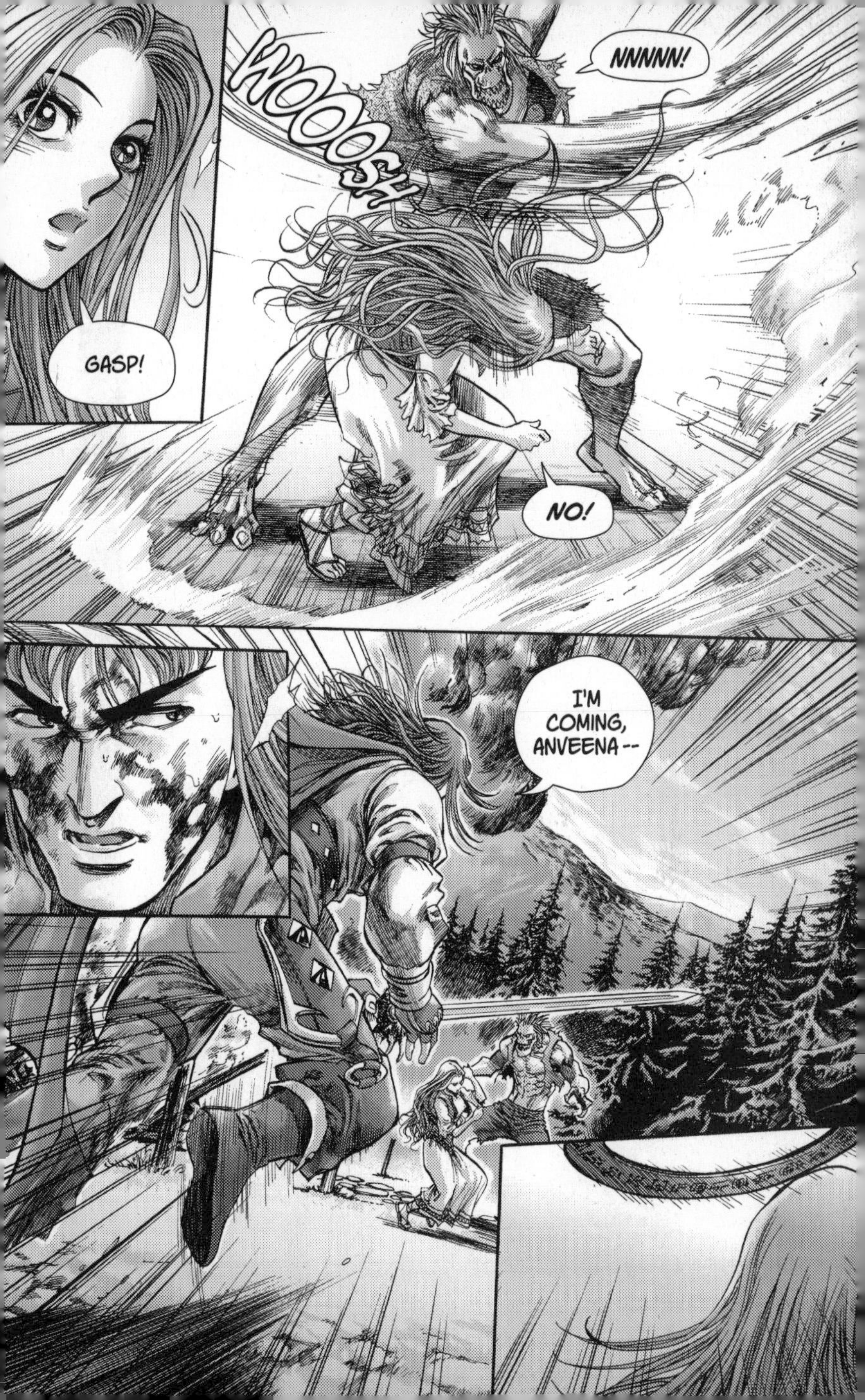
GASP!
WOOOSH
NNNNN!
NO!
I'M COMING, ANVEENA --

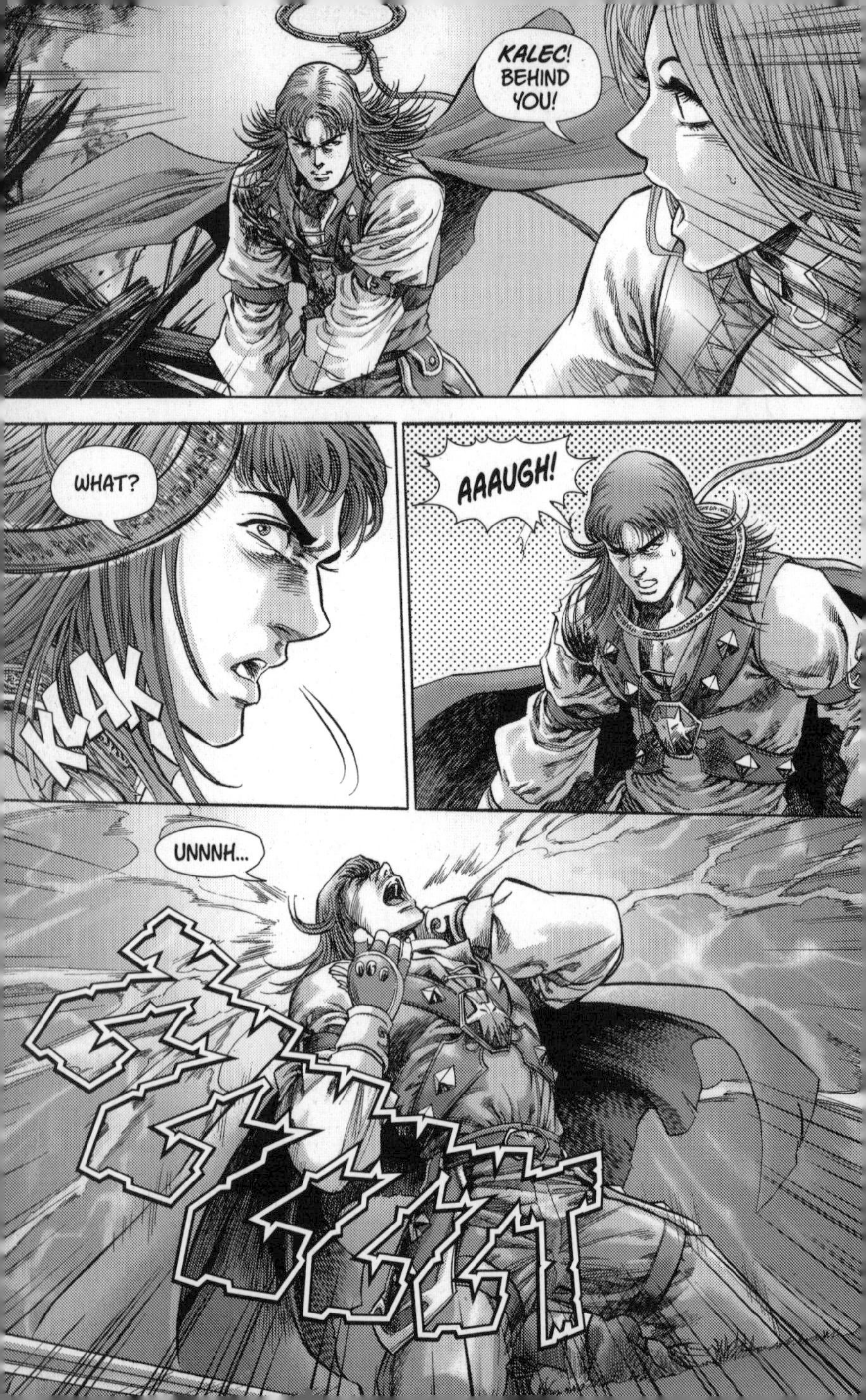
KALEC! BEHIND YOU!
WHAT?
KLAK
AAAUGH!
UNNNH...

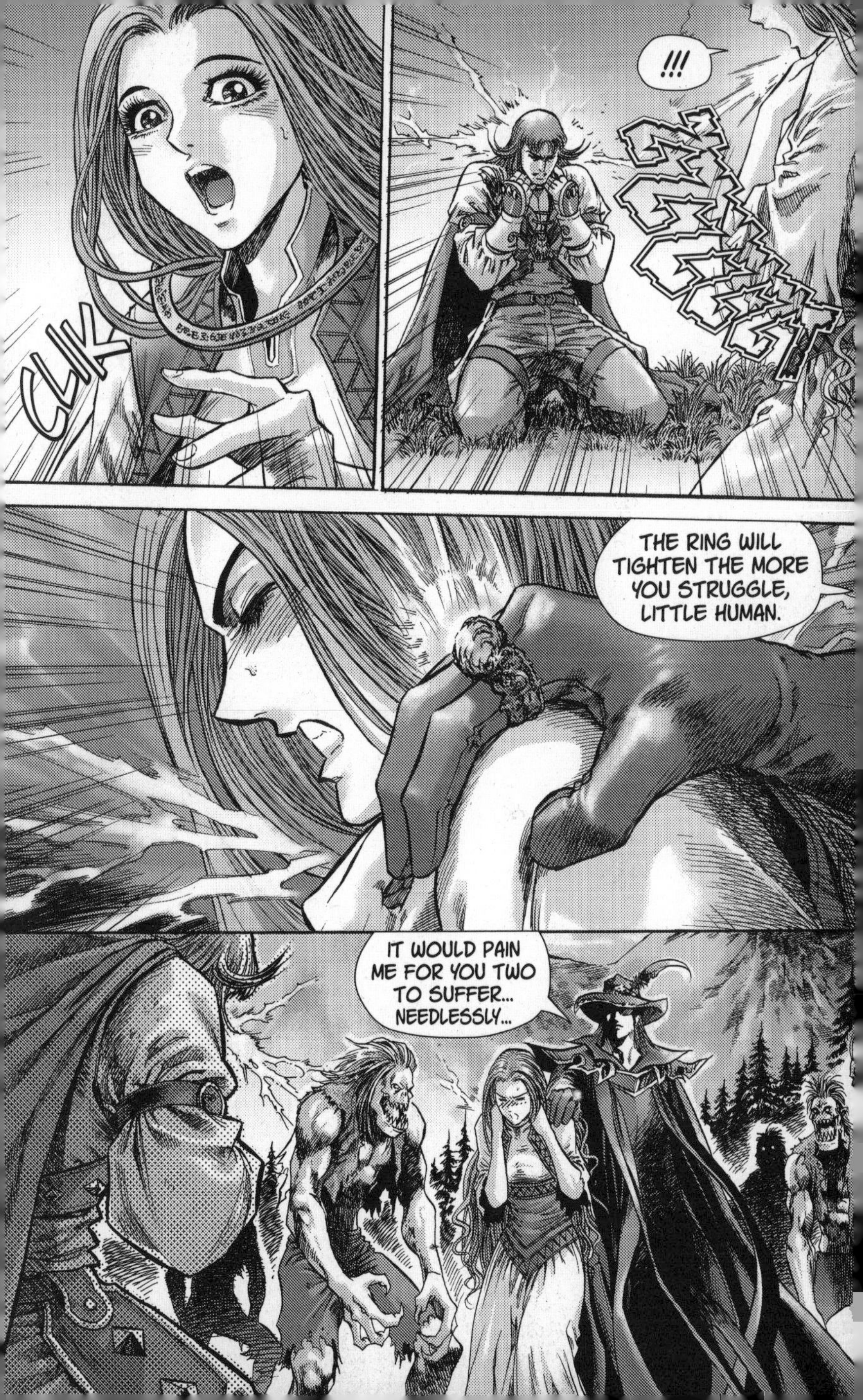
CLIK
!!!
GGGT
THE RING WILL TIGHTEN THE MORE YOU STRUGGLE, LITTLE HUMAN.
IT WOULD PAIN ME FOR YOU TWO TO SUFFER... NEEDLESSLY...

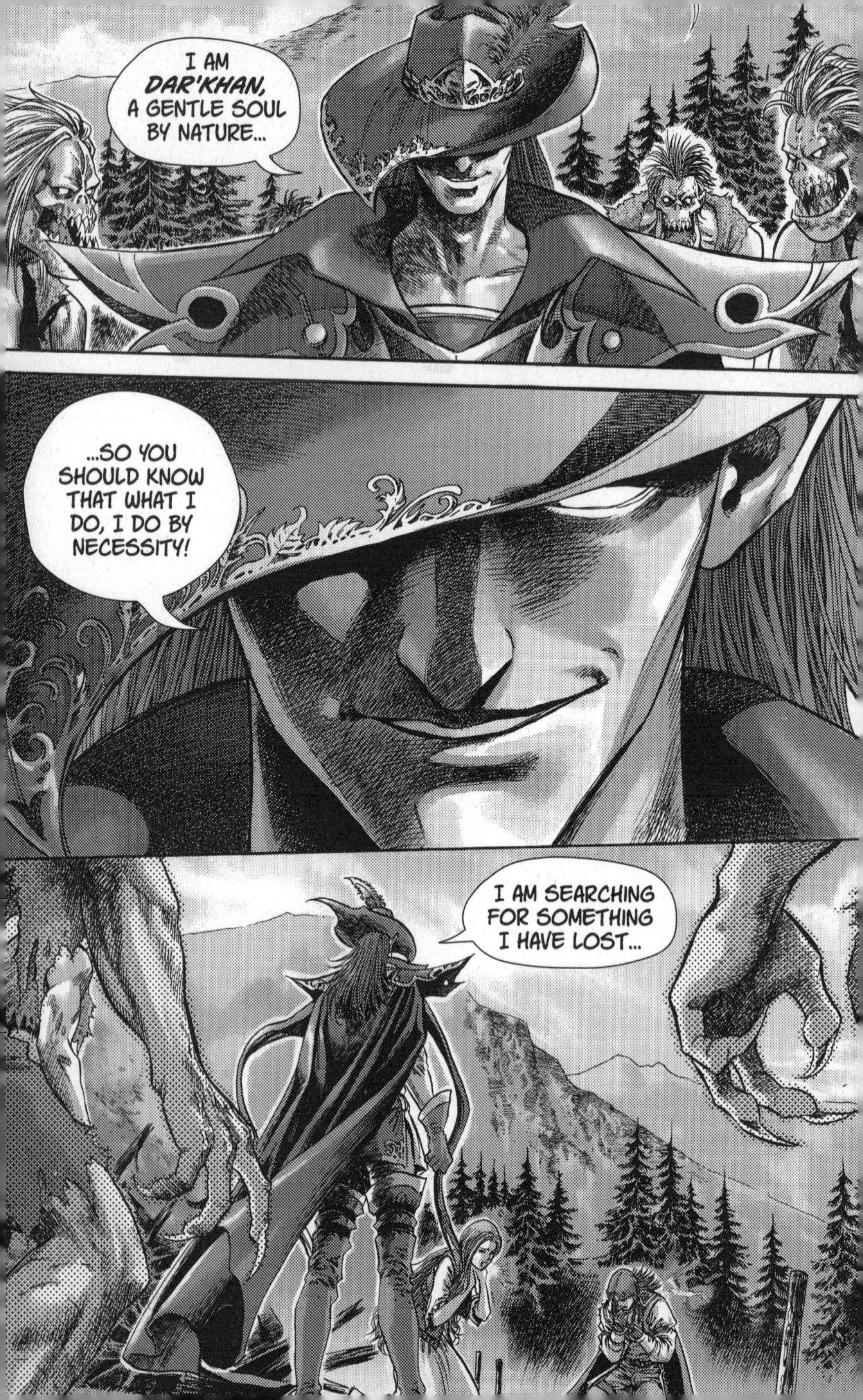
I AM DAR'KHAN, A GENTLE SOUL BY NATURE...
...SO YOU SHOULD KNOW THAT WHAT I DO, I DO BY NECESSITY!
I AM SEARCHING FOR SOMETHING I HAVE LOST...

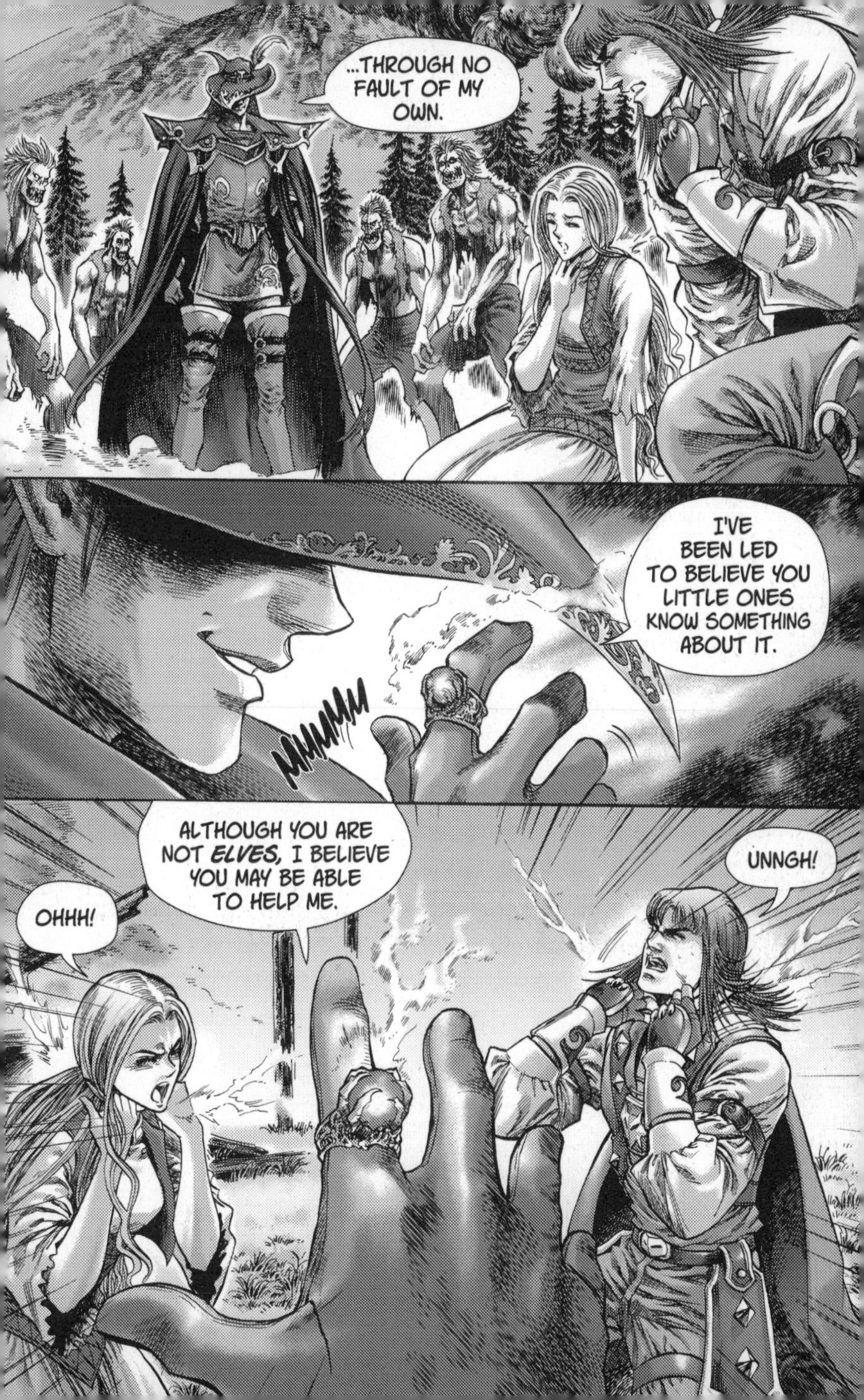
...THROUGH NO FAULT OF MY OWN.
I'VE BEEN LED TO BELIEVE YOU LITTLE ONES KNOW SOMETHING ABOUT IT.
MMMMM
OHHH!
ALTHOUGH YOU ARE NOT *ELVES,* I BELIEVE YOU MAY BE ABLE TO HELP ME.
UNNGH!

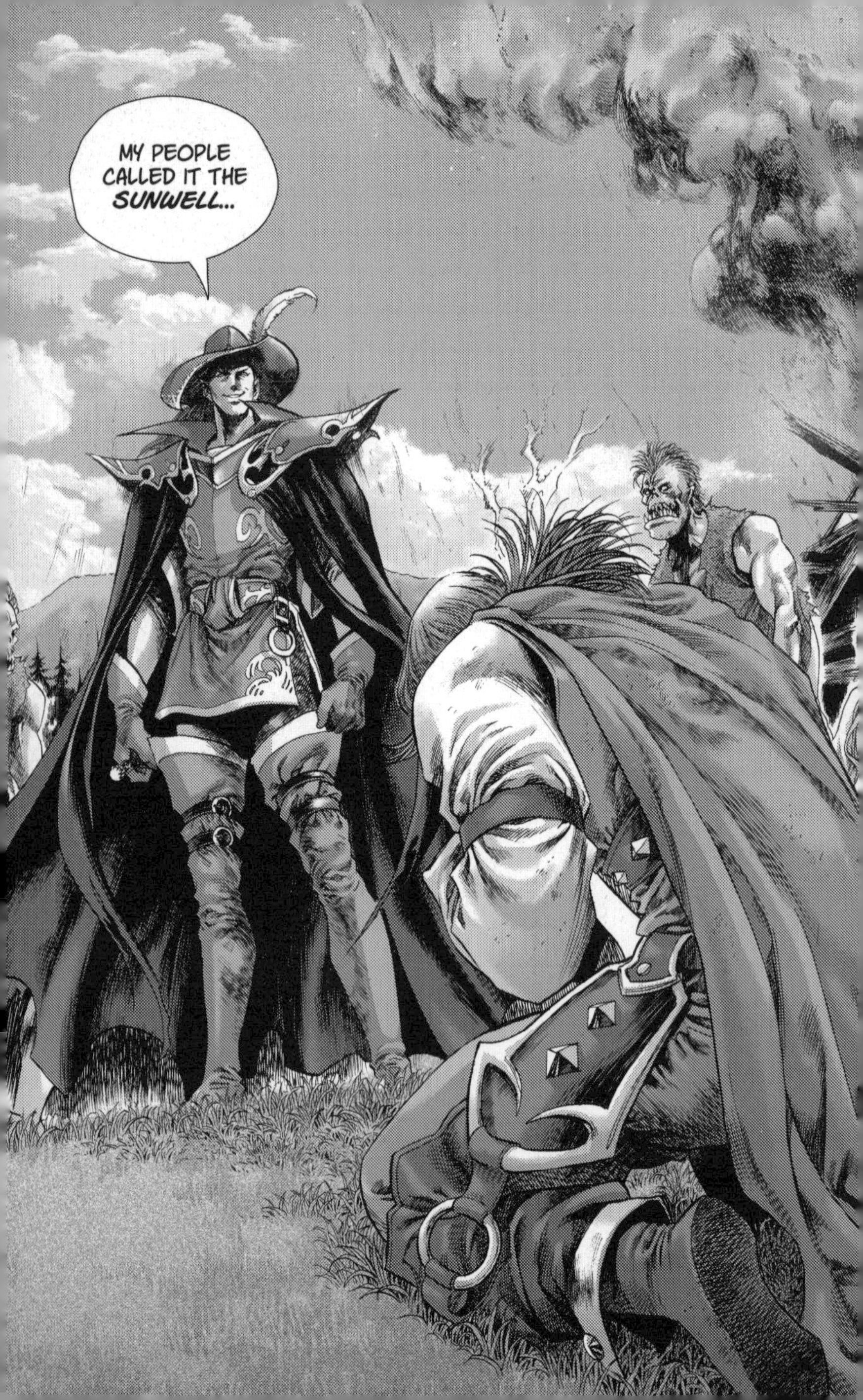
MY PEOPLE CALLED IT THE SUNWELL...

CHAPTER FOUR
LEGACY OF THE SUNWELL

IT WAS THE ESSENCE OF OUR LIVES...

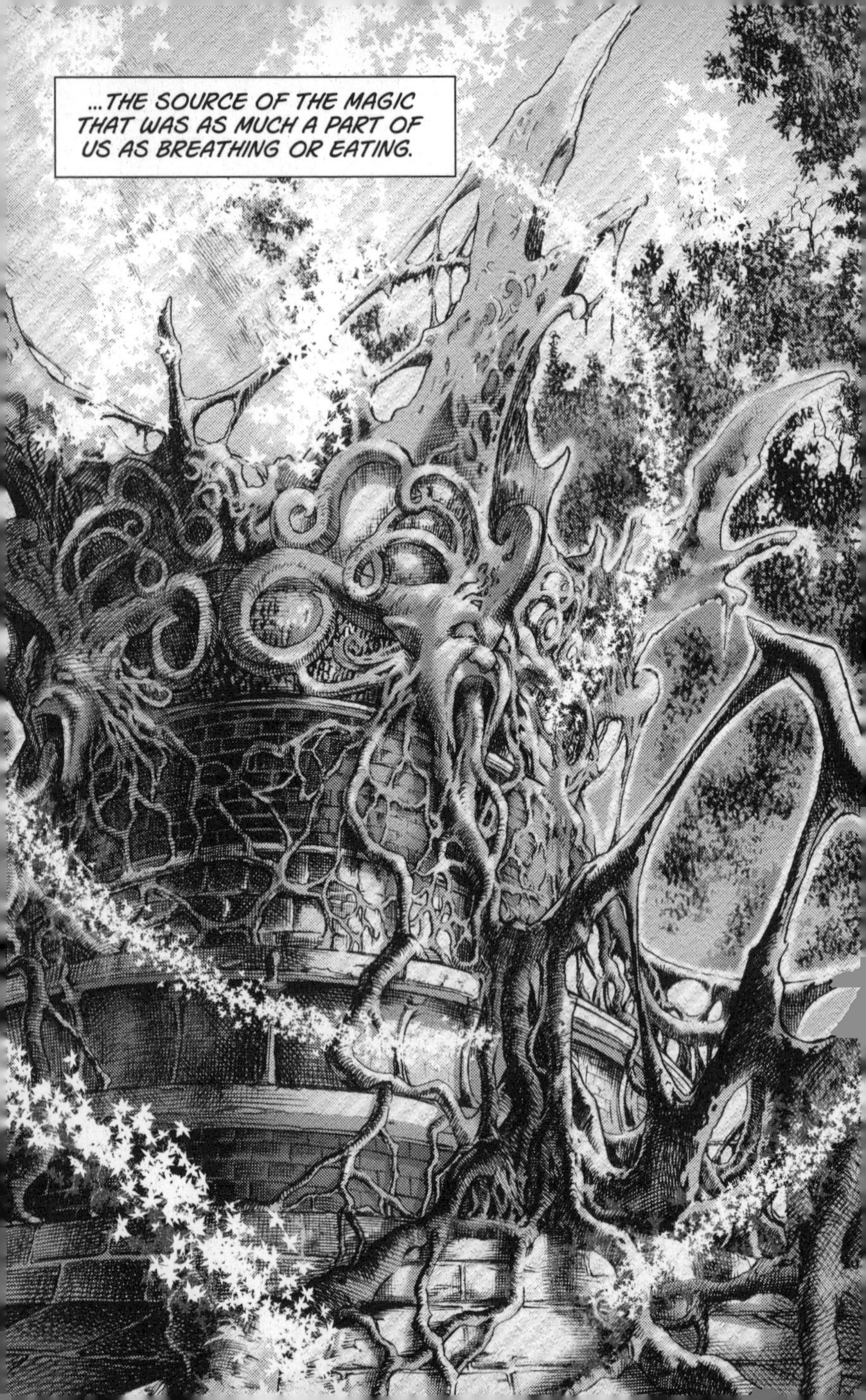
...THE SOURCE OF THE MAGIC THAT WAS AS MUCH A PART OF US AS BREATHING OR EATING.

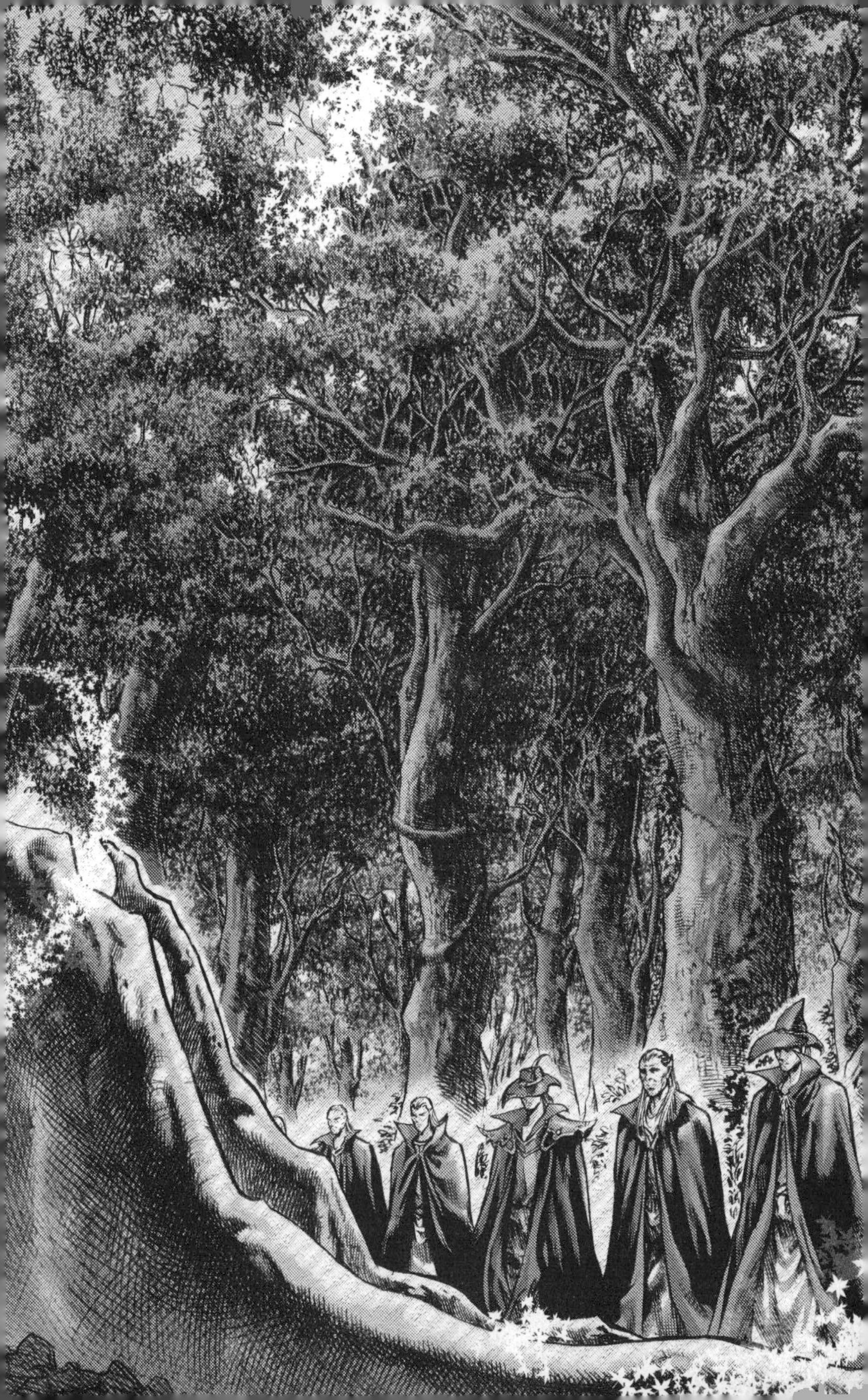

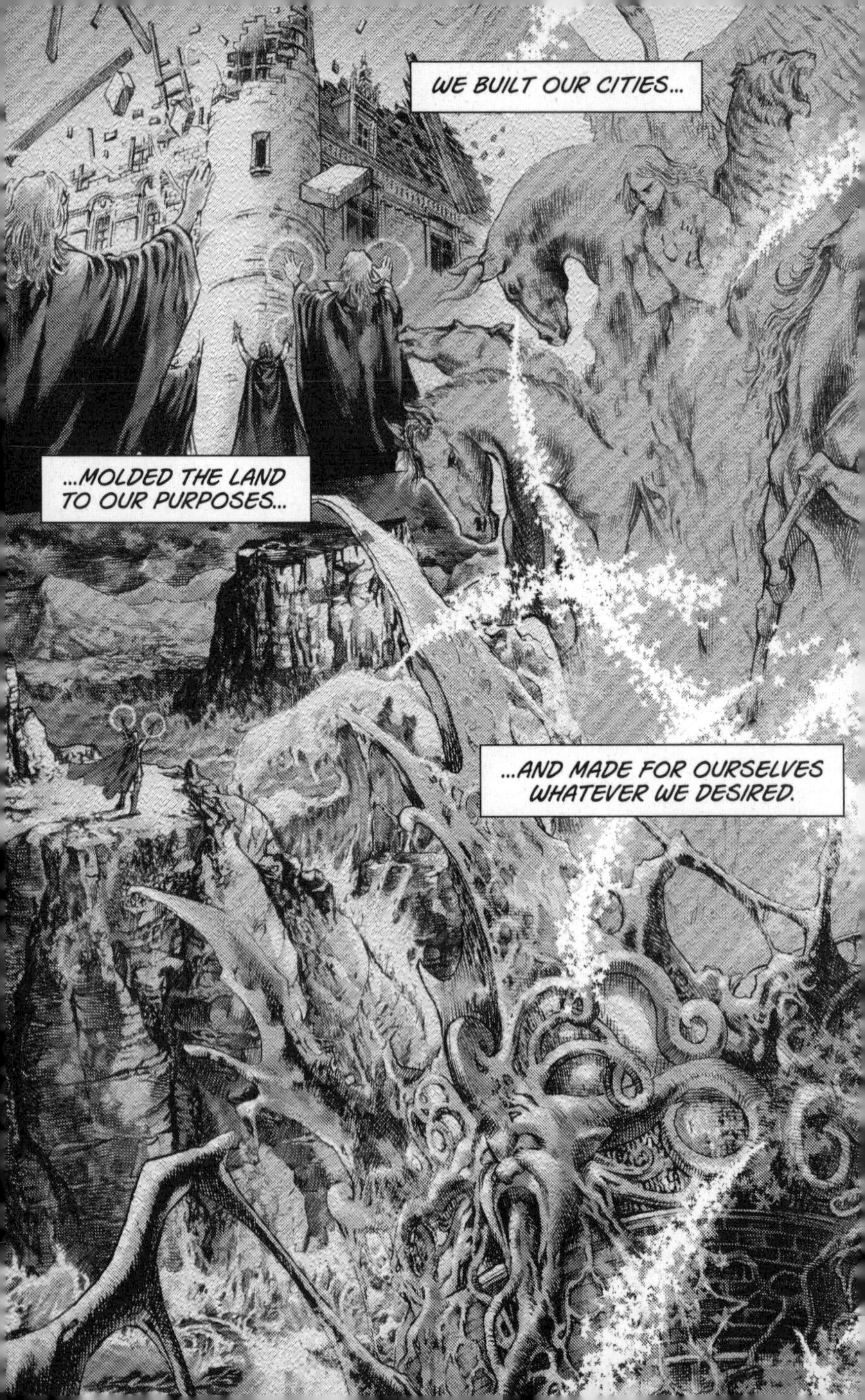
WE BUILT OUR CITIES...
...MOLDED THE LAND TO OUR PURPOSES...
...AND MADE FOR OURSELVES WHATEVER WE DESIRED.

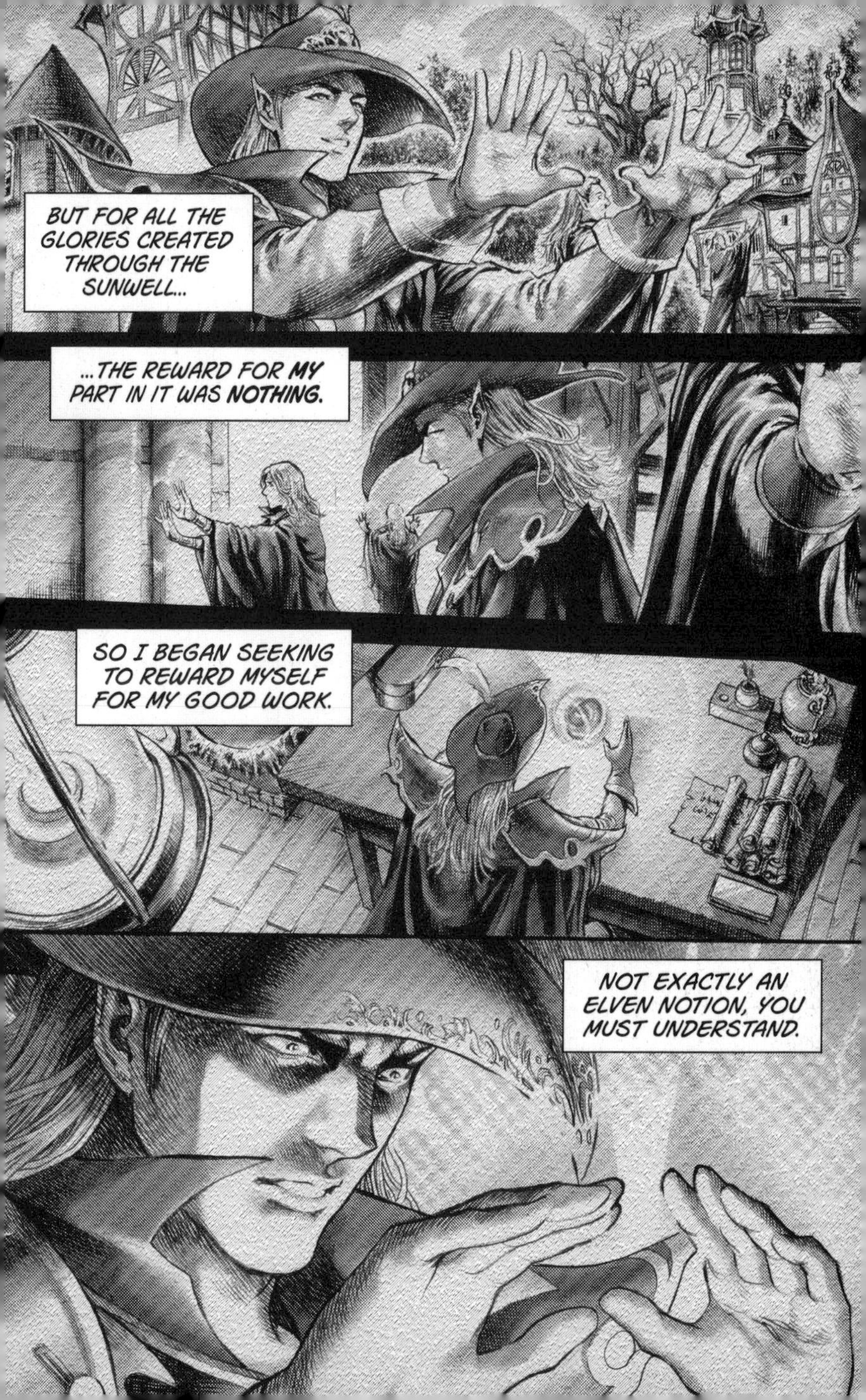
BUT FOR ALL THE GLORIES CREATED THROUGH THE SUNWELL...
...THE REWARD FOR **MY** PART IN IT WAS **NOTHING.**
SO I BEGAN SEEKING TO REWARD MYSELF FOR MY GOOD WORK.
NOT EXACTLY AN ELVEN NOTION, YOU MUST UNDERSTAND.

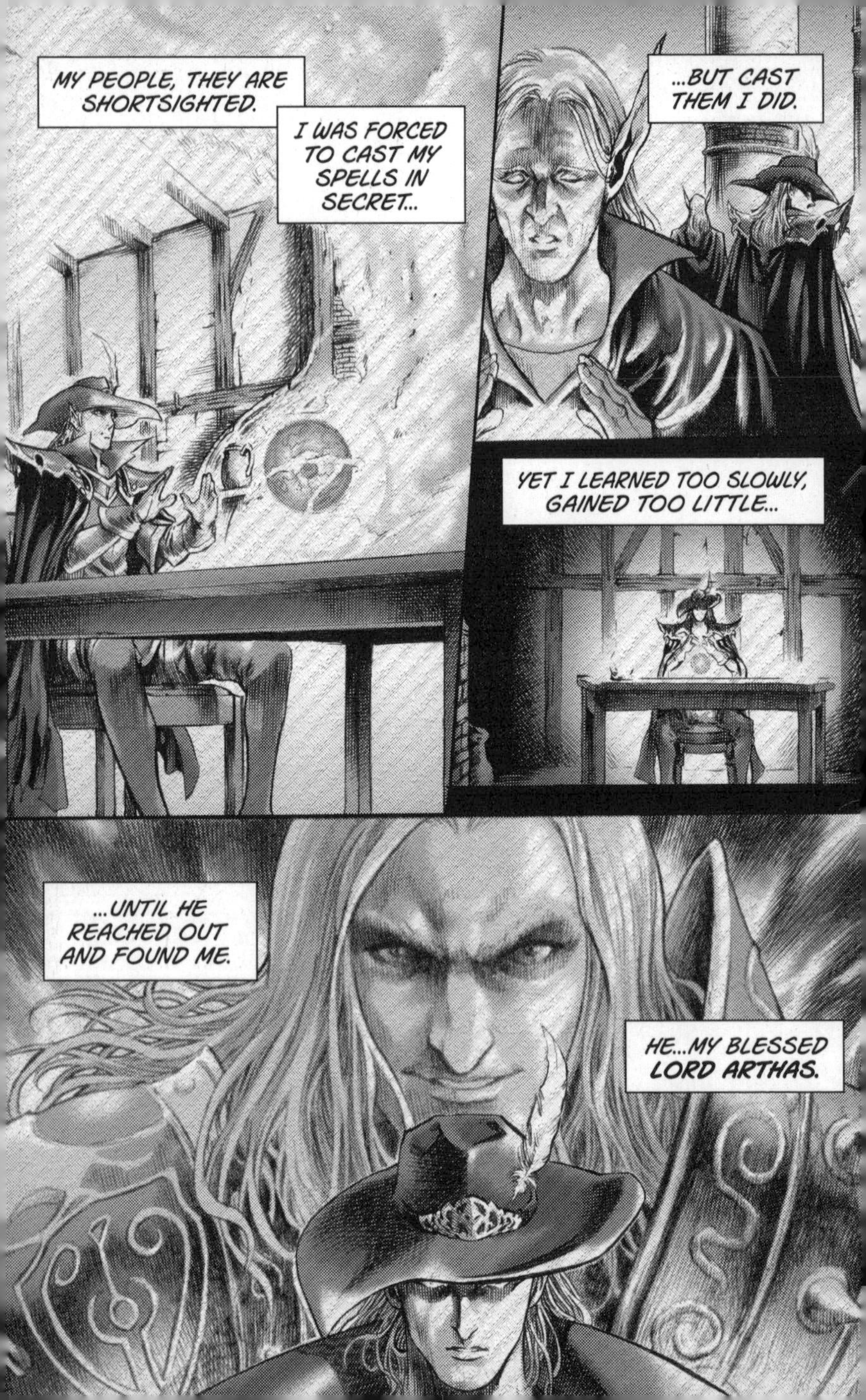
MY PEOPLE, THEY ARE SHORTSIGHTED.
I WAS FORCED TO CAST MY SPELLS IN SECRET...
...BUT CAST THEM I DID.
YET I LEARNED TOO SLOWLY, GAINED TOO LITTLE...
...UNTIL HE REACHED OUT AND FOUND ME.
HE...MY BLESSED LORD ARTHAS.

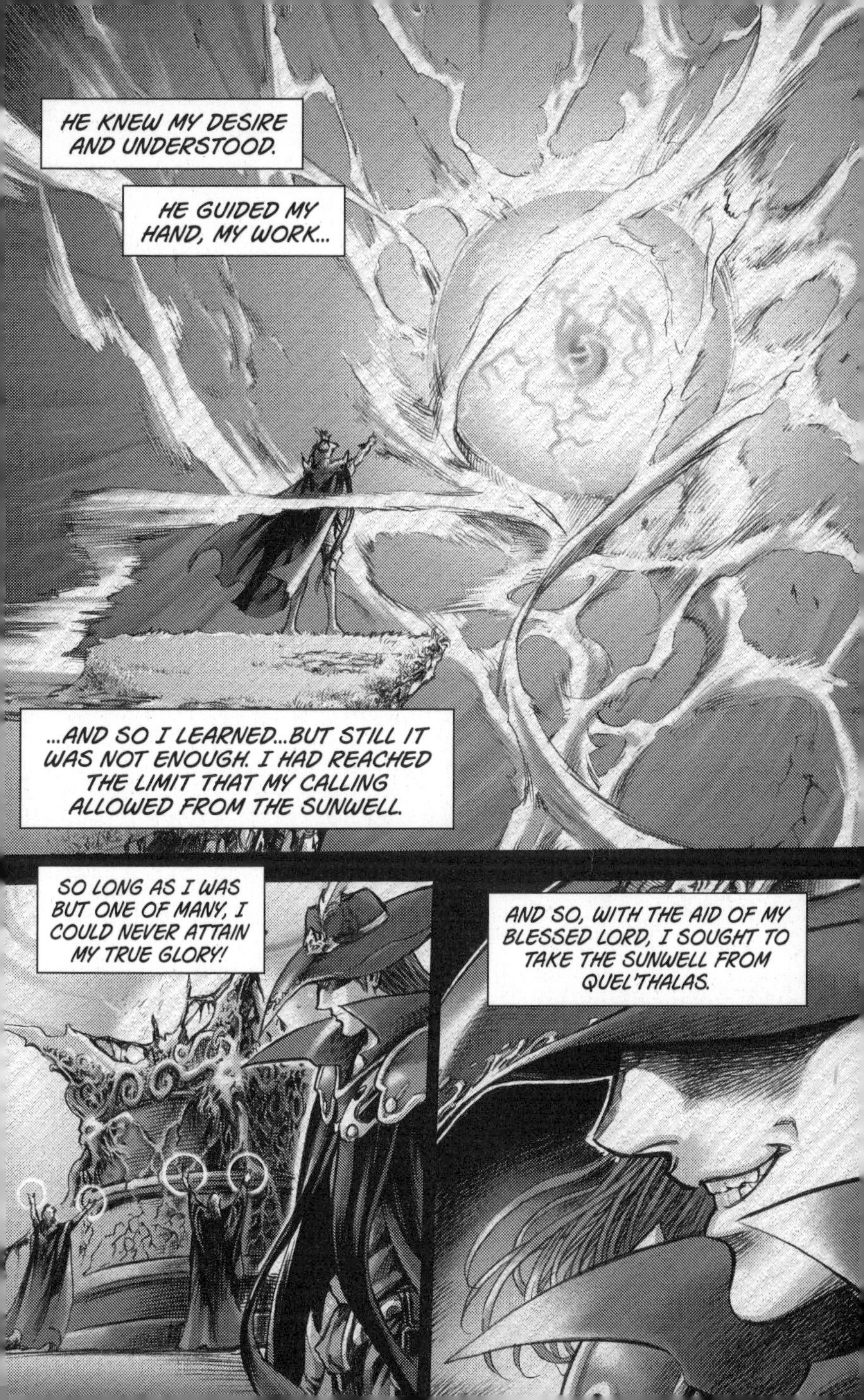
HE KNEW MY DESIRE AND UNDERSTOOD.
HE GUIDED MY HAND, MY WORK...
...AND SO I LEARNED...BUT STILL IT WAS NOT ENOUGH. I HAD REACHED THE LIMIT THAT MY CALLING ALLOWED FROM THE SUNWELL.
SO LONG AS I WAS BUT ONE OF MANY, I COULD NEVER ATTAIN MY TRUE GLORY!
AND SO, WITH THE AID OF MY BLESSED LORD, I SOUGHT TO TAKE THE SUNWELL FROM QUEL'THALAS.

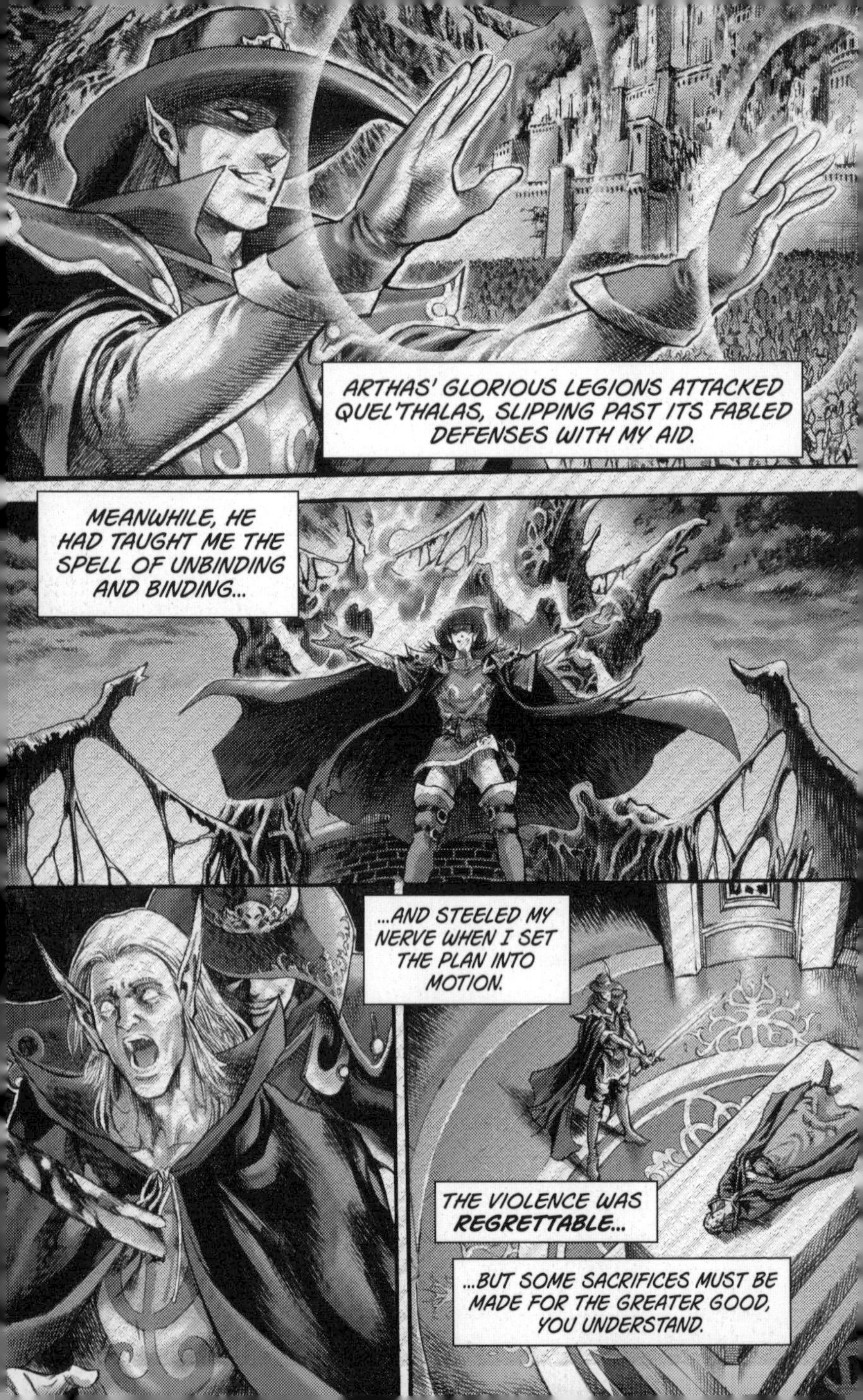
ARTHAS' GLORIOUS LEGIONS ATTACKED QUEL'THALAS, SLIPPING PAST ITS FABLED DEFENSES WITH MY AID.
MEANWHILE, HE HAD TAUGHT ME THE SPELL OF UNBINDING AND BINDING...
...AND STEELED MY NERVE WHEN I SET THE PLAN INTO MOTION.
THE VIOLENCE WAS **REGRETTABLE**...
...BUT SOME SACRIFICES MUST BE MADE FOR THE GREATER GOOD, YOU UNDERSTAND.

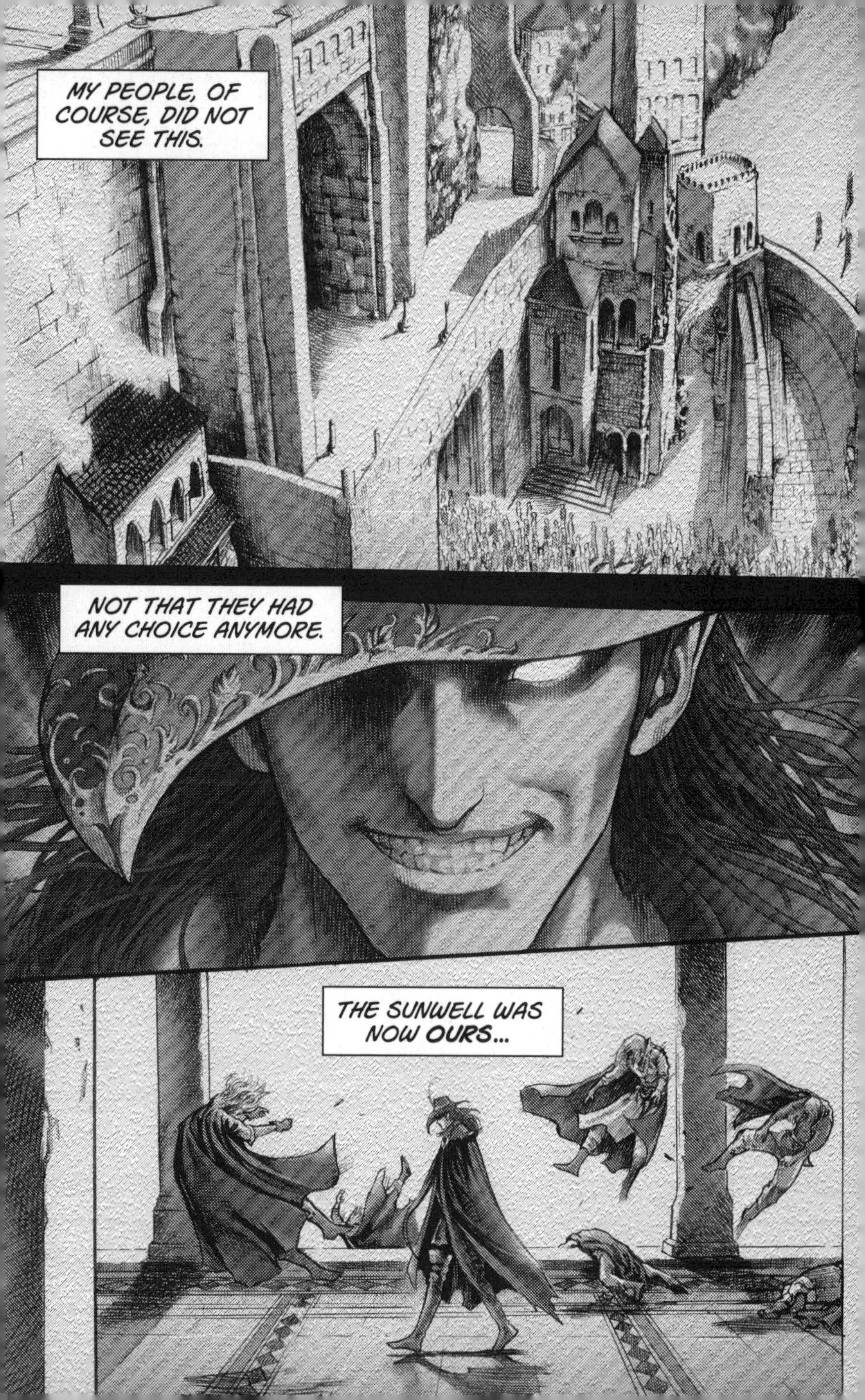
MY PEOPLE, OF COURSE, DID NOT SEE THIS.
NOT THAT THEY HAD ANY CHOICE ANYMORE.
THE SUNWELL WAS NOW OURS...

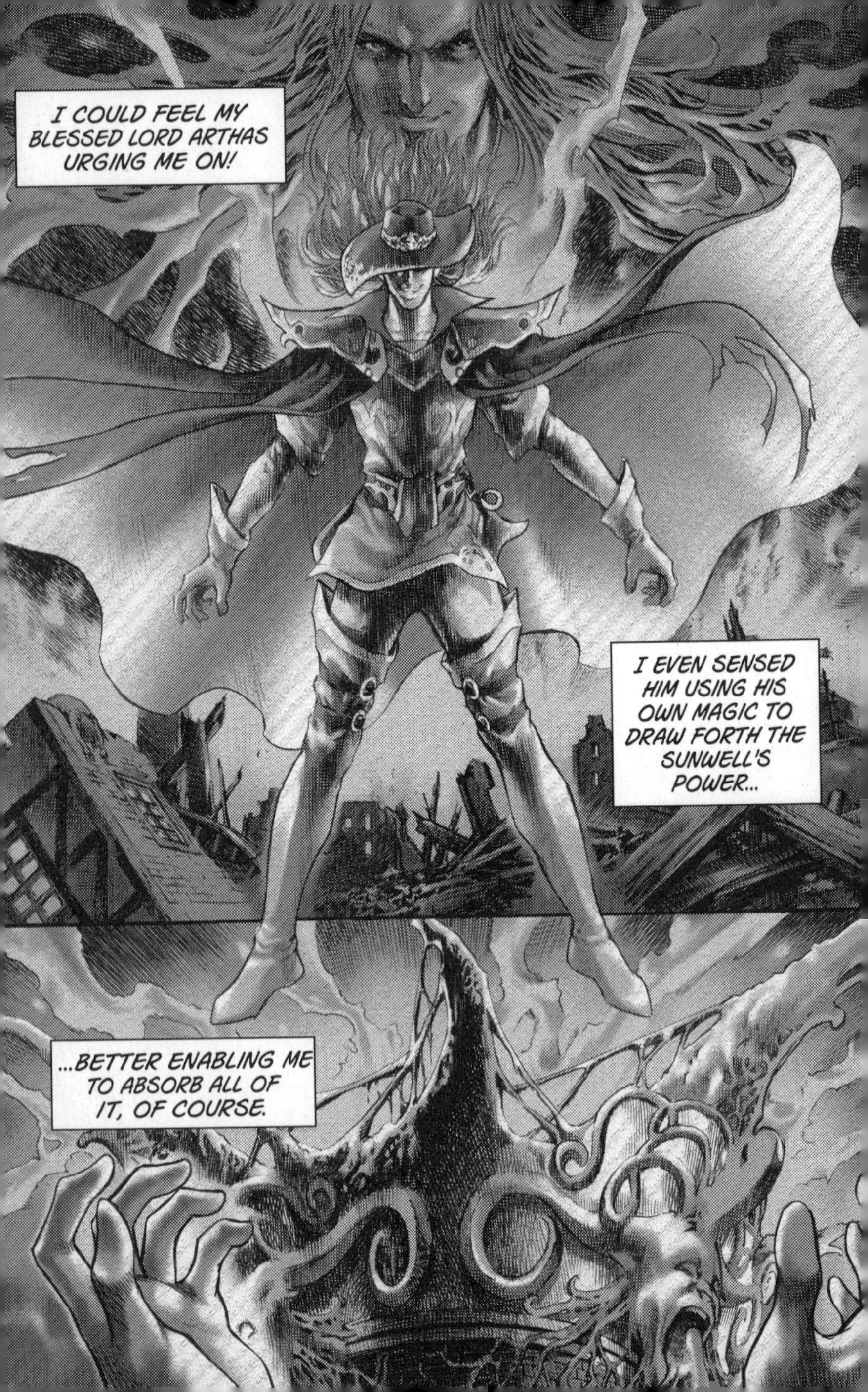
I COULD FEEL MY BLESSED LORD ARTHAS URGING ME ON!
I EVEN SENSED HIM USING HIS OWN MAGIC TO DRAW FORTH THE SUNWELL'S POWER...
...BETTER ENABLING ME TO ABSORB ALL OF IT, OF COURSE.

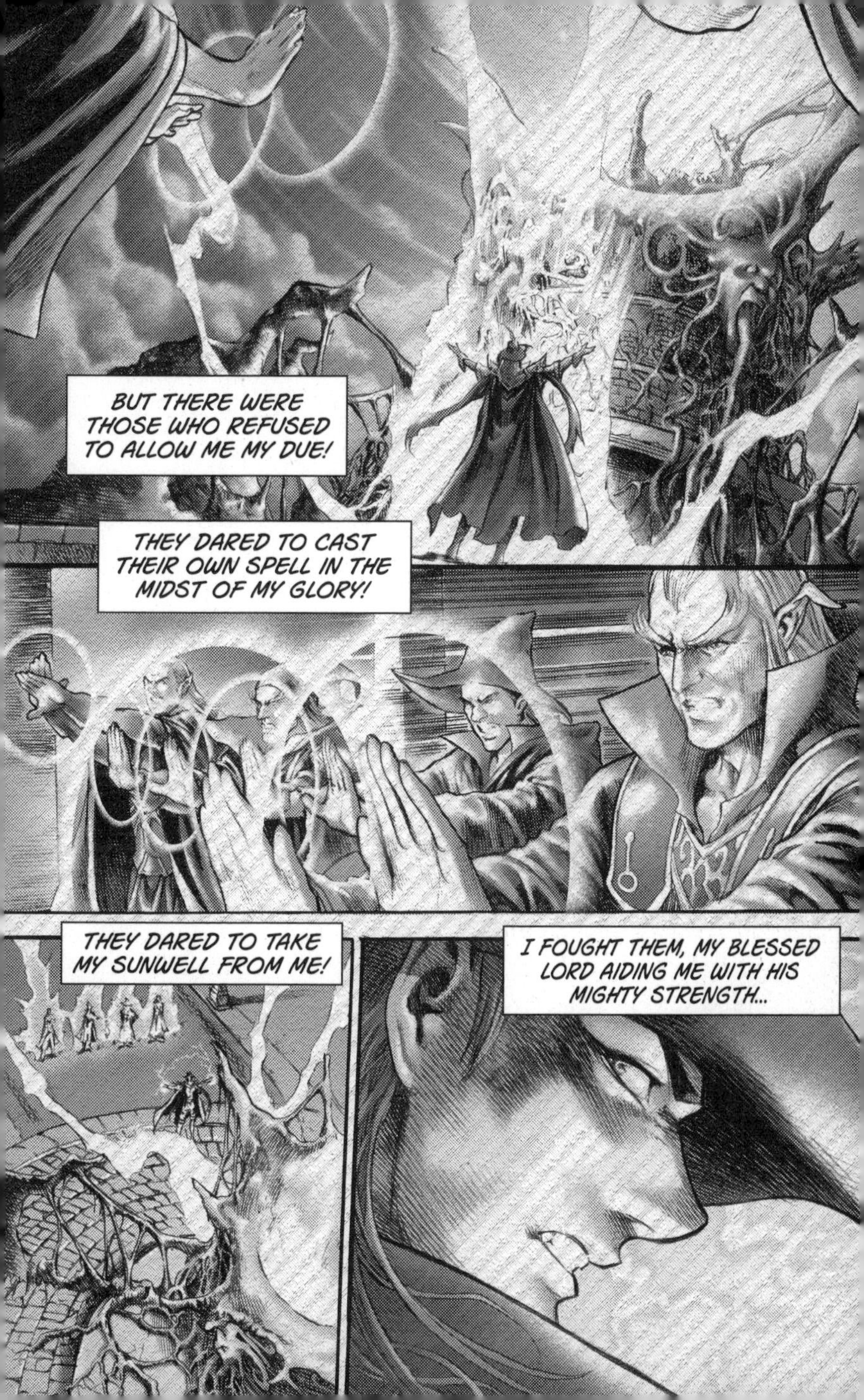
BUT THERE WERE THOSE WHO REFUSED TO ALLOW ME MY DUE!
THEY DARED TO CAST THEIR OWN SPELL IN THE MIDST OF MY GLORY!
THEY DARED TO TAKE MY SUNWELL FROM ME!
I FOUGHT THEM, MY BLESSED LORD AIDING ME WITH HIS MIGHTY STRENGTH...

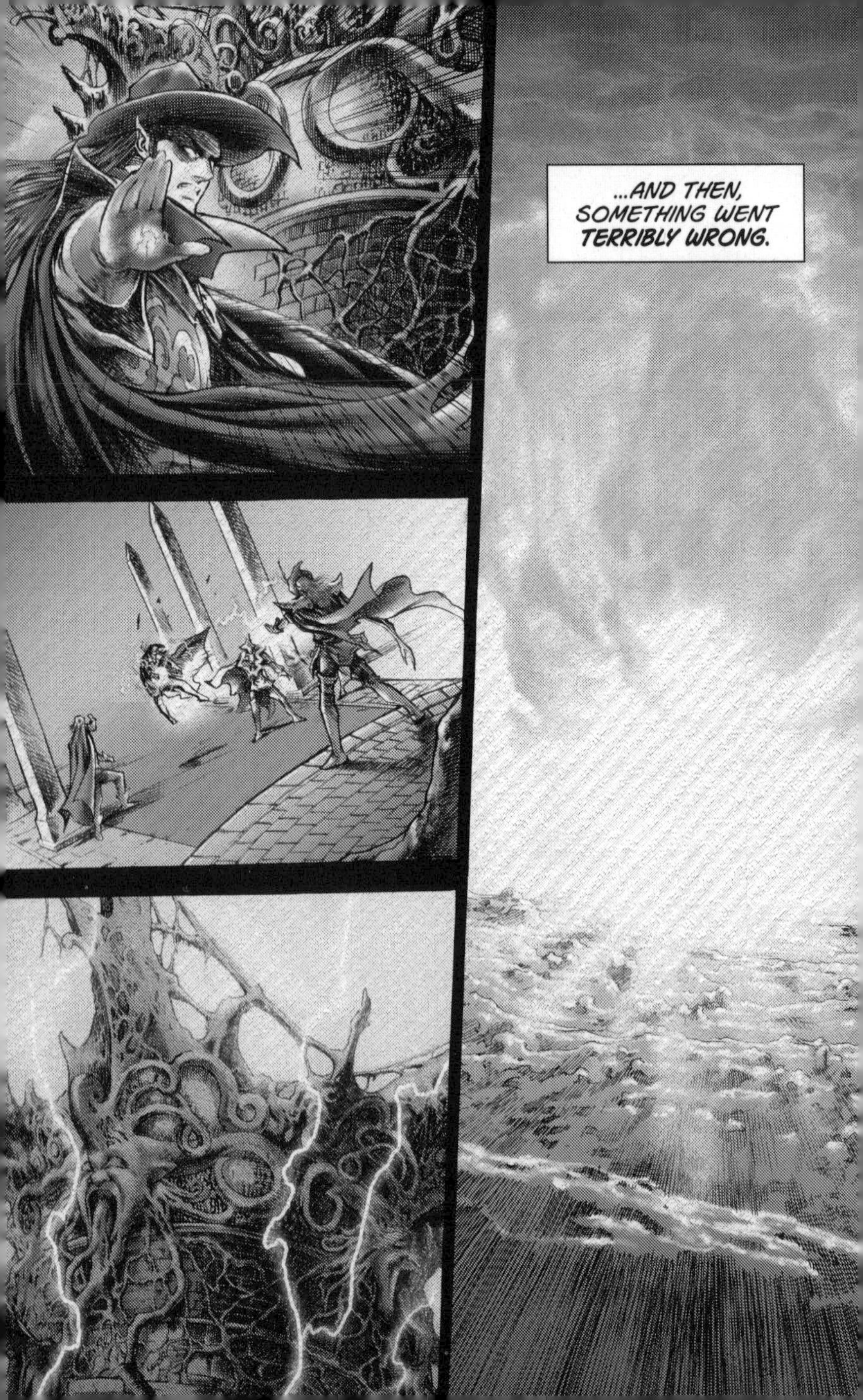
...AND THEN, SOMETHING WENT TERRIBLY WRONG.

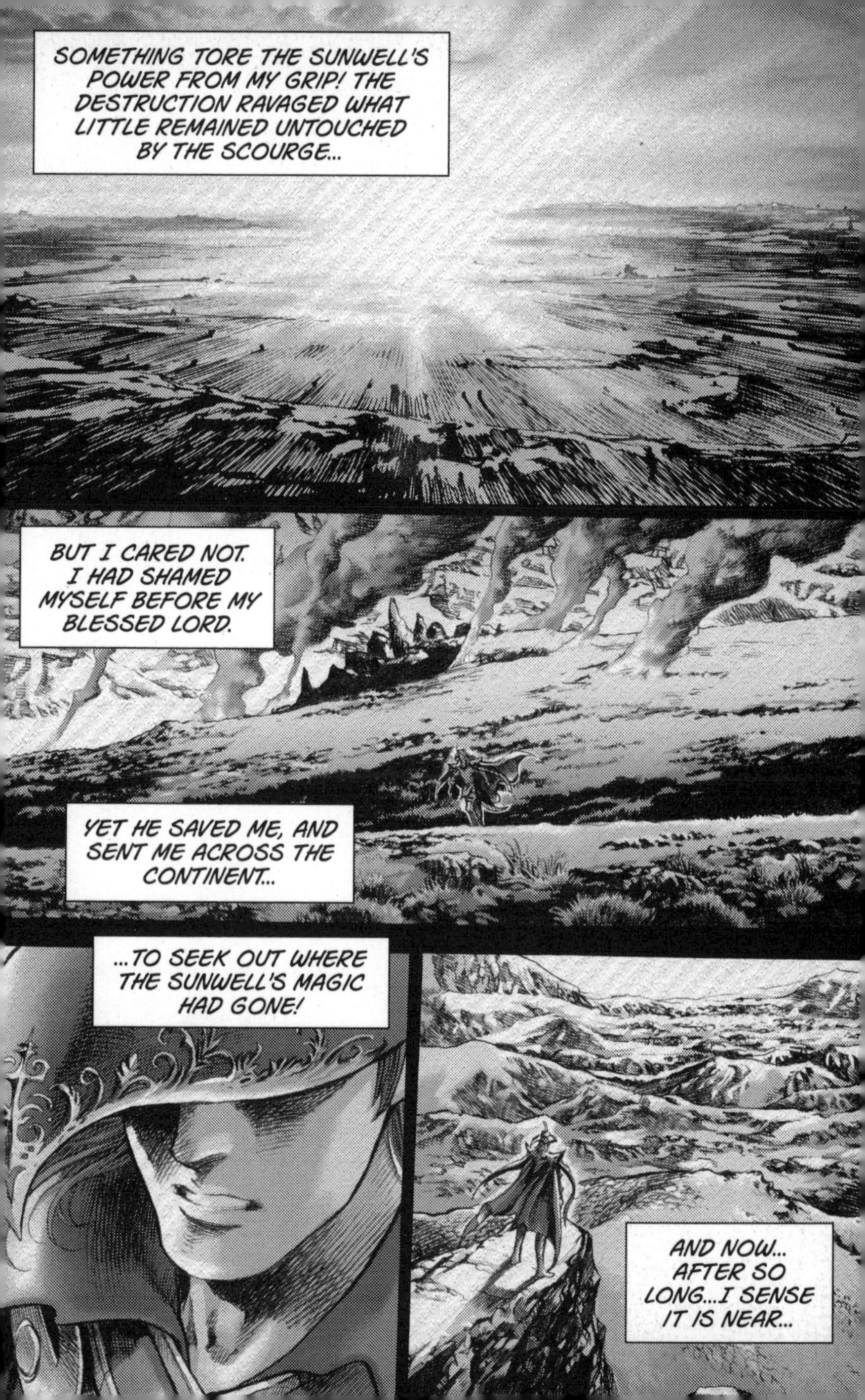
SOMETHING TORE THE SUNWELL'S POWER FROM MY GRIP! THE DESTRUCTION RAVAGED WHAT LITTLE REMAINED UNTOUCHED BY THE SCOURGE...
BUT I CARED NOT. I HAD SHAMED MYSELF BEFORE MY BLESSED LORD.
YET HE SAVED ME, AND SENT ME ACROSS THE CONTINENT...
...TO SEEK OUT WHERE THE SUNWELL'S MAGIC HAD GONE!
AND NOW... AFTER SO LONG...I SENSE IT IS NEAR...

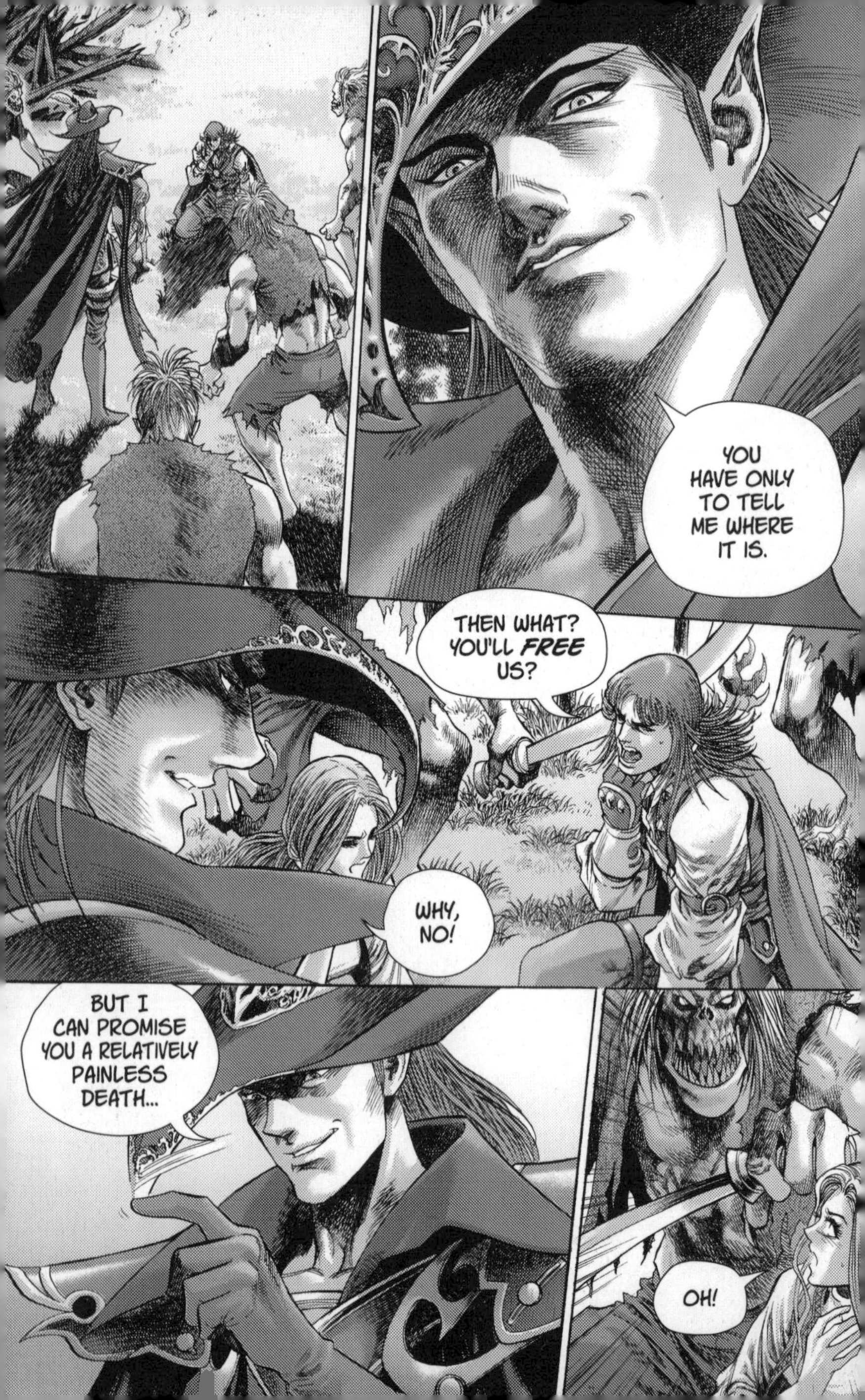
YOU HAVE ONLY TO TELL ME WHERE IT IS.
THEN WHAT? YOU'LL ***FREE*** US?
WHY, NO!
BUT I CAN PROMISE YOU A RELATIVELY PAINLESS DEATH...
OH!

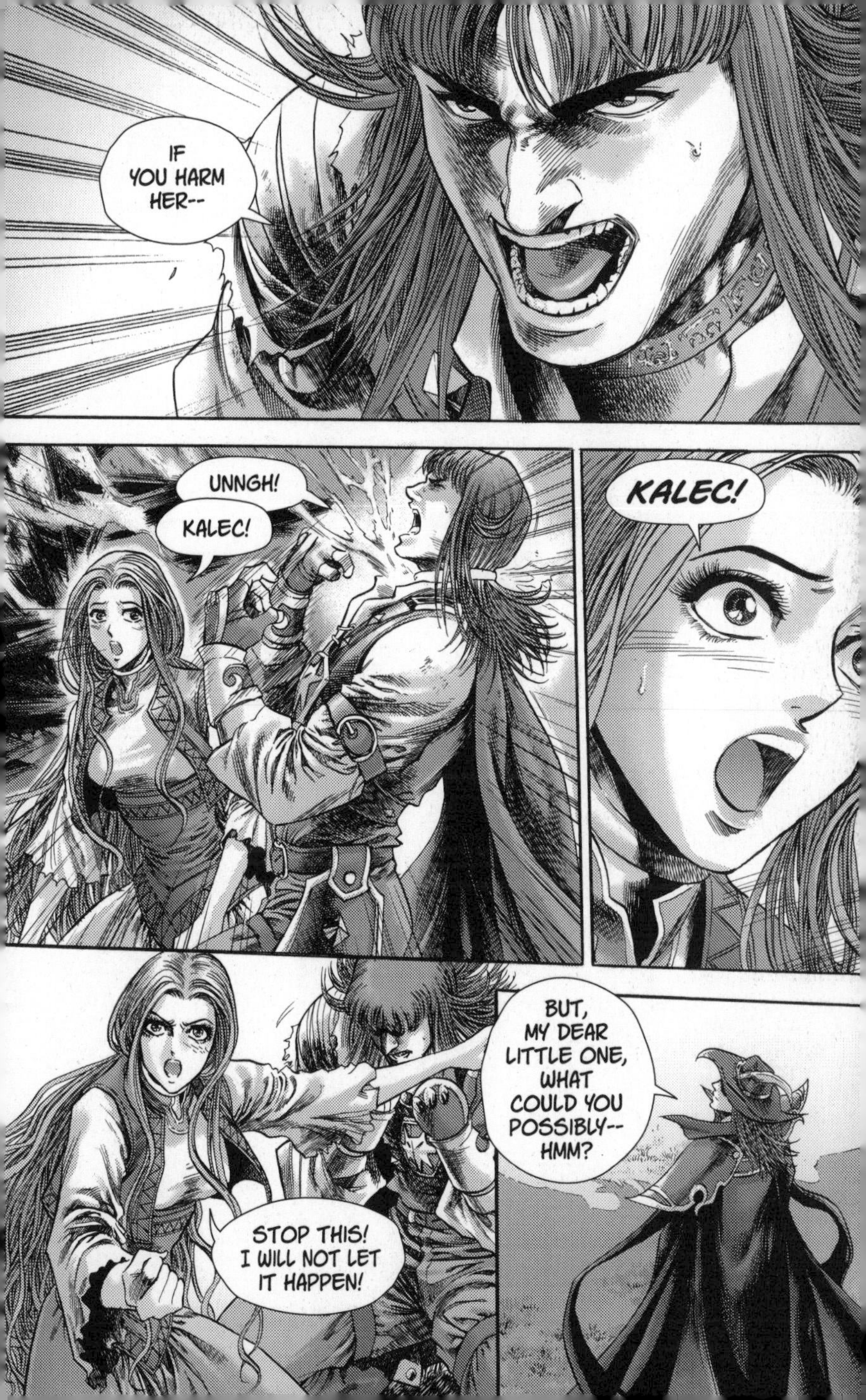
IF YOU HARM HER--
UNNGH!
KALEC!
KALEC!
STOP THIS! I WILL NOT LET IT HAPPEN!
BUT, MY DEAR LITTLE ONE, WHAT COULD YOU POSSIBLY-- HMM?

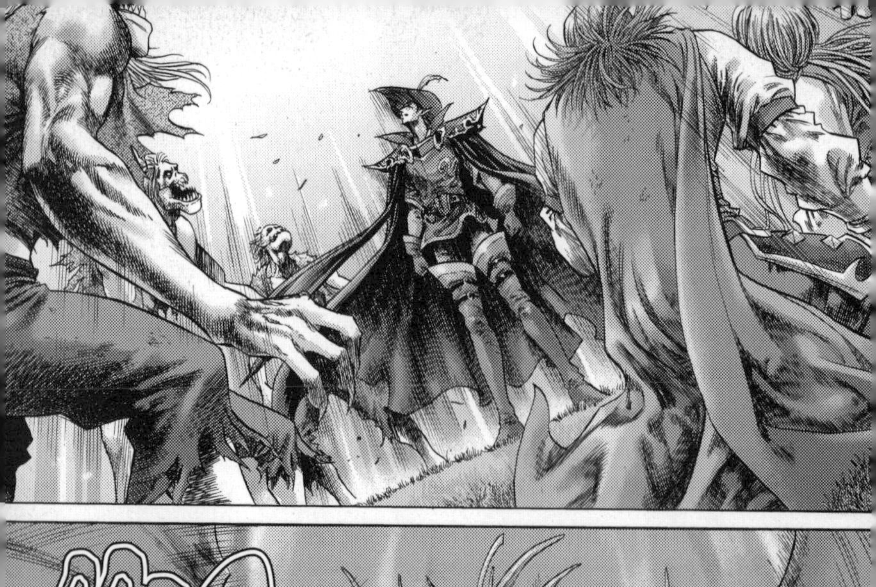

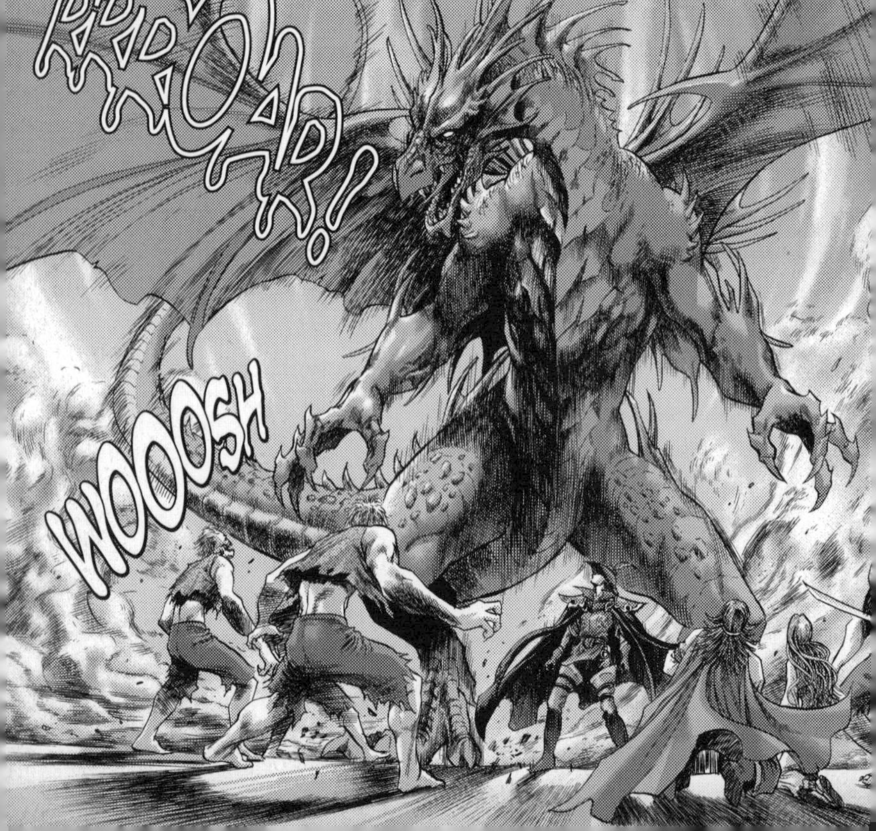
RRROAR!
WOOOSH

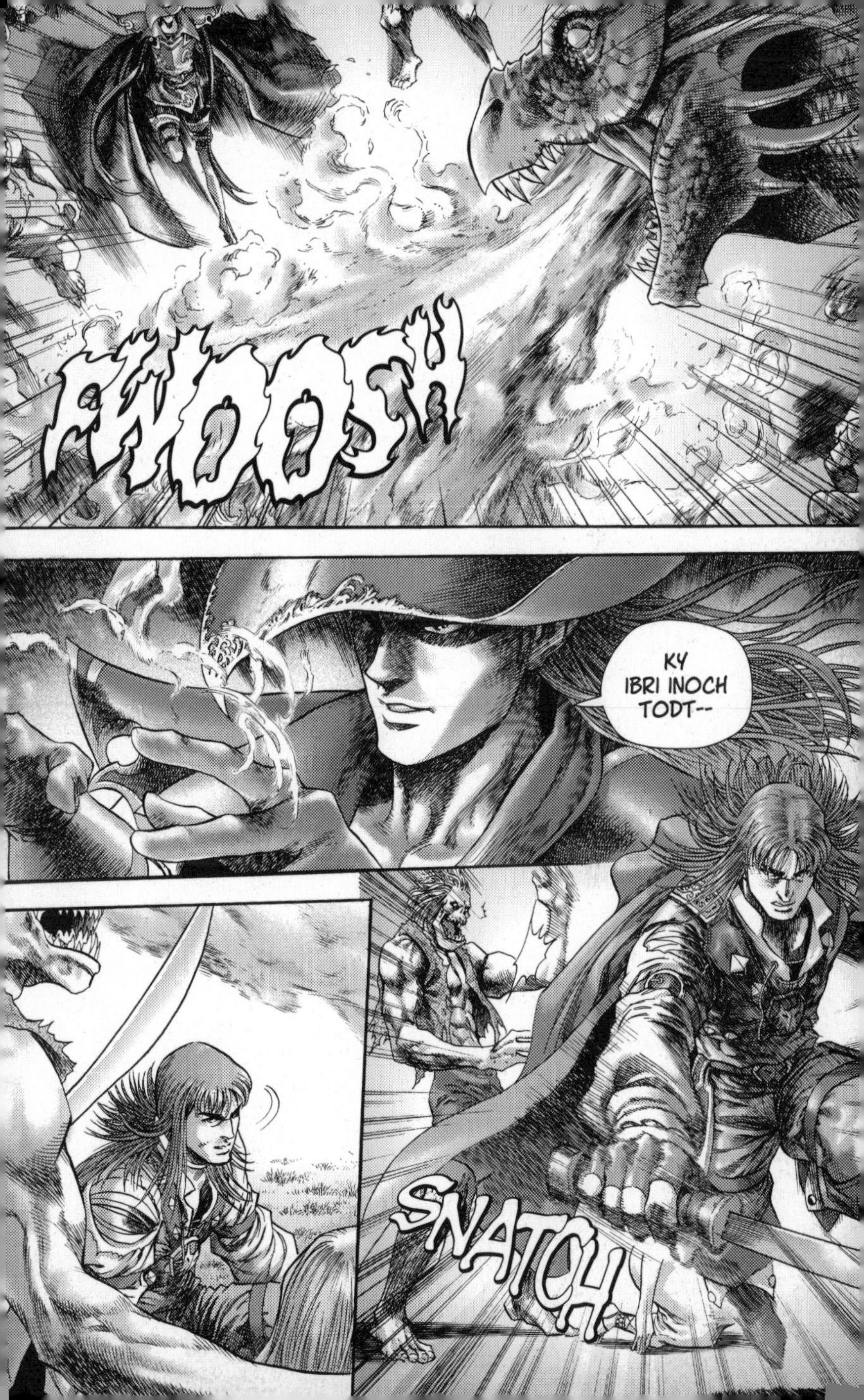
FWOOSH
KY IBRI INOCH TODT--
SNATCH

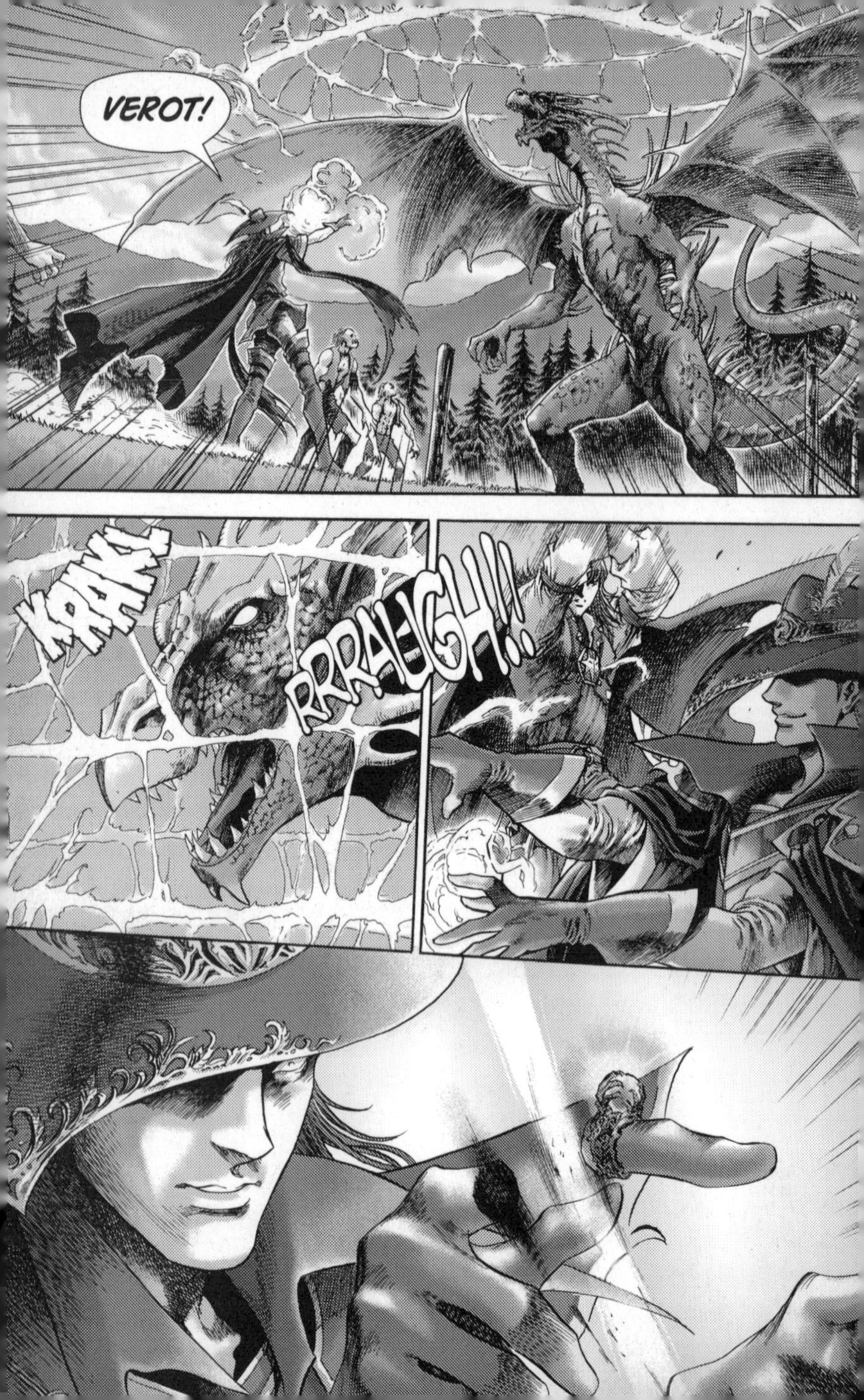
VEROT!
KRAK!
RRRAUGH!!!

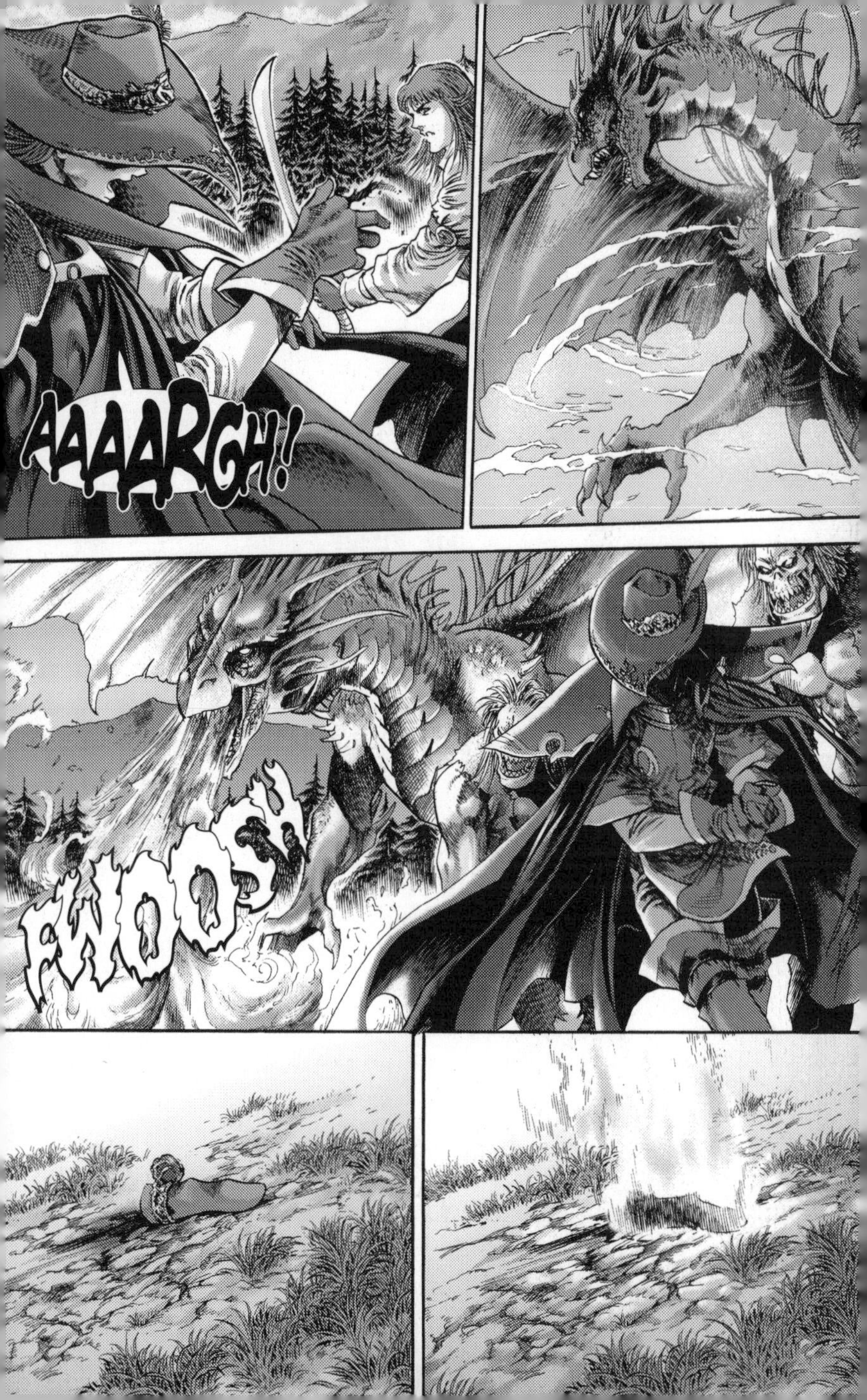
AAAARGH!
FWOOSH

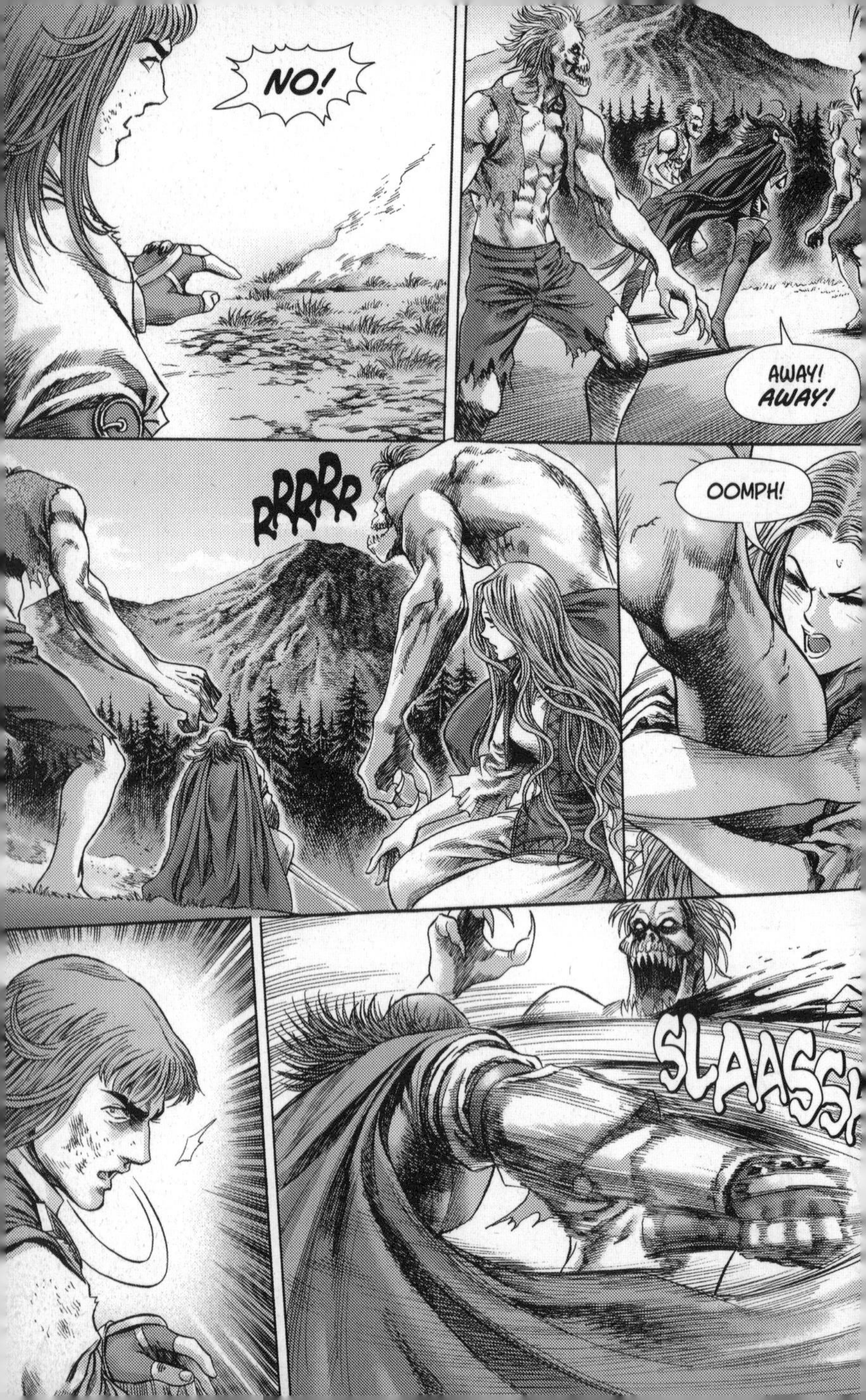
NO!
AWAY! AWAY!
RRRRR
OOMPH!
SLAASSH

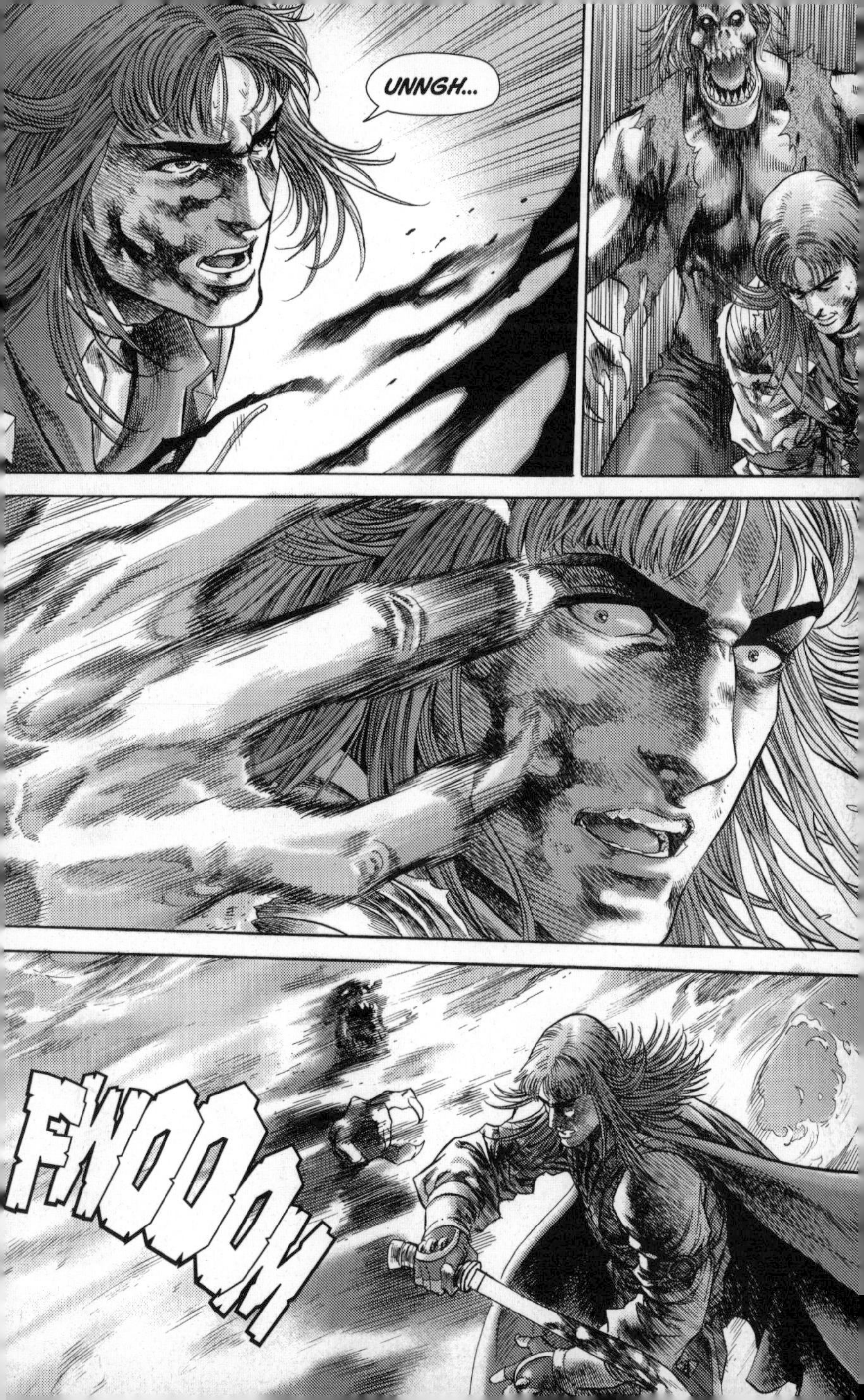
UNNGH...
FWOOOM

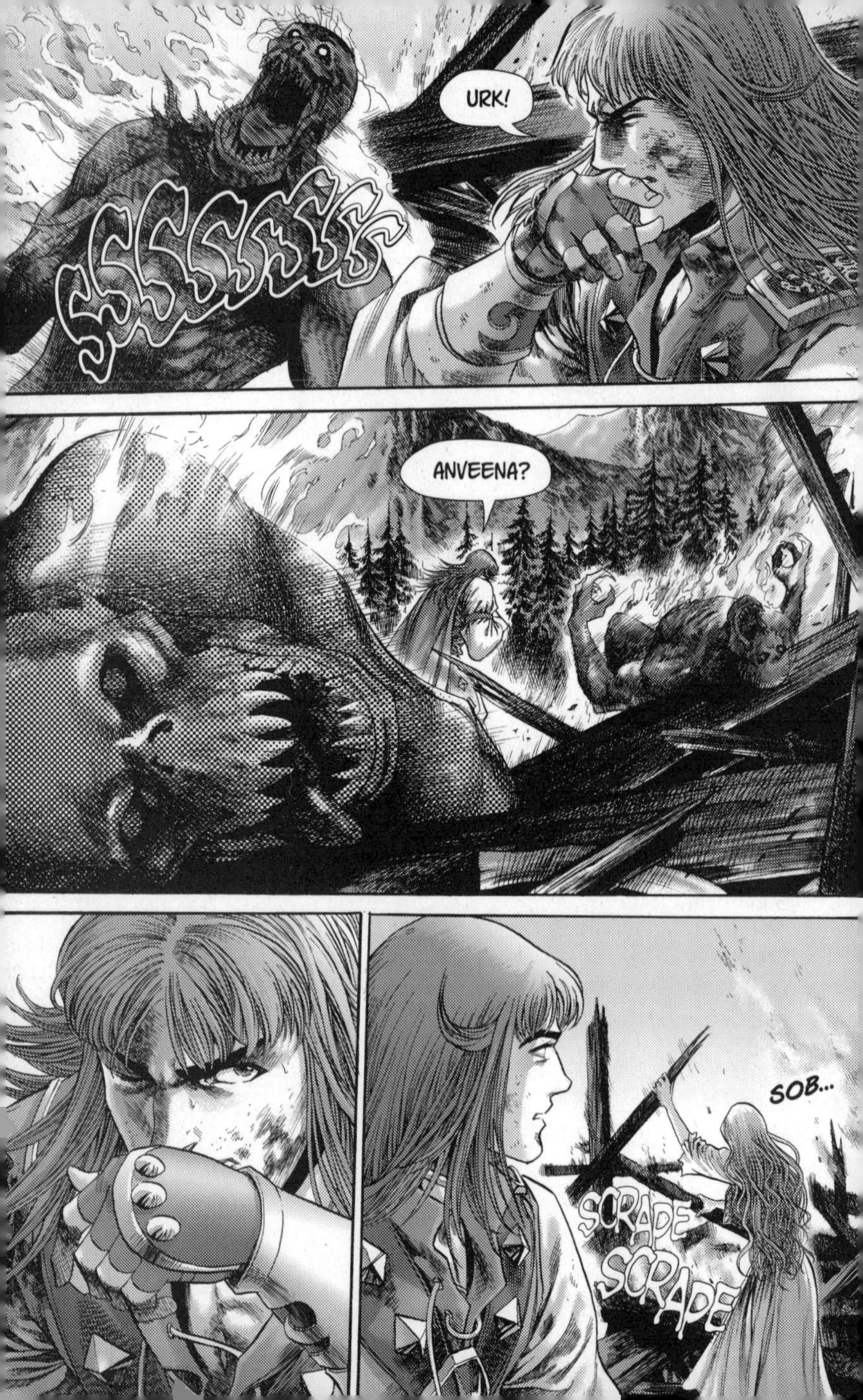
URK!
ANVEENA?
SOB...
SCRAPE
SCRAPE

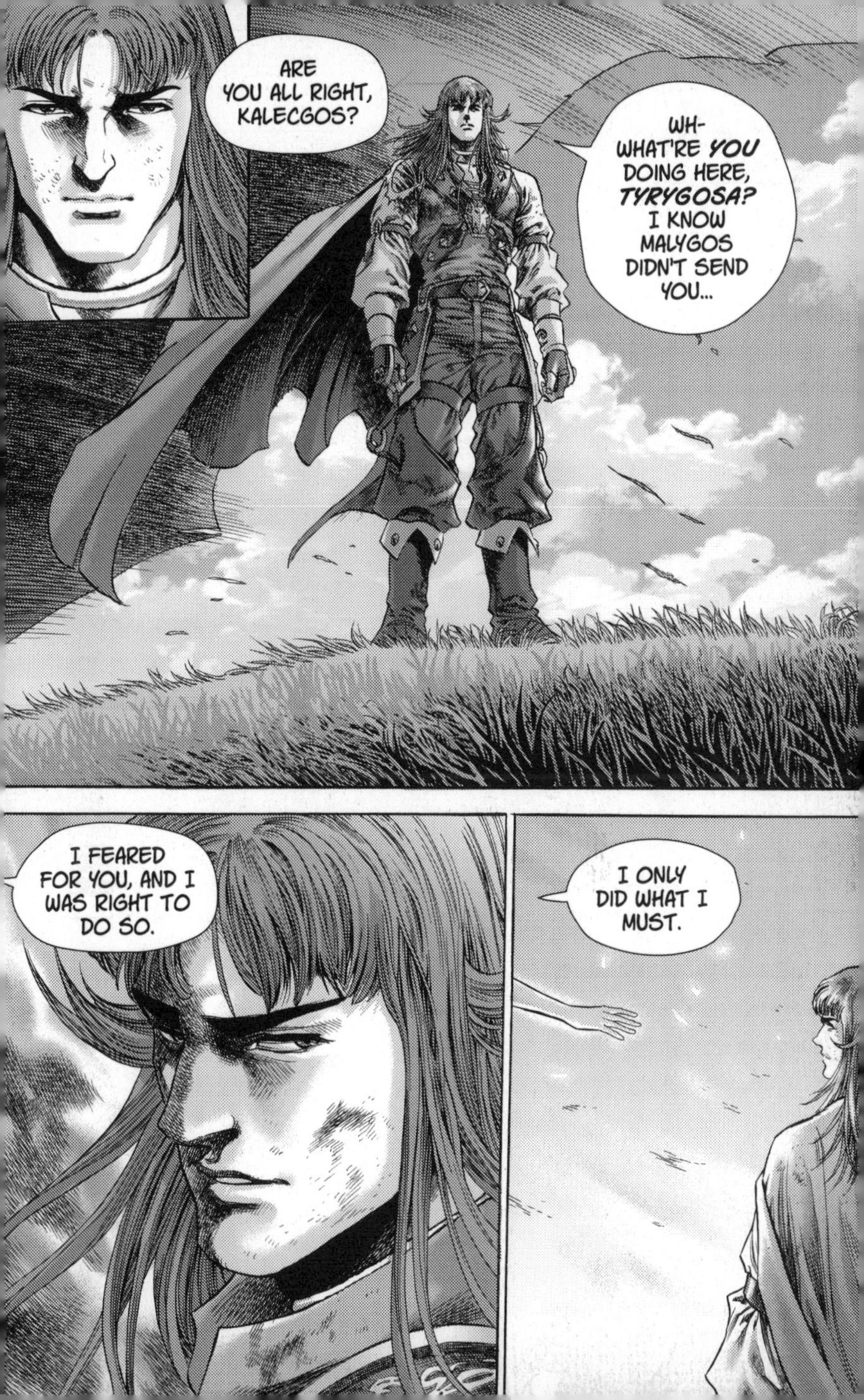
ARE YOU ALL RIGHT, KALECGOS?
WH- WHAT'RE *YOU* DOING HERE, *TYRYGOSA?* I KNOW MALYGOS DIDN'T SEND YOU...
I FEARED FOR YOU, AND I WAS RIGHT TO DO SO.
I ONLY DID WHAT I MUST.

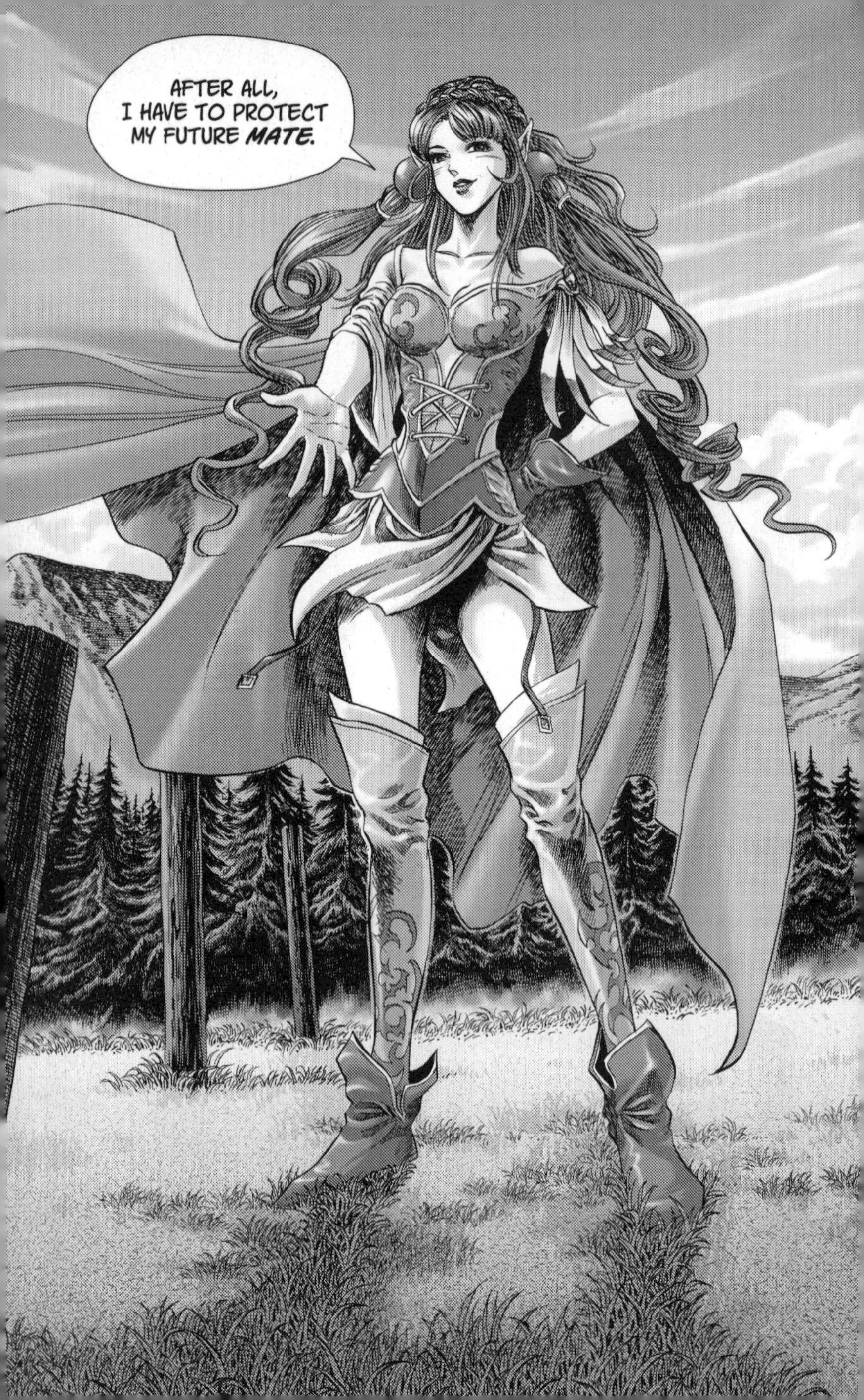
AFTER ALL, I HAVE TO PROTECT MY FUTURE ***MATE***.

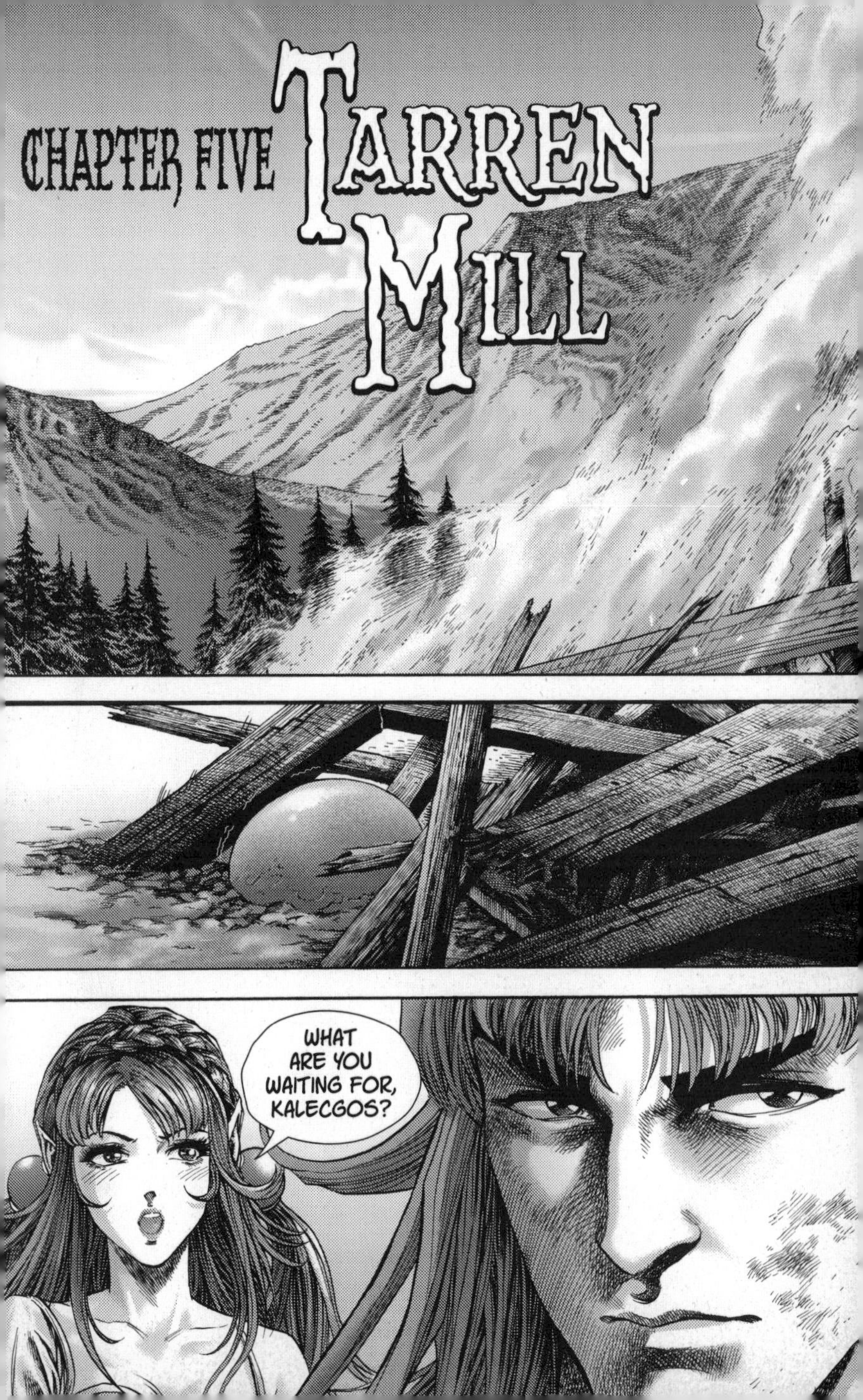
CHAPTER FIVE
TARREN MILL
WHAT ARE YOU WAITING FOR, KALECGOS?

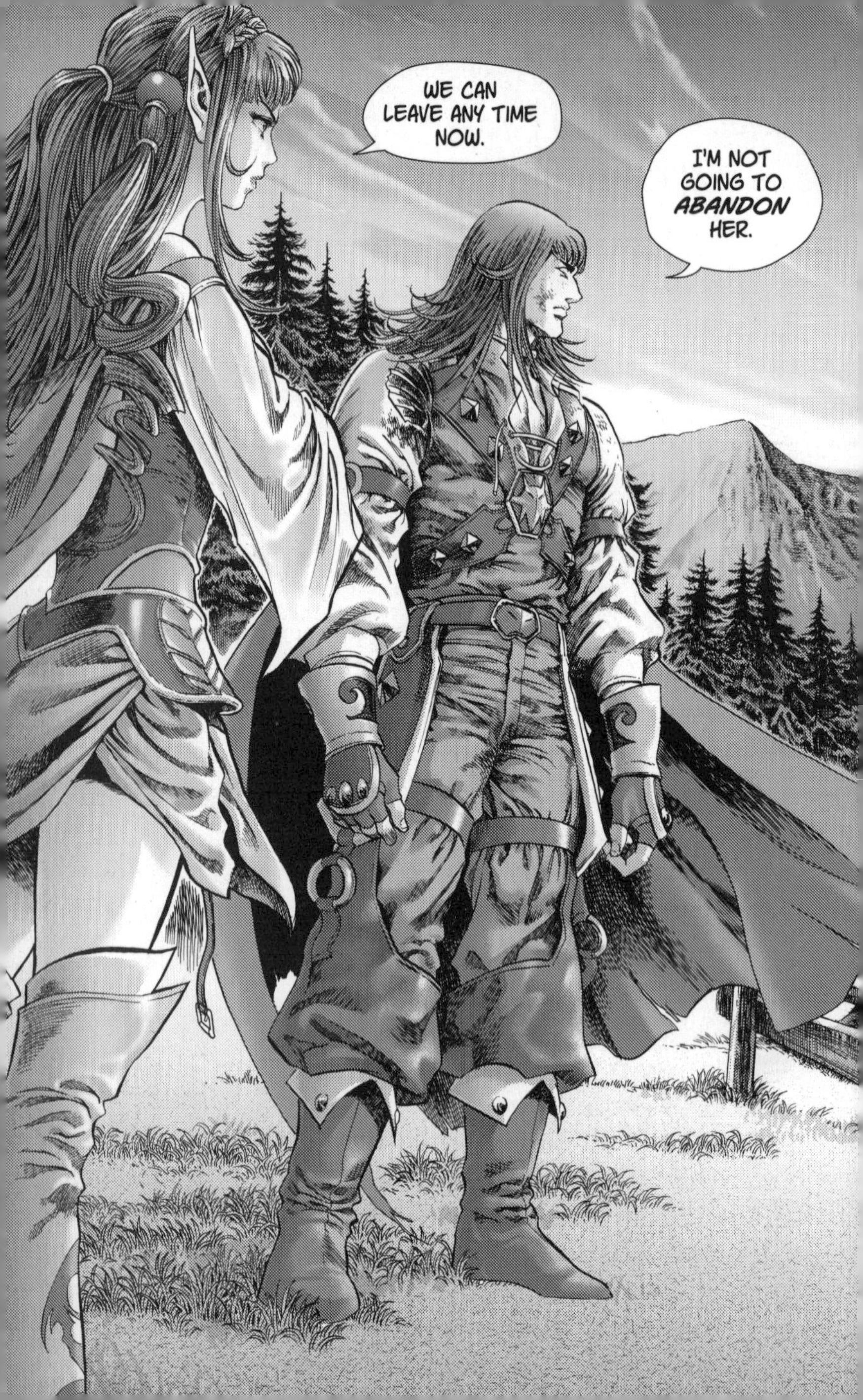
WE CAN LEAVE ANY TIME NOW.
I'M NOT GOING TO *ABANDON* HER.

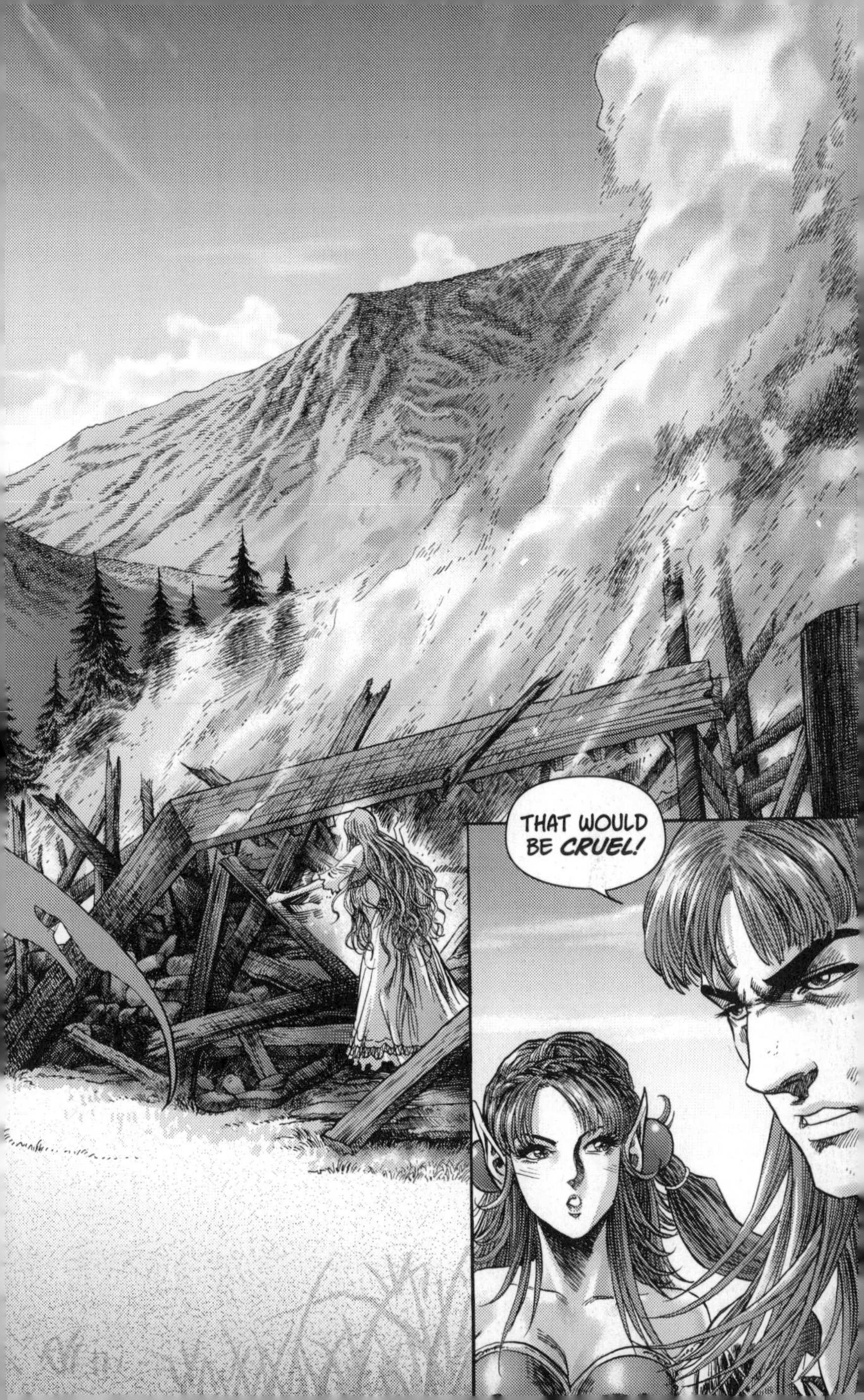
THAT WOULD BE CRUEL!

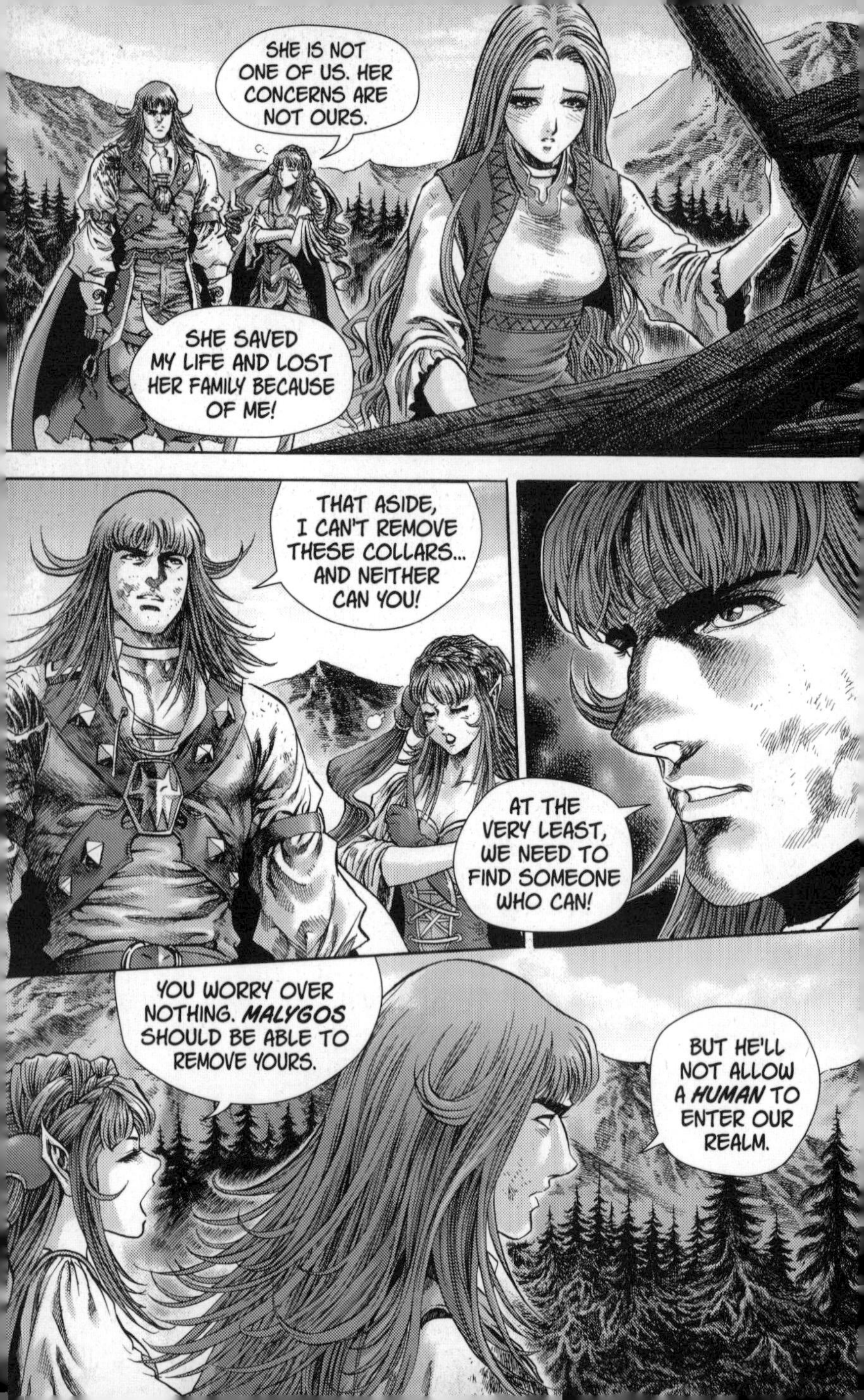
SHE IS NOT ONE OF US. HER CONCERNS ARE NOT OURS.
SHE SAVED MY LIFE AND LOST HER FAMILY BECAUSE OF ME!
THAT ASIDE, I CAN'T REMOVE THESE COLLARS... AND NEITHER CAN YOU!
AT THE VERY LEAST, WE NEED TO FIND SOMEONE WHO CAN!
YOU WORRY OVER NOTHING. *MALYGOS* SHOULD BE ABLE TO REMOVE YOURS.
BUT HE'LL NOT ALLOW A *HUMAN* TO ENTER OUR REALM.

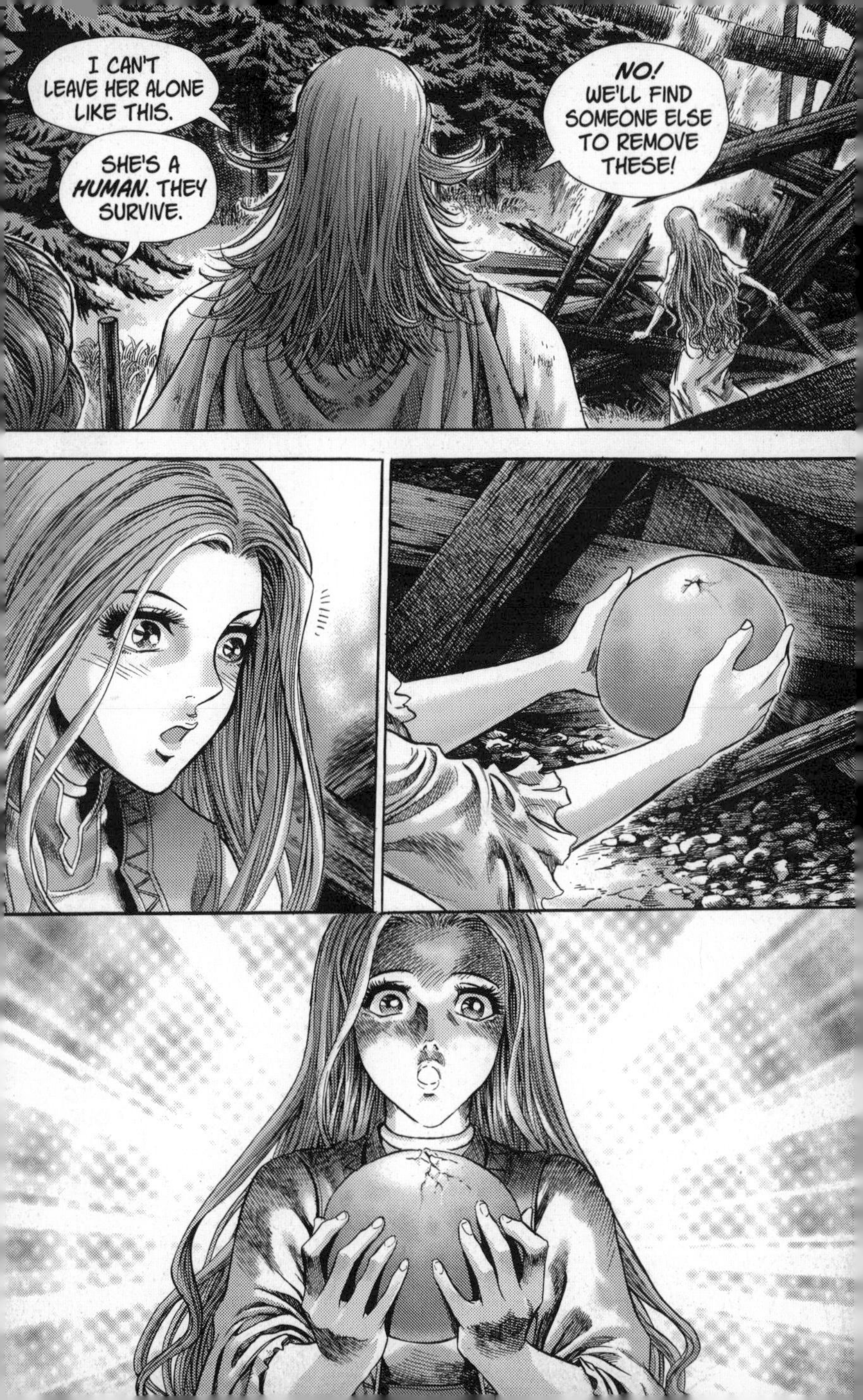
I CAN'T LEAVE HER ALONE LIKE THIS.
SHE'S A *HUMAN*. THEY SURVIVE.
NO! WE'LL FIND SOMEONE ELSE TO REMOVE THESE!

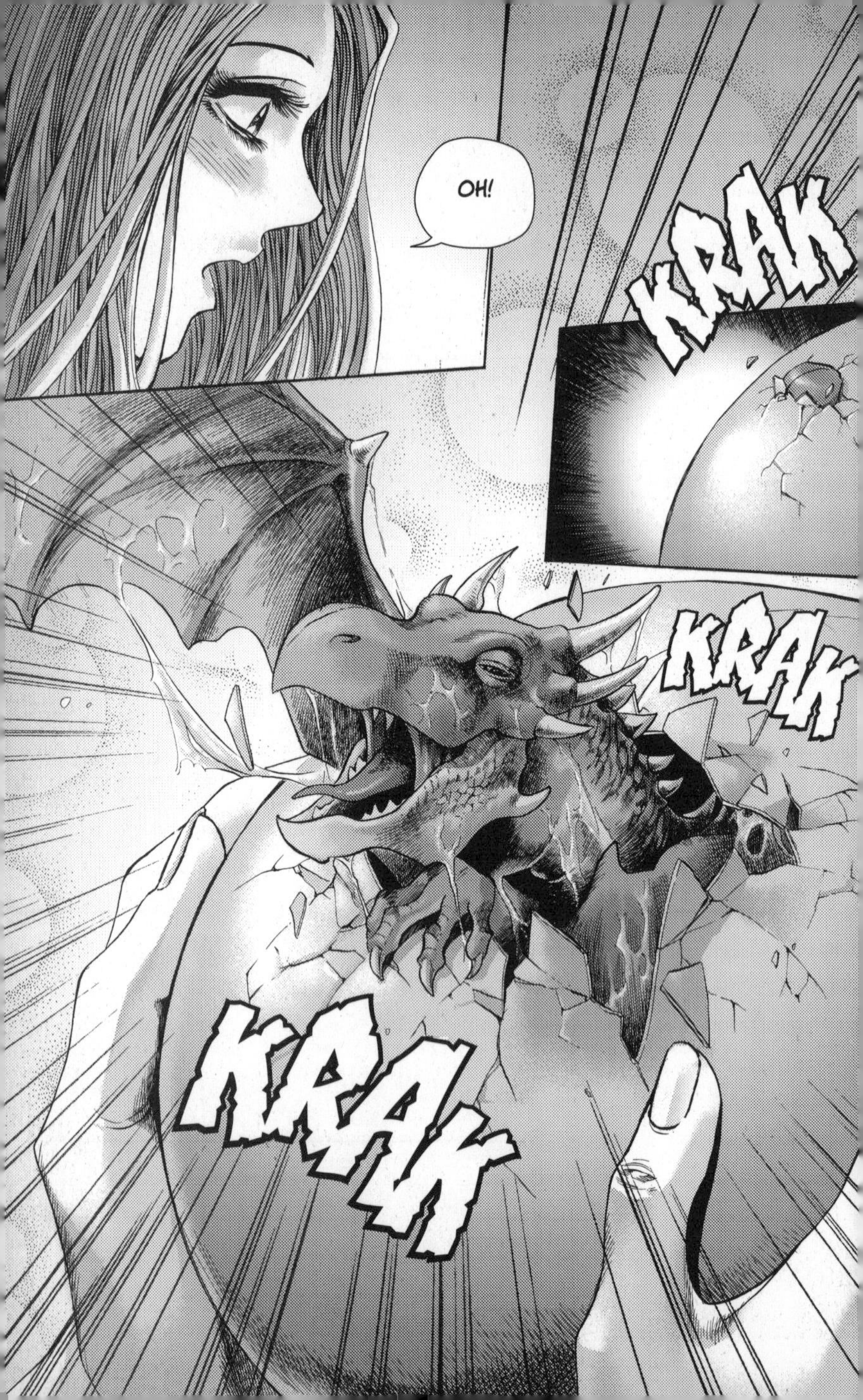
OH!
KRAK
KRAK
KRAK

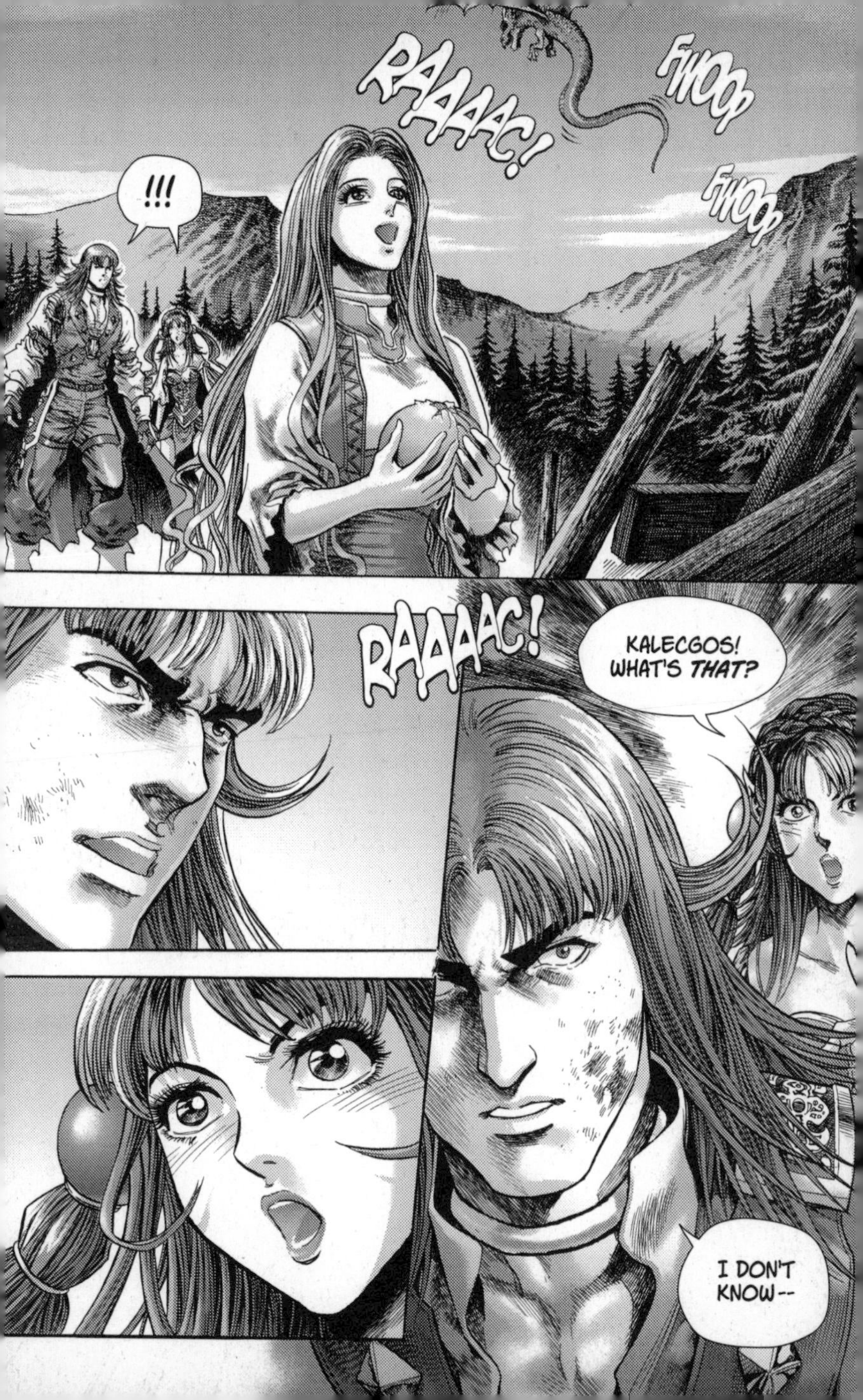
RAAAAC!
FWOOP
FWOOP
!!!
RAAAAC!
KALECGOS! WHAT'S *THAT*?
I DON'T KNOW--

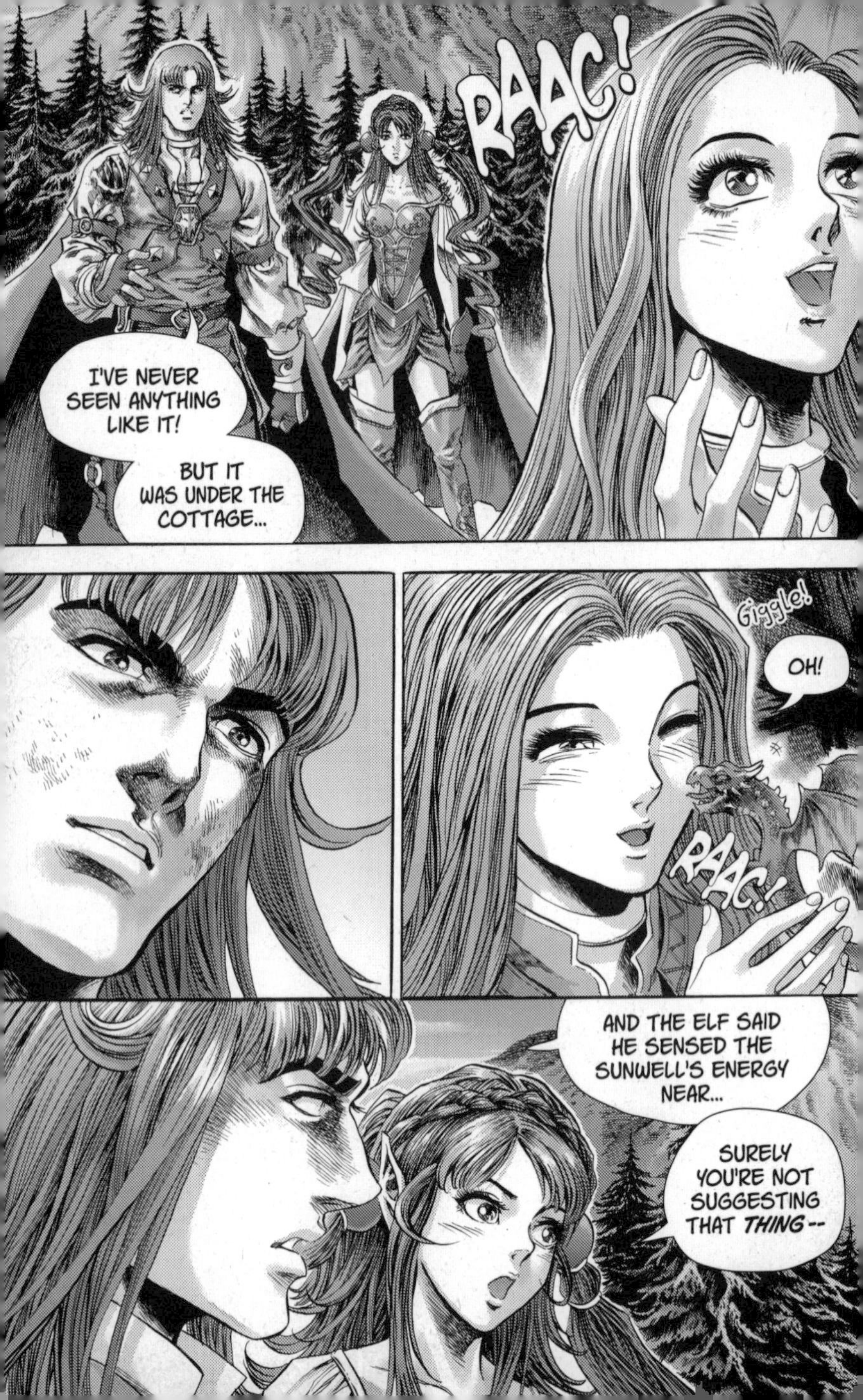
RAAC!
I'VE NEVER SEEN ANYTHING LIKE IT!
BUT IT WAS UNDER THE COTTAGE...
Giggle!
OH!
RAAC!
AND THE ELF SAID HE SENSED THE SUNWELL'S ENERGY NEAR...
SURELY YOU'RE NOT SUGGESTING THAT *THING*--

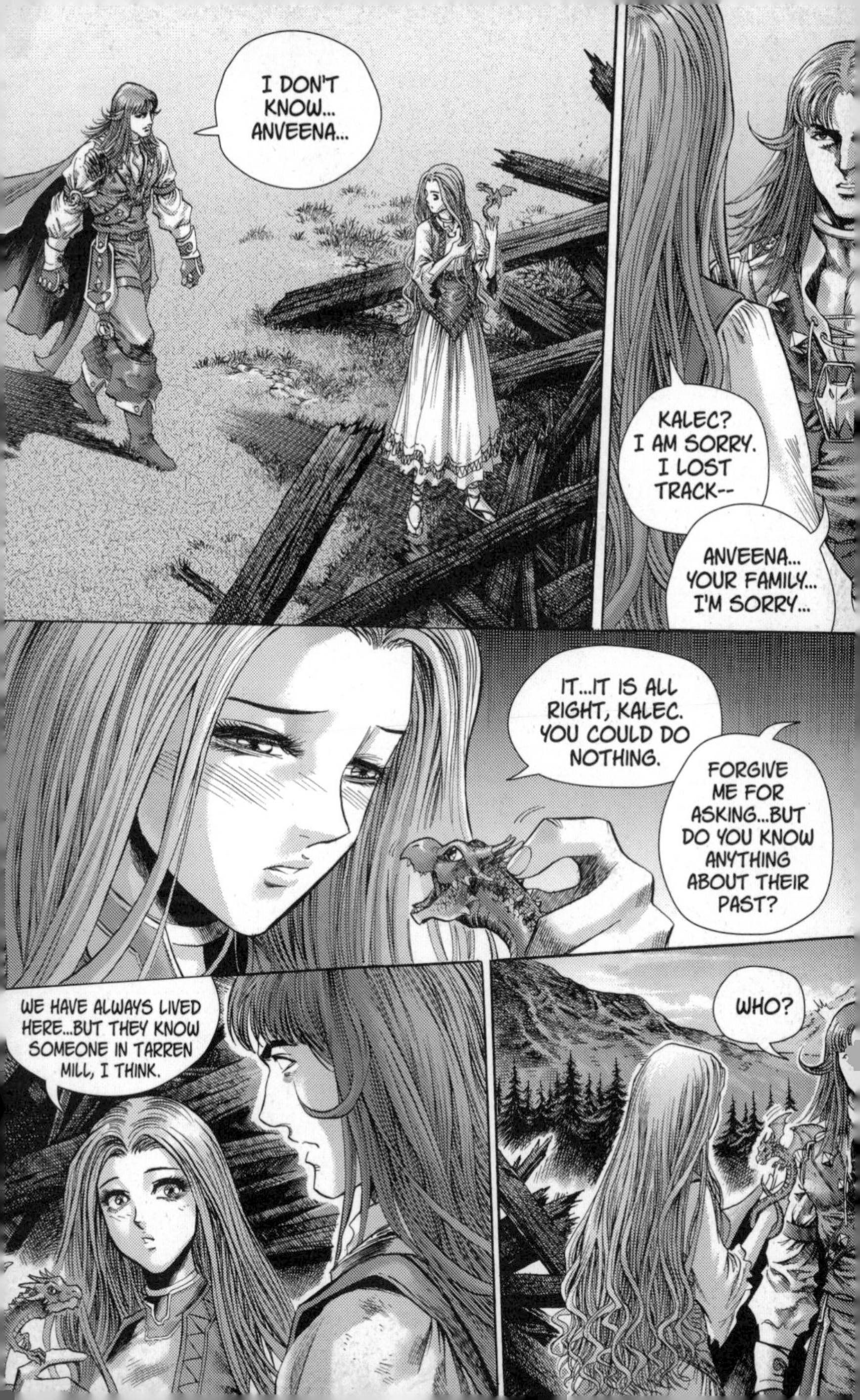
I DON'T KNOW... ANVEENA...
KALEC? I AM SORRY. I LOST TRACK--
ANVEENA... YOUR FAMILY... I'M SORRY...
IT...IT IS ALL RIGHT, KALEC. YOU COULD DO NOTHING.
FORGIVE ME FOR ASKING...BUT DO YOU KNOW ANYTHING ABOUT THEIR PAST?
WE HAVE ALWAYS LIVED HERE...BUT THEY KNOW SOMEONE IN TARREN MILL, I THINK.
WHO?

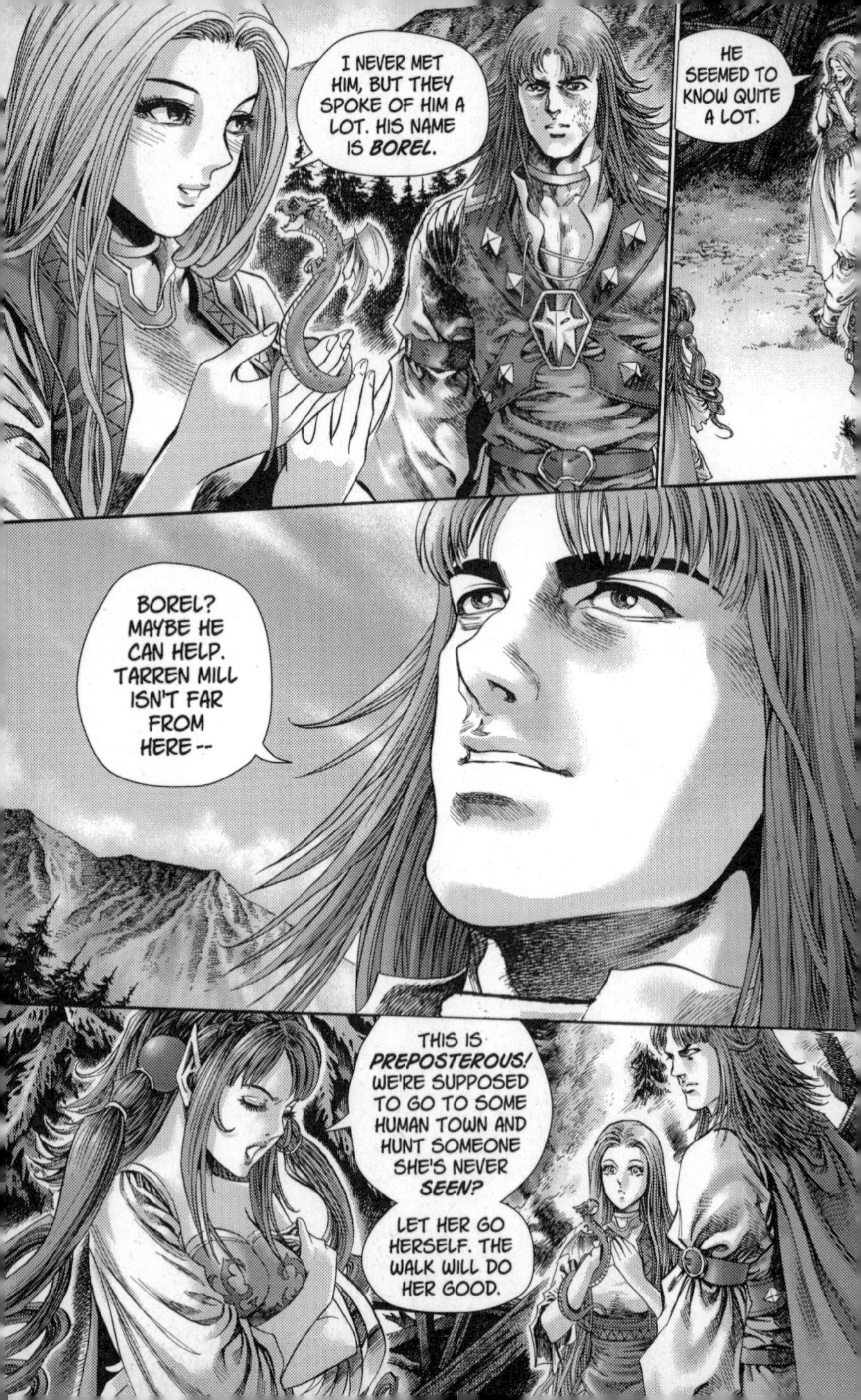
I NEVER MET HIM, BUT THEY SPOKE OF HIM A LOT. HIS NAME IS *BOREL.*
HE SEEMED TO KNOW QUITE A LOT.
BOREL? MAYBE HE CAN HELP. TARREN MILL ISN'T FAR FROM HERE--
THIS IS *PREPOSTEROUS!* WE'RE SUPPOSED TO GO TO SOME HUMAN TOWN AND HUNT SOMEONE SHE'S NEVER *SEEN?*
LET HER GO HERSELF. THE WALK WILL DO HER GOOD.

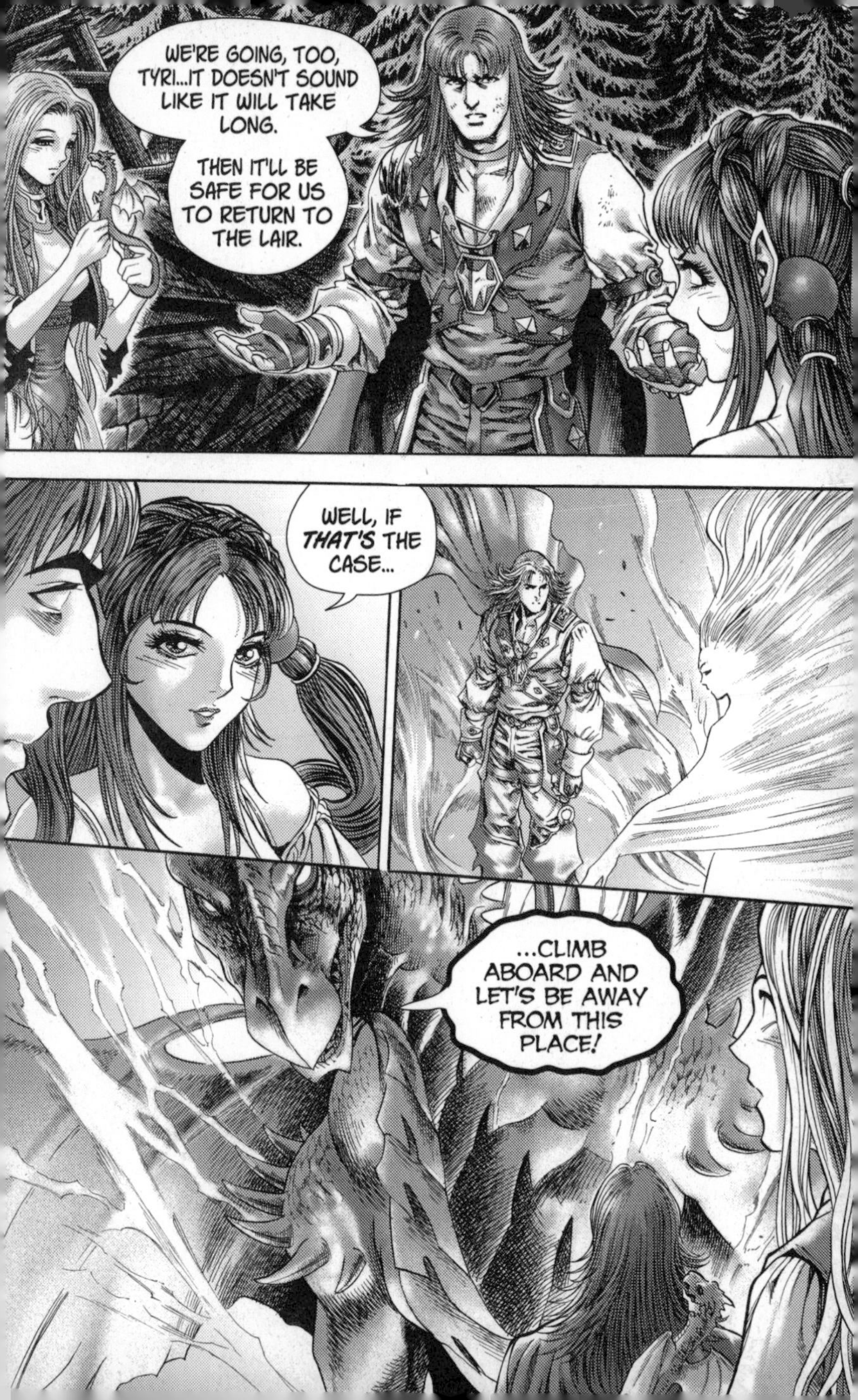
WE'RE GOING, TOO, TYRI...IT DOESN'T SOUND LIKE IT WILL TAKE LONG.
THEN IT'LL BE SAFE FOR US TO RETURN TO THE LAIR.
WELL, IF *THAT'S* THE CASE...
...CLIMB ABOARD AND LET'S BE AWAY FROM THIS PLACE!

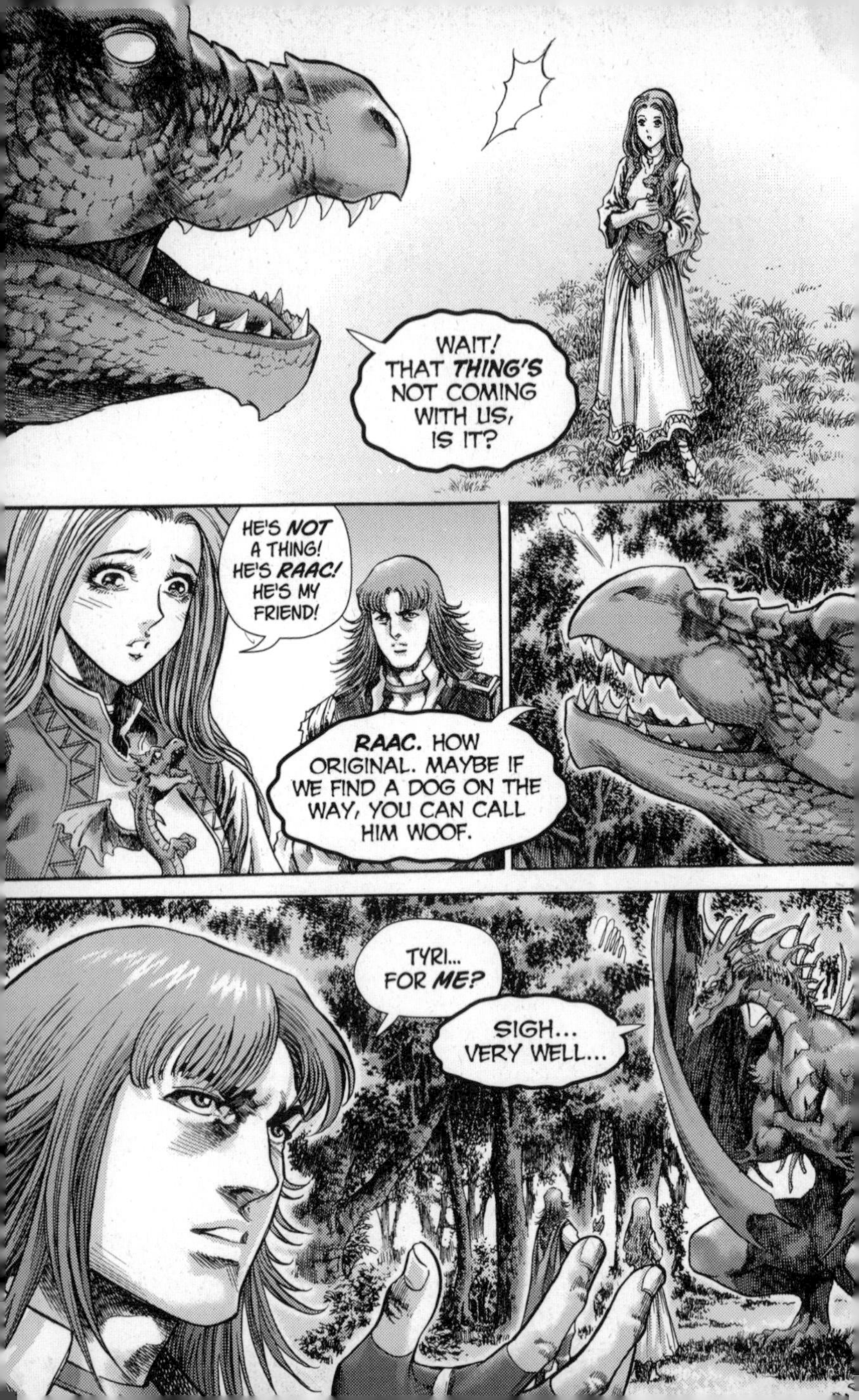
WAIT! THAT *THING'S* NOT COMING WITH US, IS IT?
HE'S *NOT* A THING! HE'S *RAAC!* HE'S MY FRIEND!
RAAC. HOW ORIGINAL. MAYBE IF WE FIND A DOG ON THE WAY, YOU CAN CALL HIM WOOF.
TYRI... FOR *ME?*
SIGH... VERY WELL...

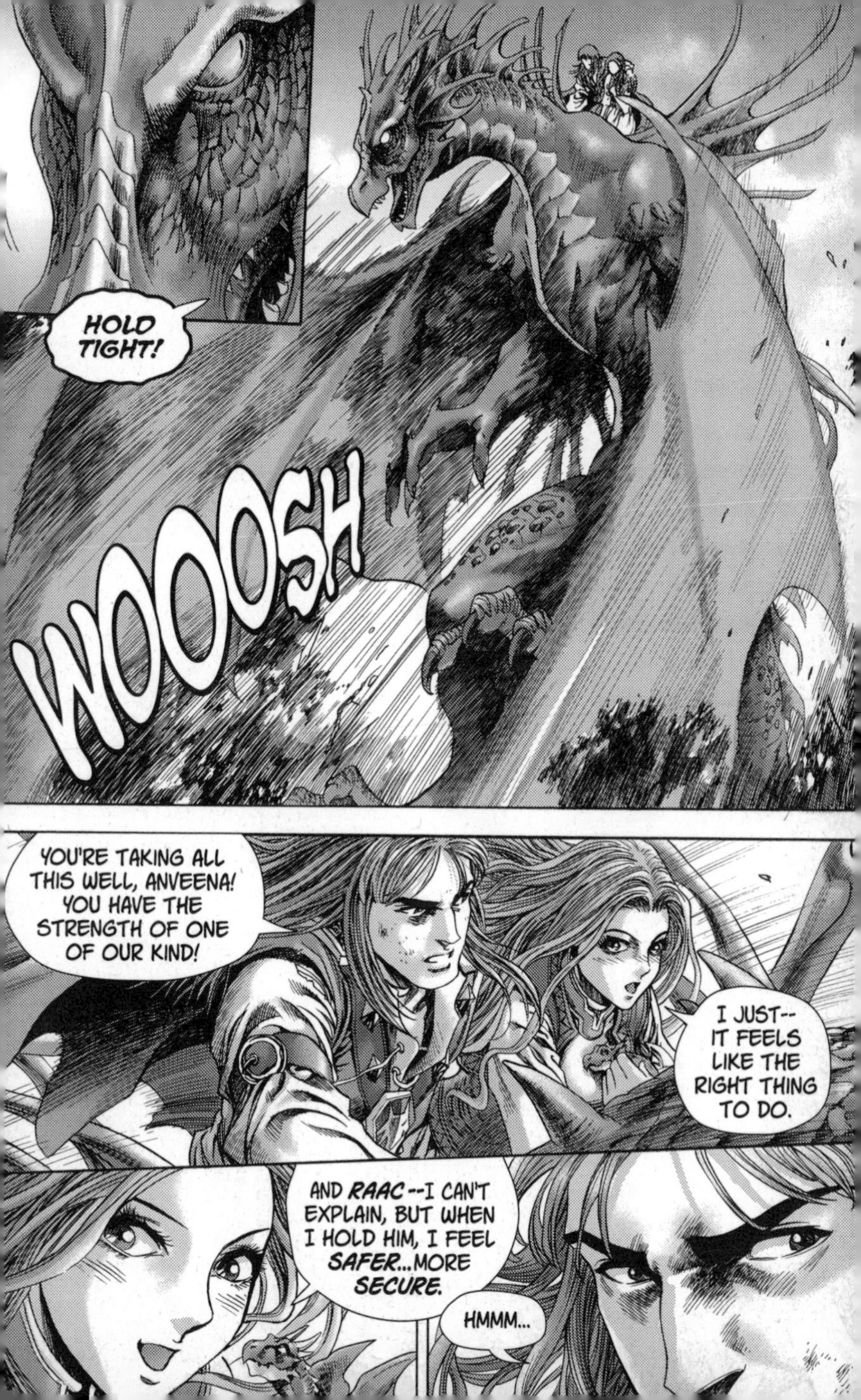
HOLD TIGHT!
WOOOSH
YOU'RE TAKING ALL THIS WELL, ANVEENA! YOU HAVE THE STRENGTH OF ONE OF OUR KIND!
I JUST-- IT FEELS LIKE THE RIGHT THING TO DO.
AND RAAC--I CAN'T EXPLAIN, BUT WHEN I HOLD HIM, I FEEL SAFER...MORE SECURE.
HMMM...

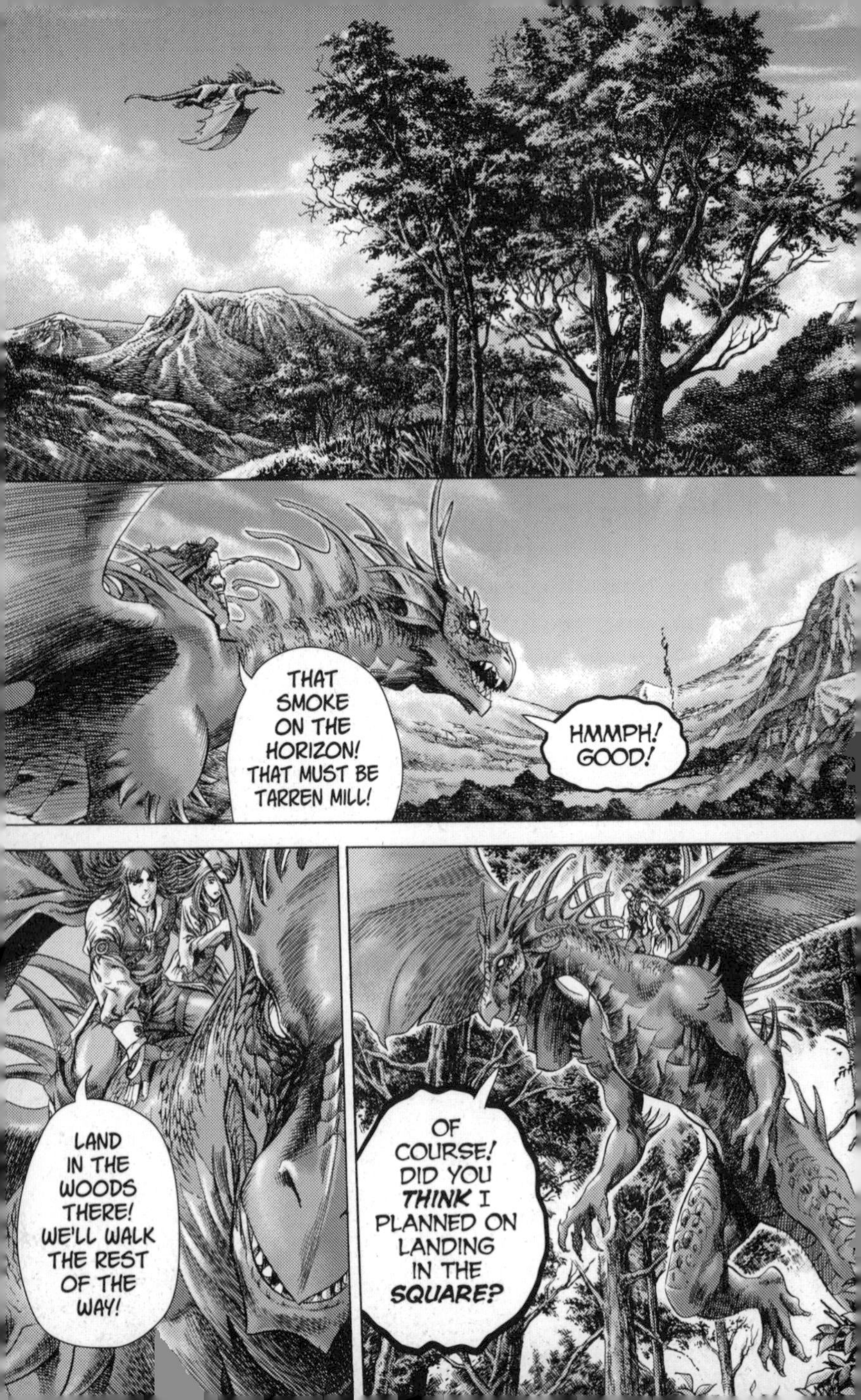
THAT SMOKE ON THE HORIZON! THAT MUST BE TARREN MILL!
HMMPH! GOOD!
LAND IN THE WOODS THERE! WE'LL WALK THE REST OF THE WAY!
OF COURSE! DID YOU *THINK* I PLANNED ON LANDING IN THE **SQUARE?**

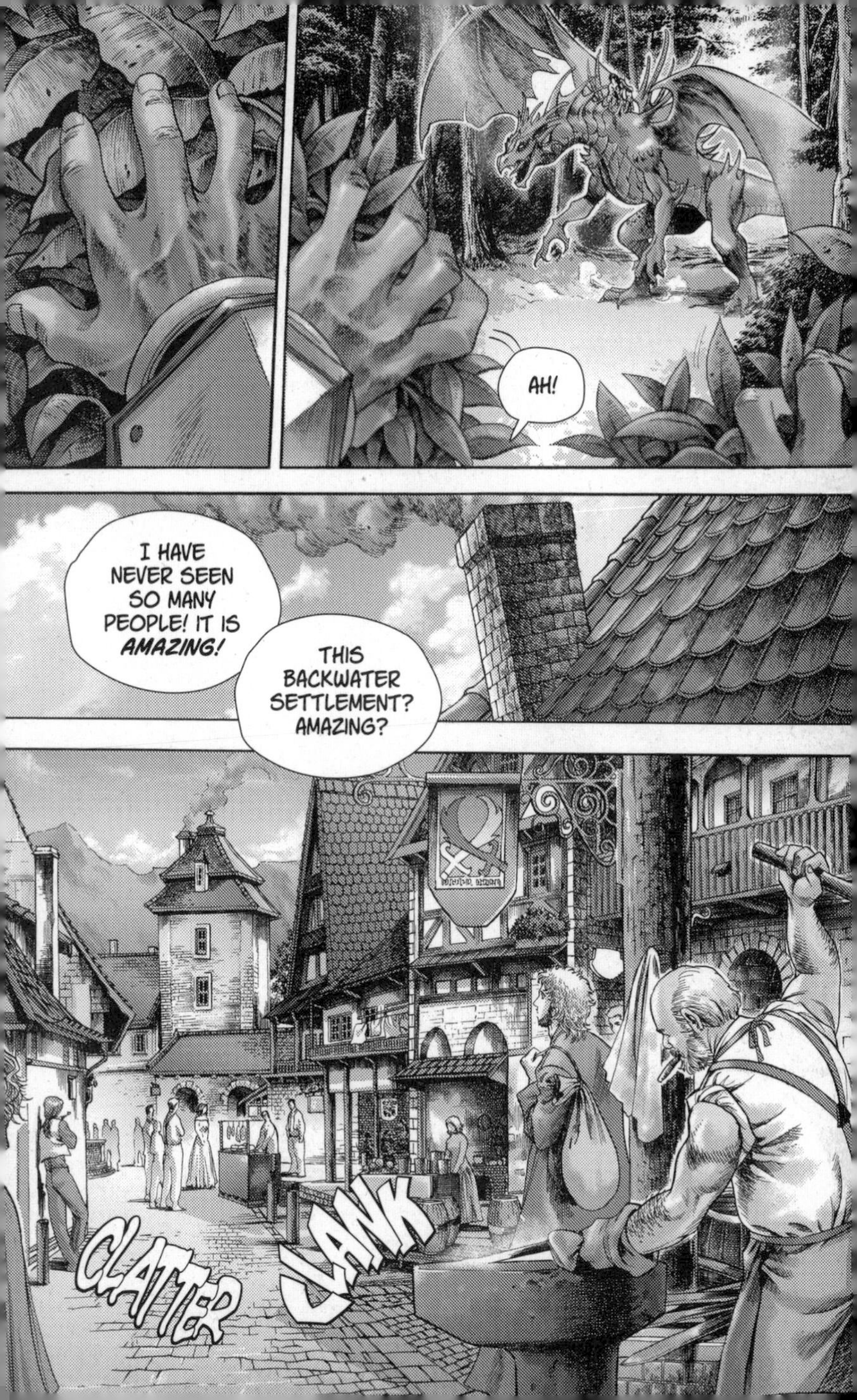
AH!
I HAVE NEVER SEEN SO MANY PEOPLE! IT IS AMAZING!
THIS BACKWATER SETTLEMENT? AMAZING?
CLATTER
CLANK

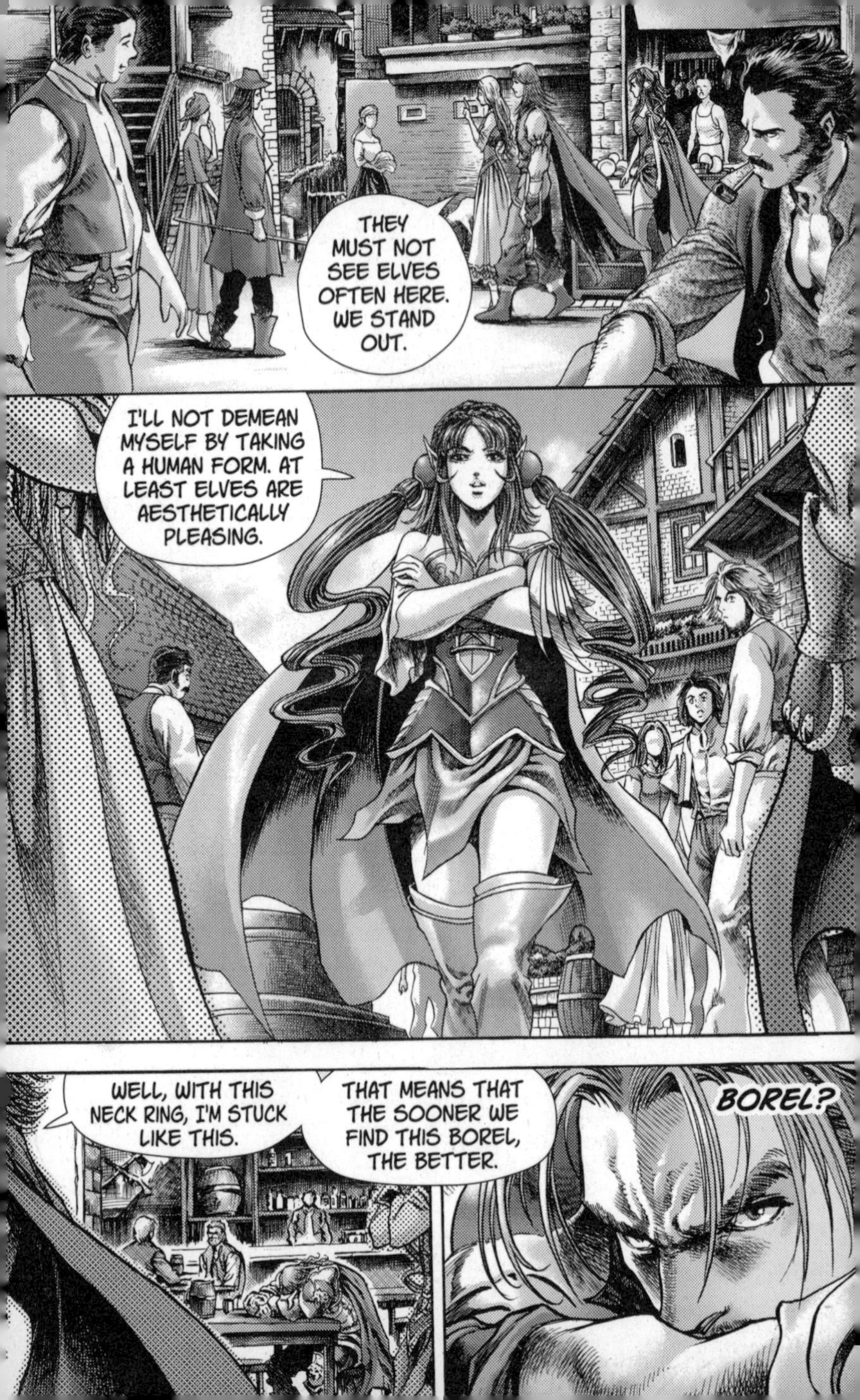
THEY MUST NOT SEE ELVES OFTEN HERE. WE STAND OUT.
I'LL NOT DEMEAN MYSELF BY TAKING A HUMAN FORM. AT LEAST ELVES ARE AESTHETICALLY PLEASING.
WELL, WITH THIS NECK RING, I'M STUCK LIKE THIS.
THAT MEANS THAT THE SOONER WE FIND THIS BOREL, THE BETTER.
BOREL?

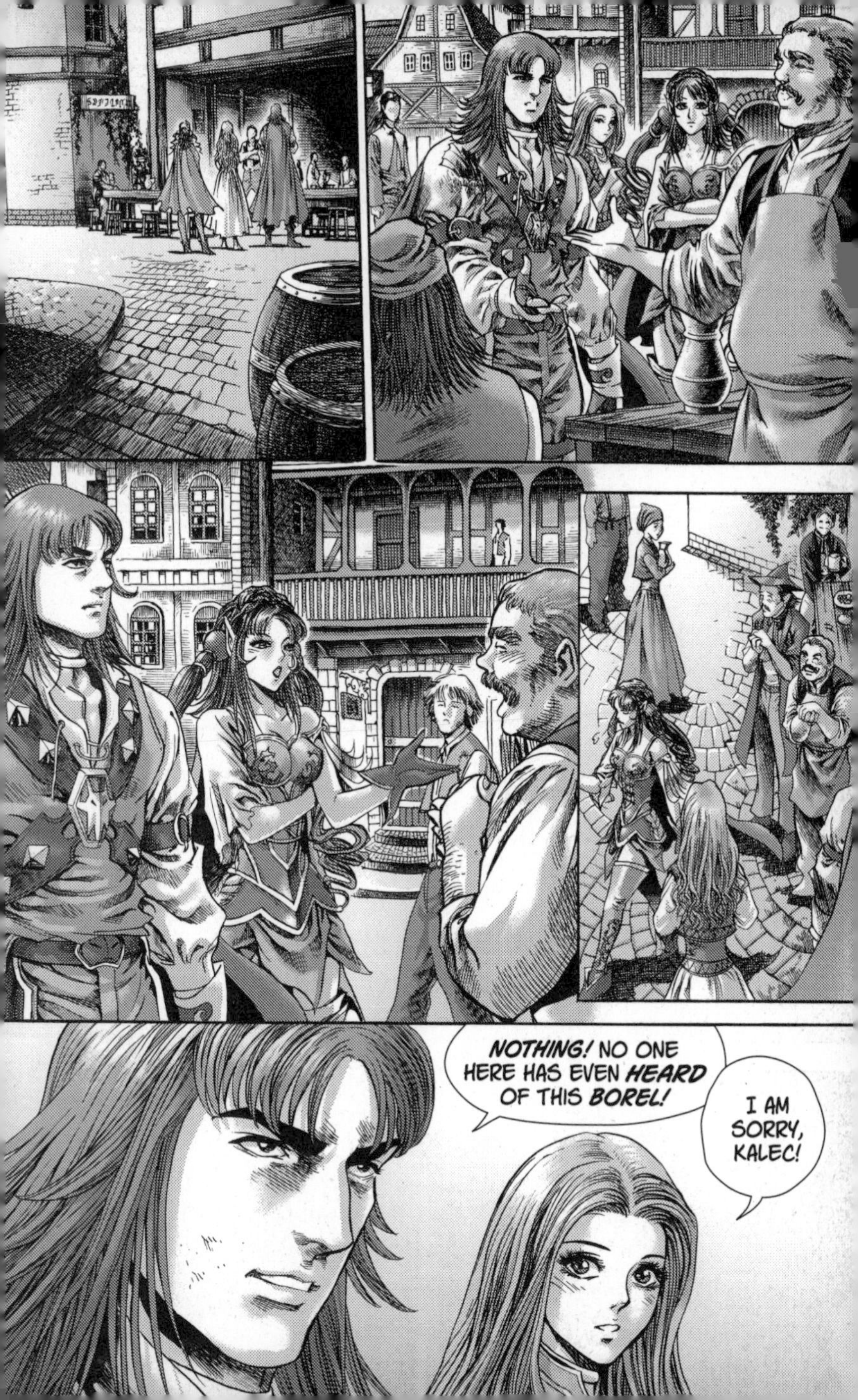
NOTHING! NO ONE HERE HAS EVEN HEARD OF THIS BOREL!
I AM SORRY, KALEC!

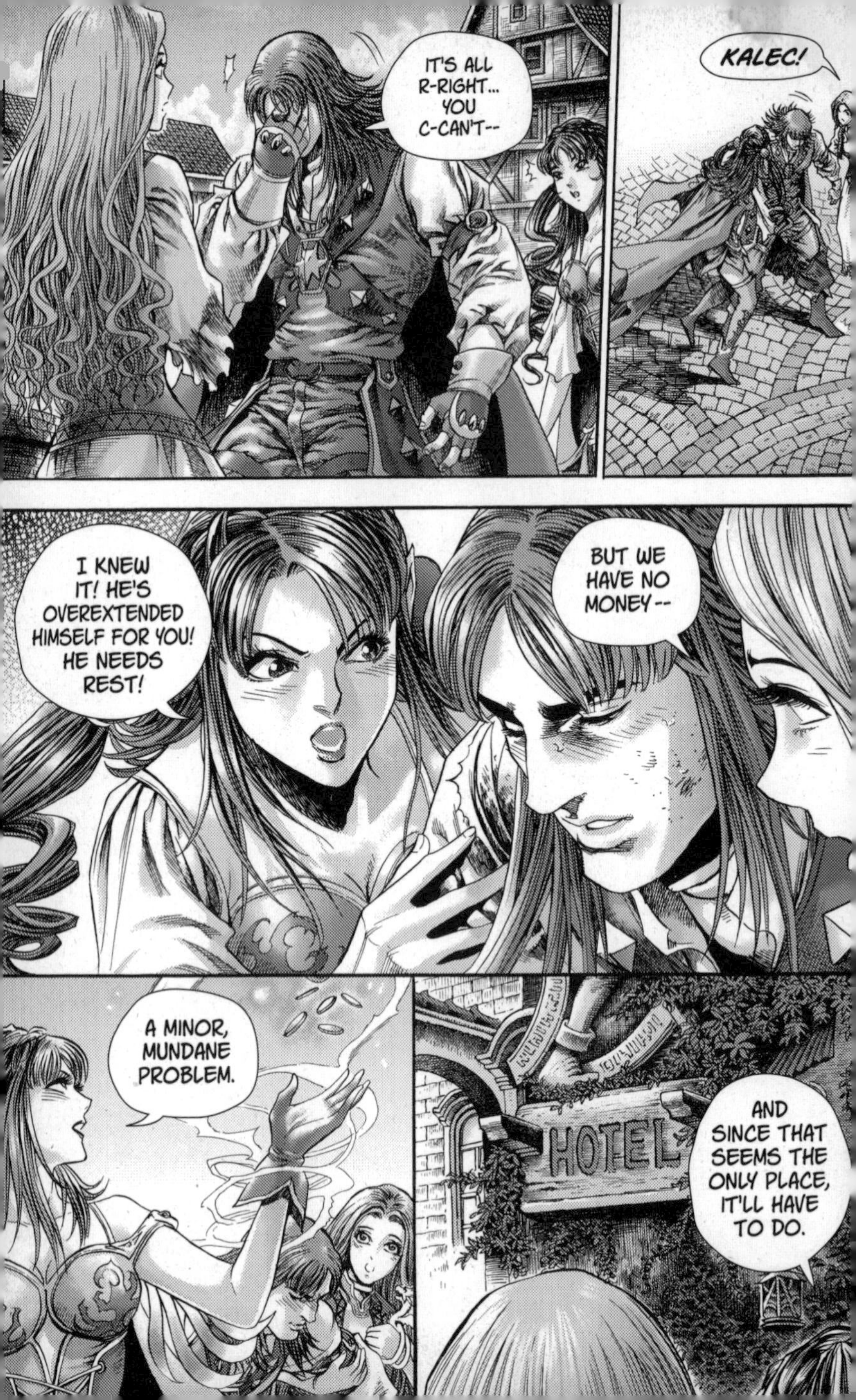
IT'S ALL R-RIGHT... YOU C-CAN'T--
KALEC!
I KNEW IT! HE'S OVEREXTENDED HIMSELF FOR YOU! HE NEEDS REST!
BUT WE HAVE NO MONEY--
A MINOR, MUNDANE PROBLEM.
HOTEL
AND SINCE THAT SEEMS THE ONLY PLACE, IT'LL HAVE TO DO.

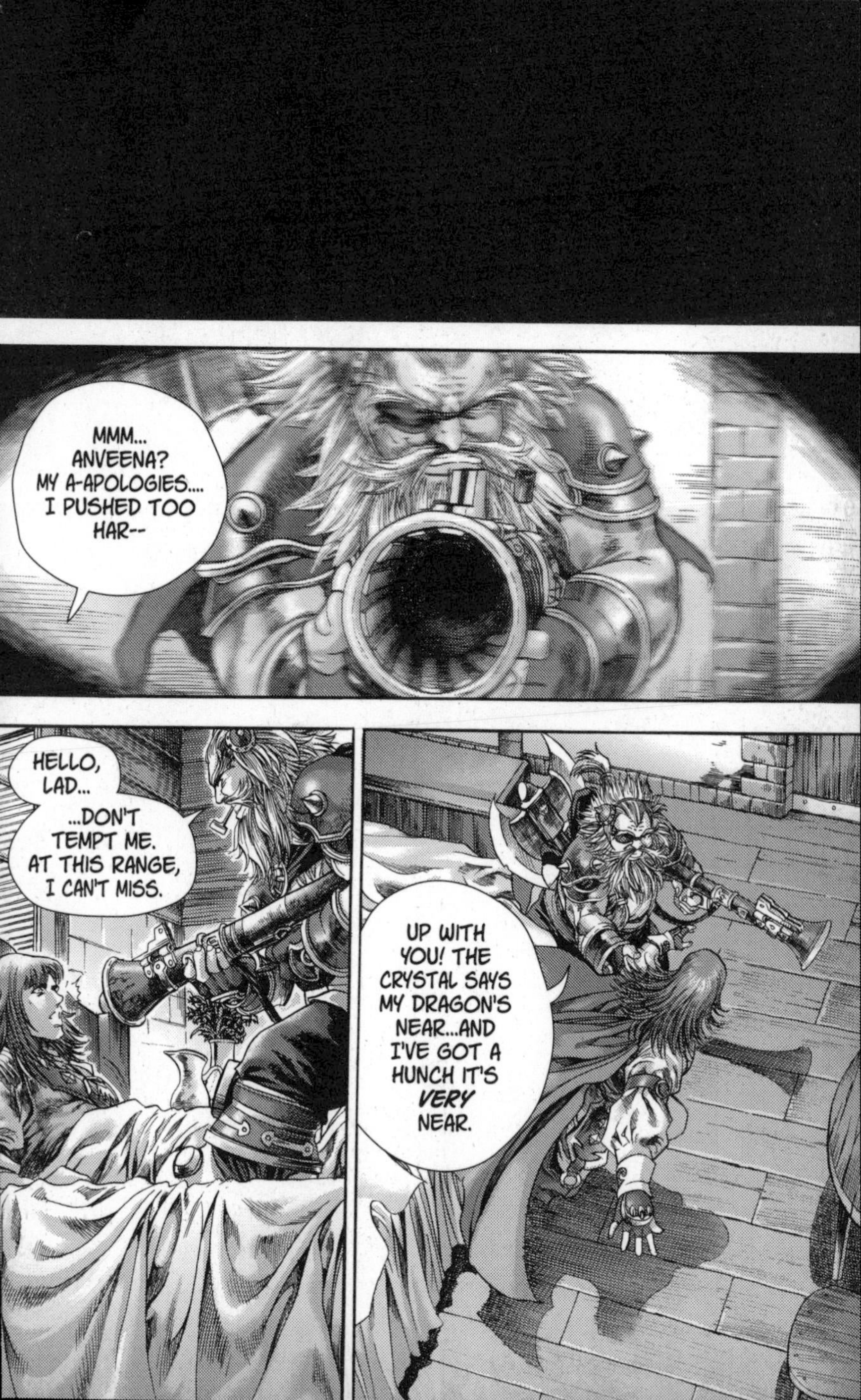
MMM... ANVEENA? MY A-APOLOGIES.... I PUSHED TOO HAR--
HELLO, LAD...
...DON'T TEMPT ME. AT THIS RANGE, I CAN'T MISS.
UP WITH YOU! THE CRYSTAL SAYS MY DRAGON'S NEAR...AND I'VE GOT A HUNCH IT'S *VERY* NEAR.

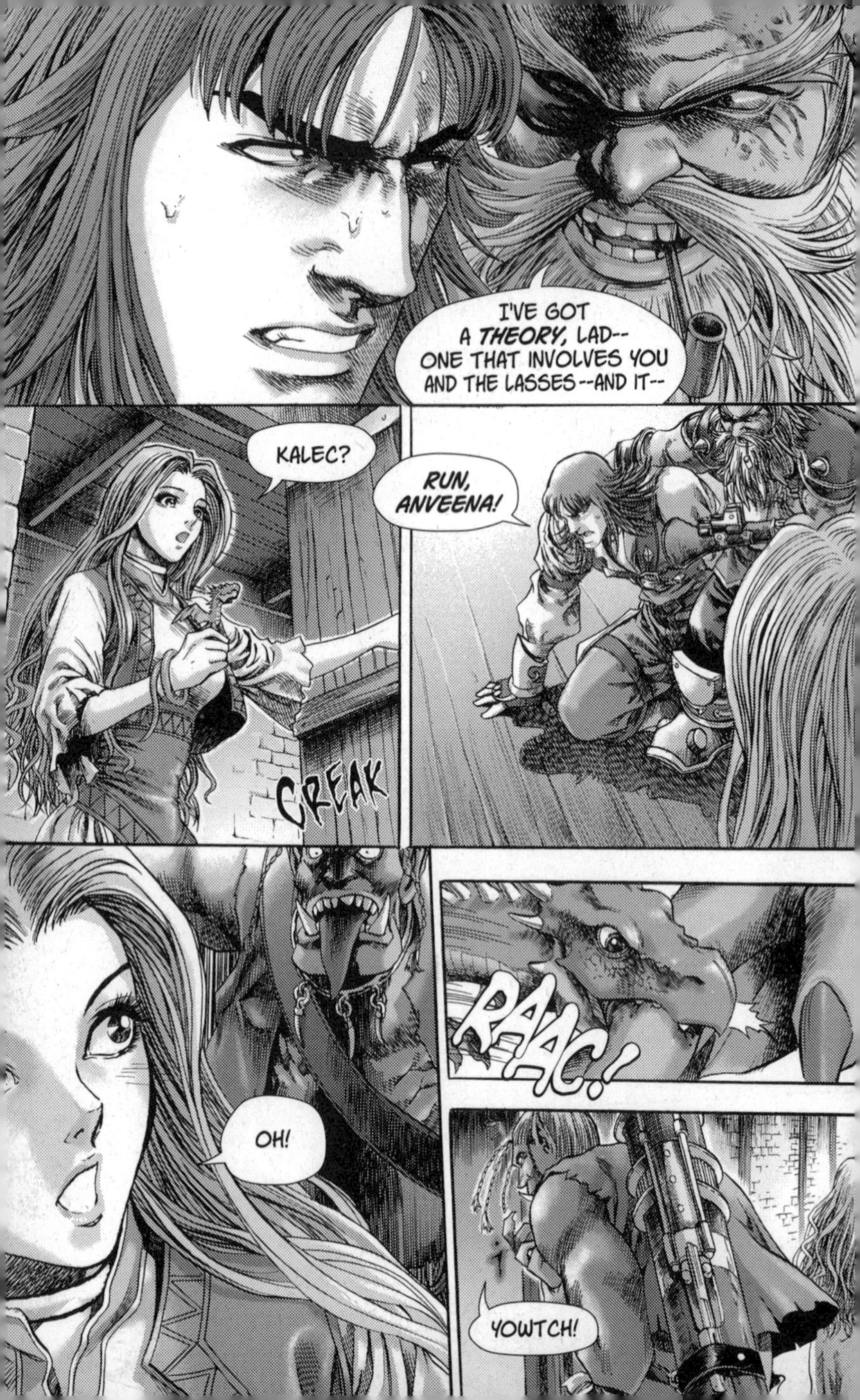
I'VE GOT A THEORY, LAD-- ONE THAT INVOLVES YOU AND THE LASSES--AND IT--
KALEC?
CREAK
RUN, ANVEENA!
OH!
RAAAC!
YOWTCH!

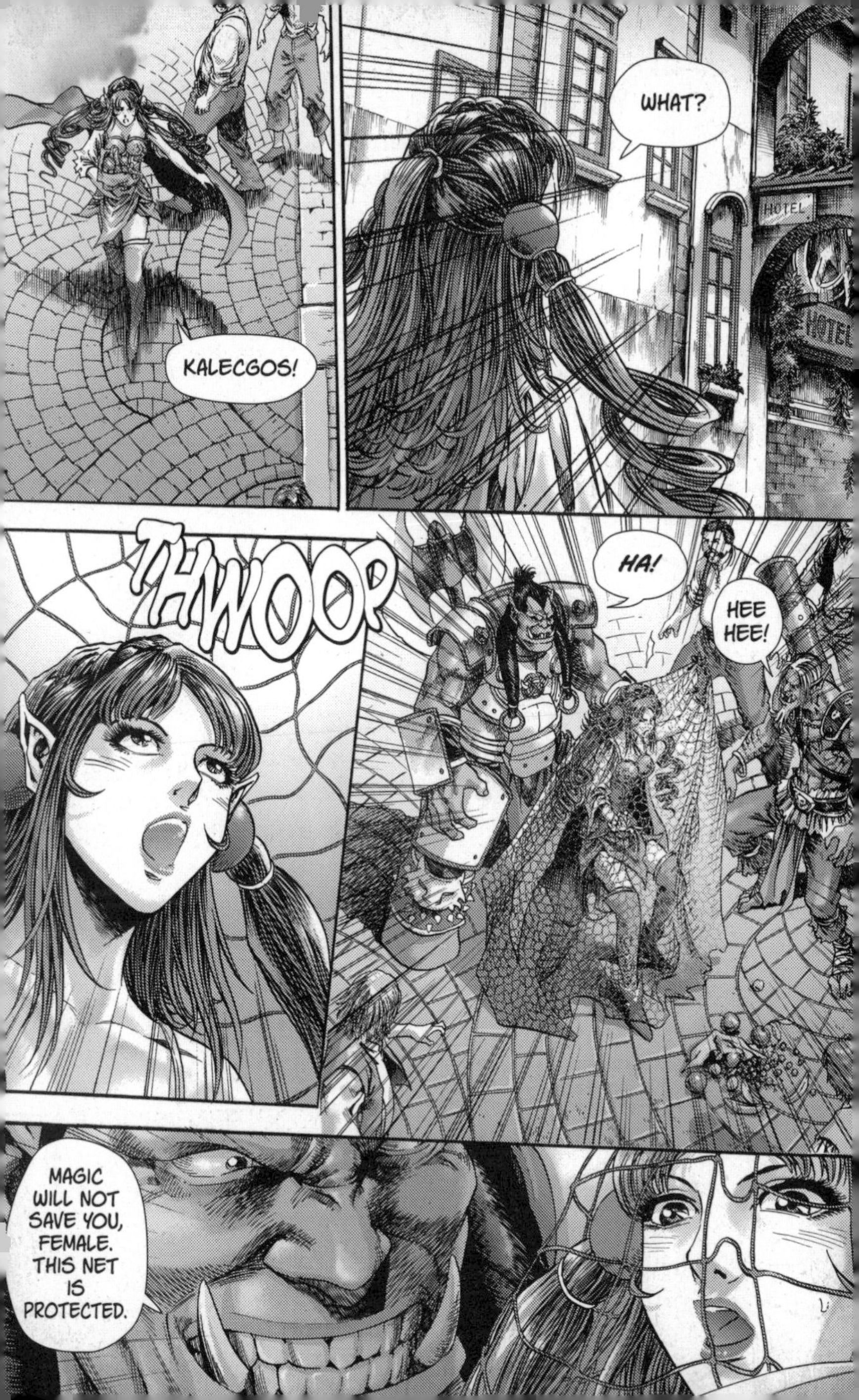
KALECGOS!
WHAT?
THWOOP
HA!
HEE HEE!
MAGIC WILL NOT SAVE YOU, FEMALE. THIS NET IS PROTECTED.

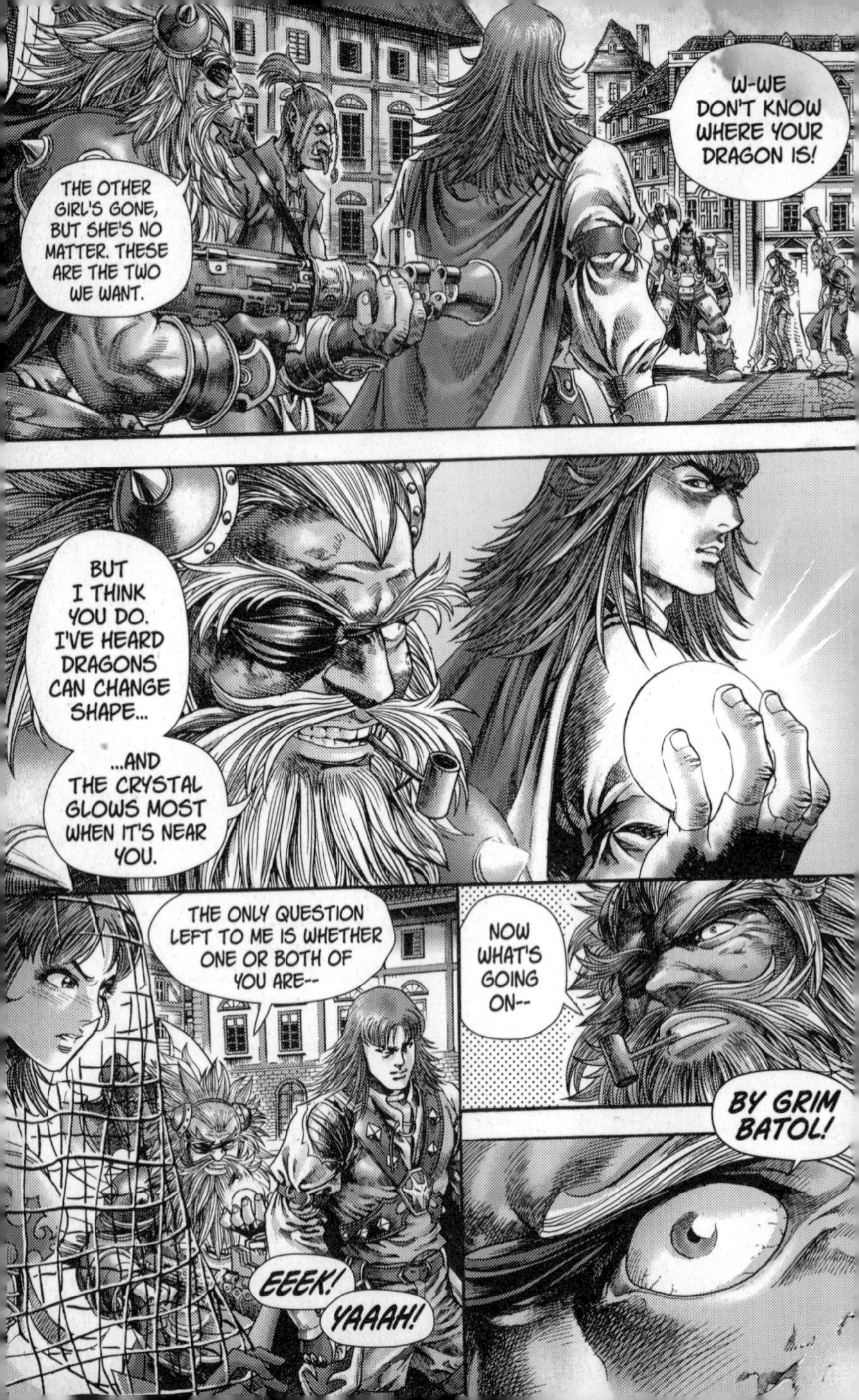
THE OTHER GIRL'S GONE, BUT SHE'S NO MATTER. THESE ARE THE TWO WE WANT.
W-WE DON'T KNOW WHERE YOUR DRAGON IS!
BUT I THINK YOU DO. I'VE HEARD DRAGONS CAN CHANGE SHAPE...
...AND THE CRYSTAL GLOWS MOST WHEN IT'S NEAR YOU.
THE ONLY QUESTION LEFT TO ME IS WHETHER ONE OR BOTH OF YOU ARE--
EEEK!
YAAAH!
NOW WHAT'S GOING ON--
BY GRIM BATOL!

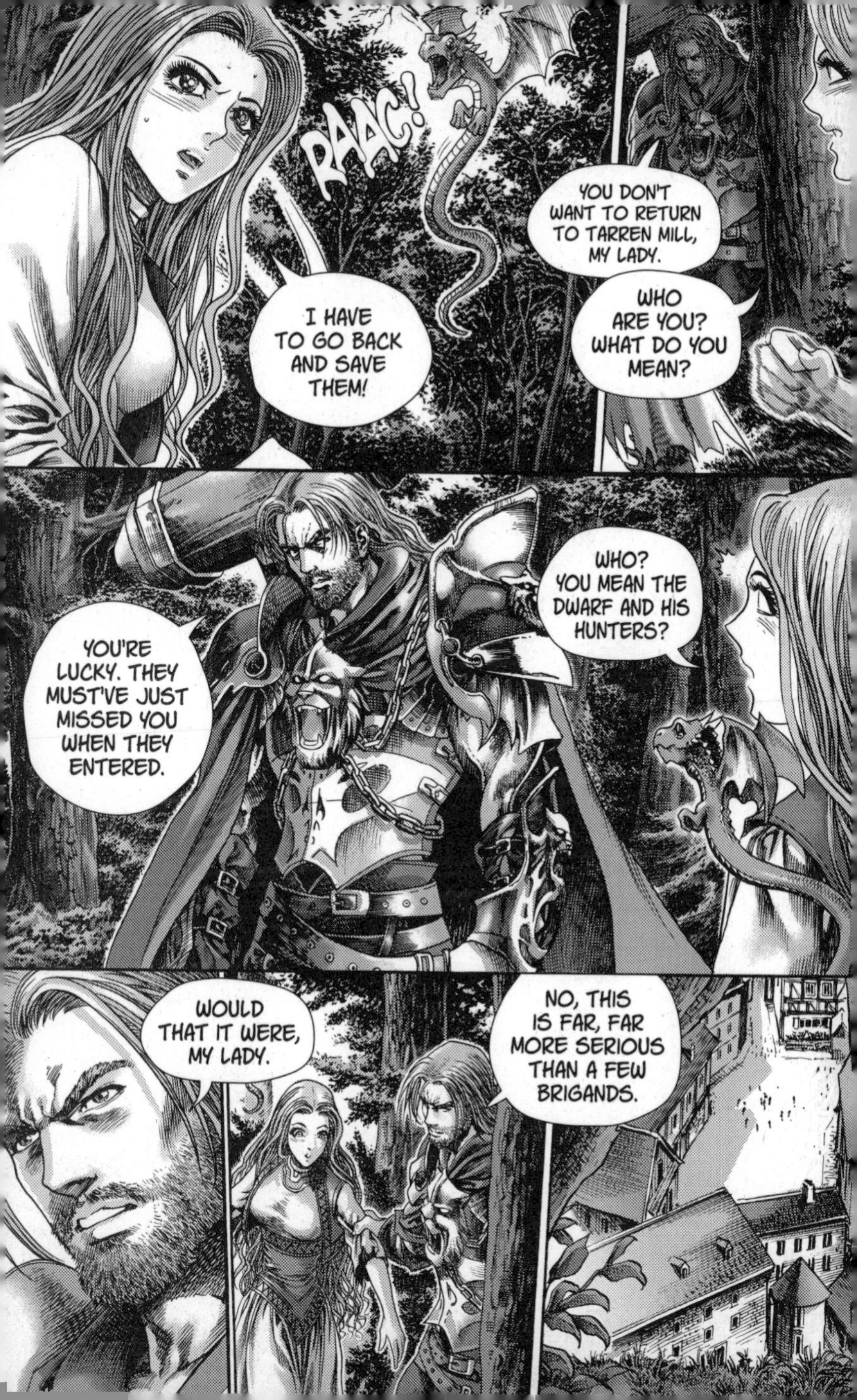
RAAC!
I HAVE TO GO BACK AND SAVE THEM!
YOU DON'T WANT TO RETURN TO TARREN MILL, MY LADY.
WHO ARE YOU? WHAT DO YOU MEAN?
YOU'RE LUCKY. THEY MUST'VE JUST MISSED YOU WHEN THEY ENTERED.
WHO? YOU MEAN THE DWARF AND HIS HUNTERS?
WOULD THAT IT WERE, MY LADY.
NO, THIS IS FAR, FAR MORE SERIOUS THAN A FEW BRIGANDS.

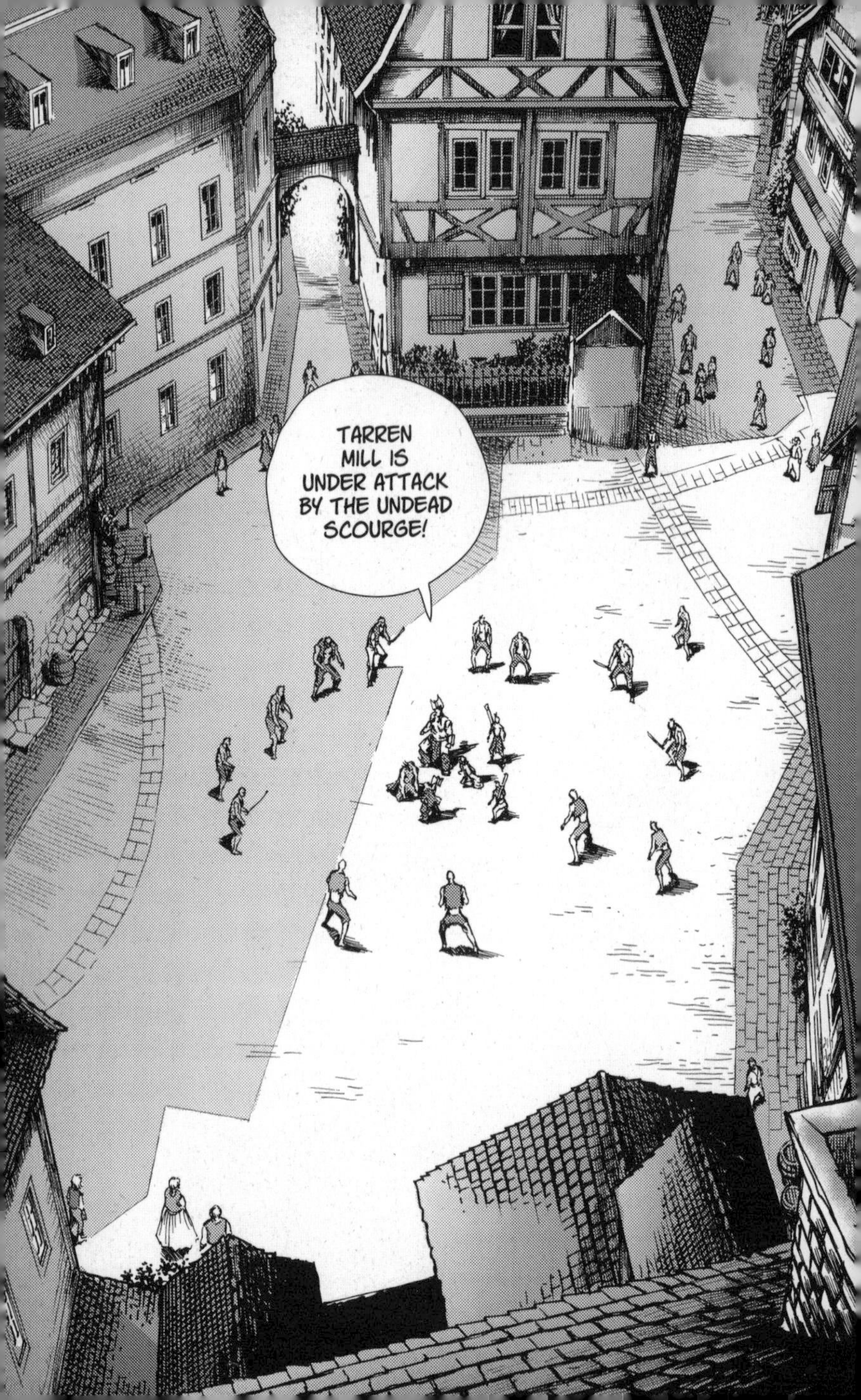
TARREN MILL IS UNDER ATTACK BY THE UNDEAD SCOURGE!

CHAPTER SIX
Against the Scourge

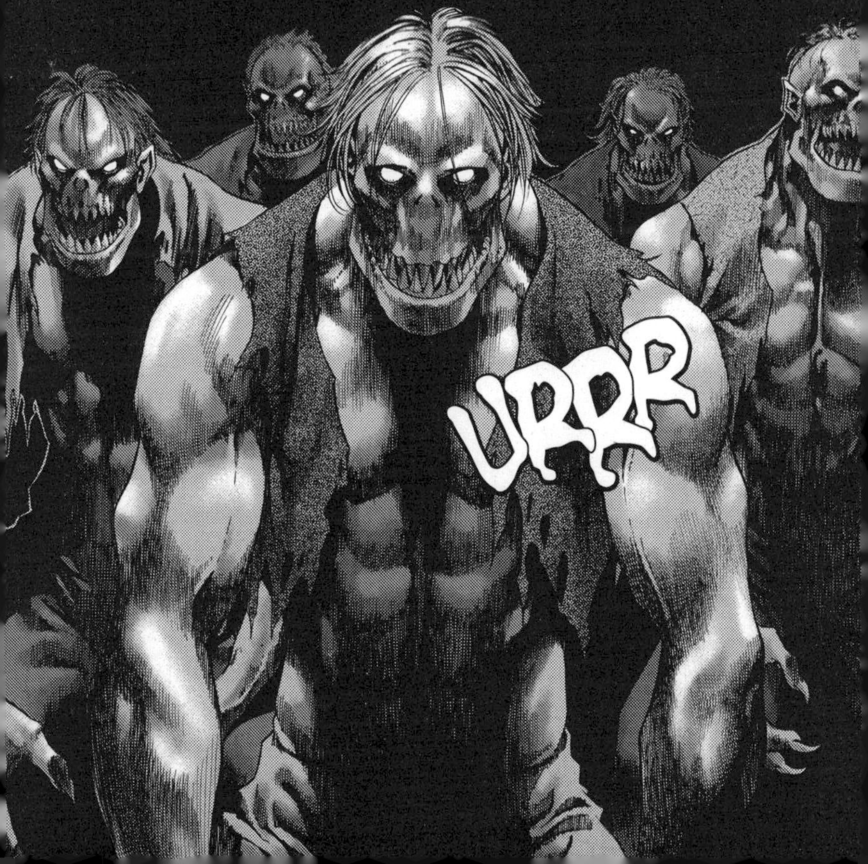
URRR

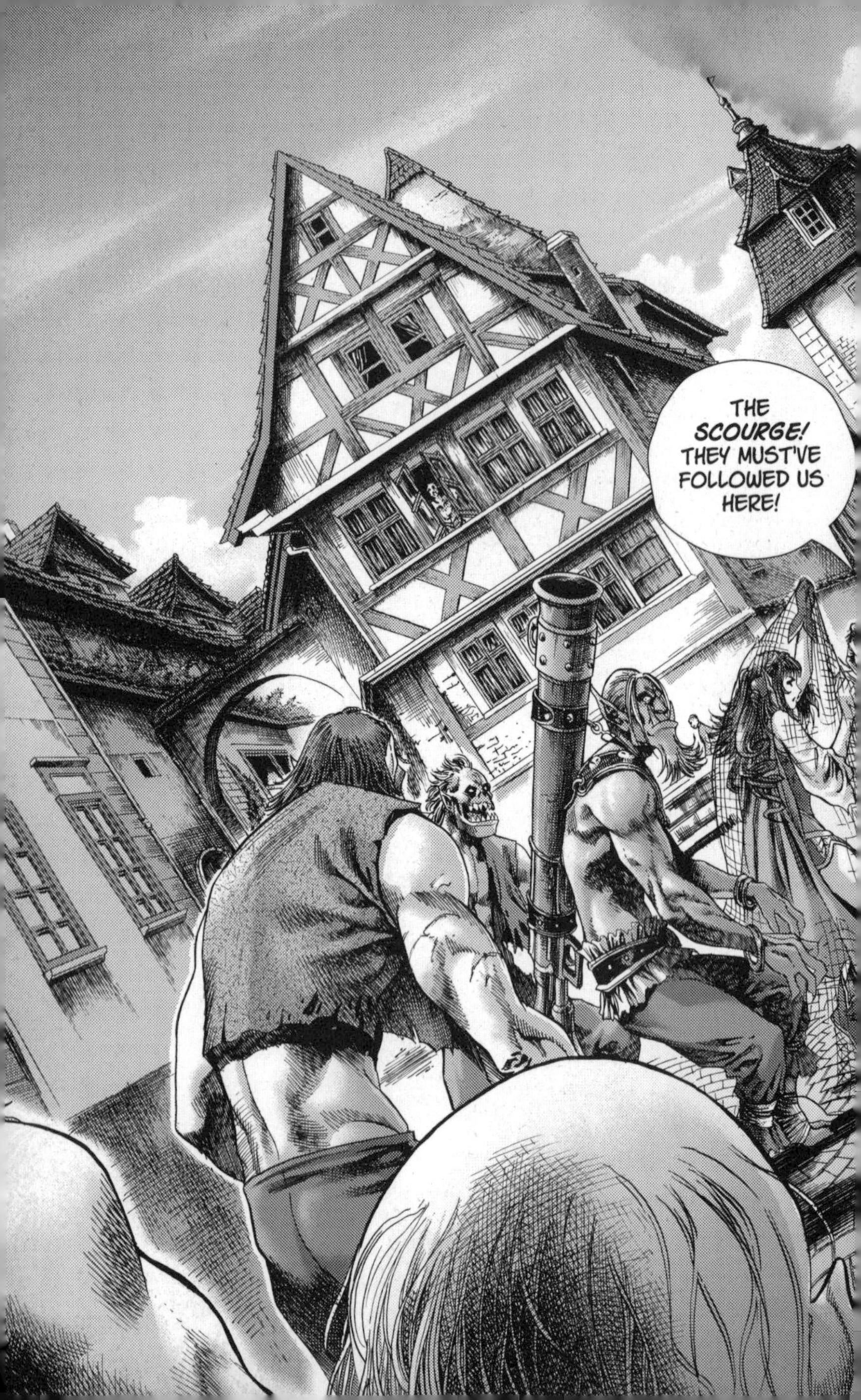
THE SCOURGE! THEY MUST'VE FOLLOWED US HERE!

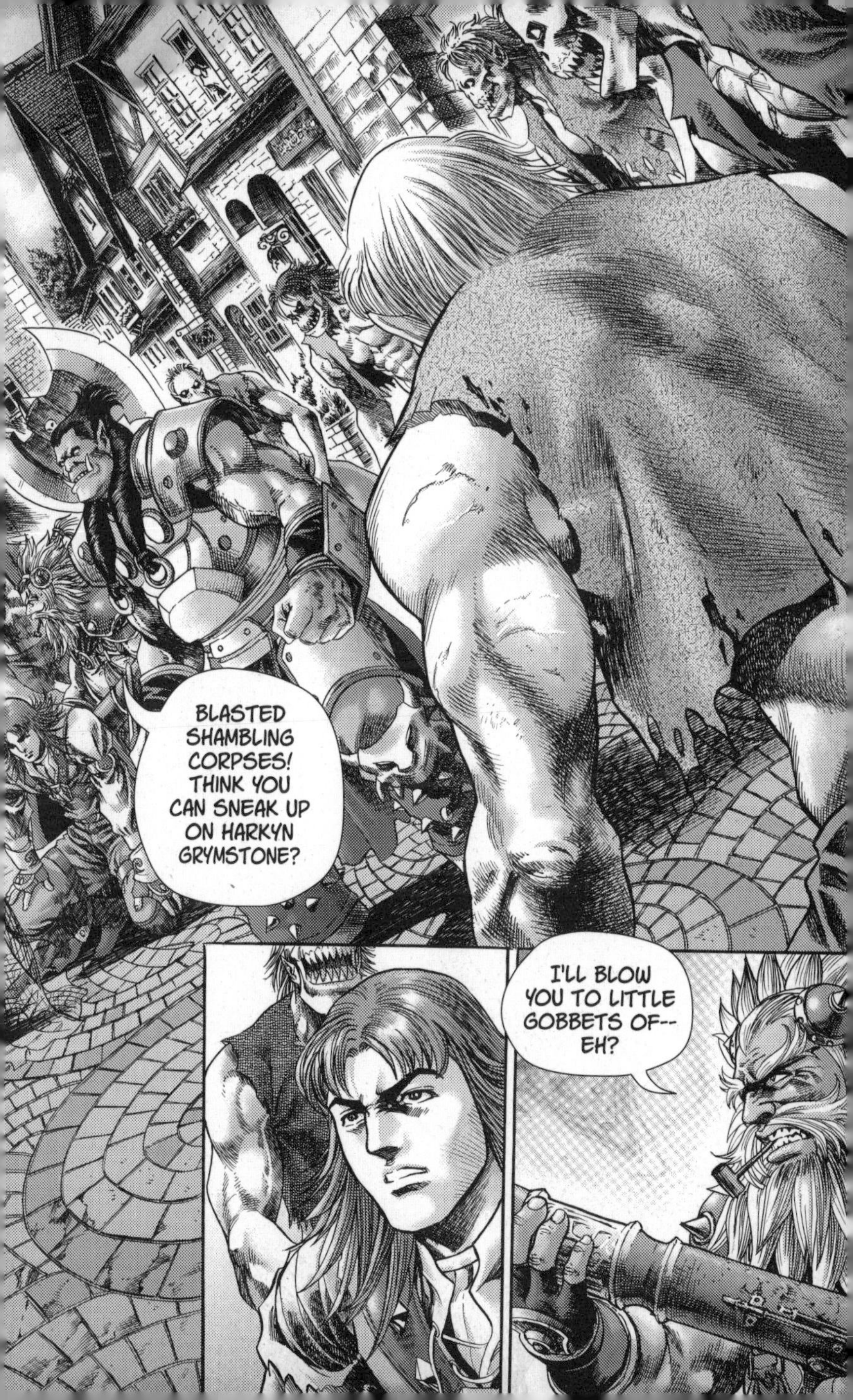
BLASTED SHAMBLING CORPSES! THINK YOU CAN SNEAK UP ON HARKYN GRYMSTONE?
I'LL BLOW YOU TO LITTLE GOBBETS OF-- EH?

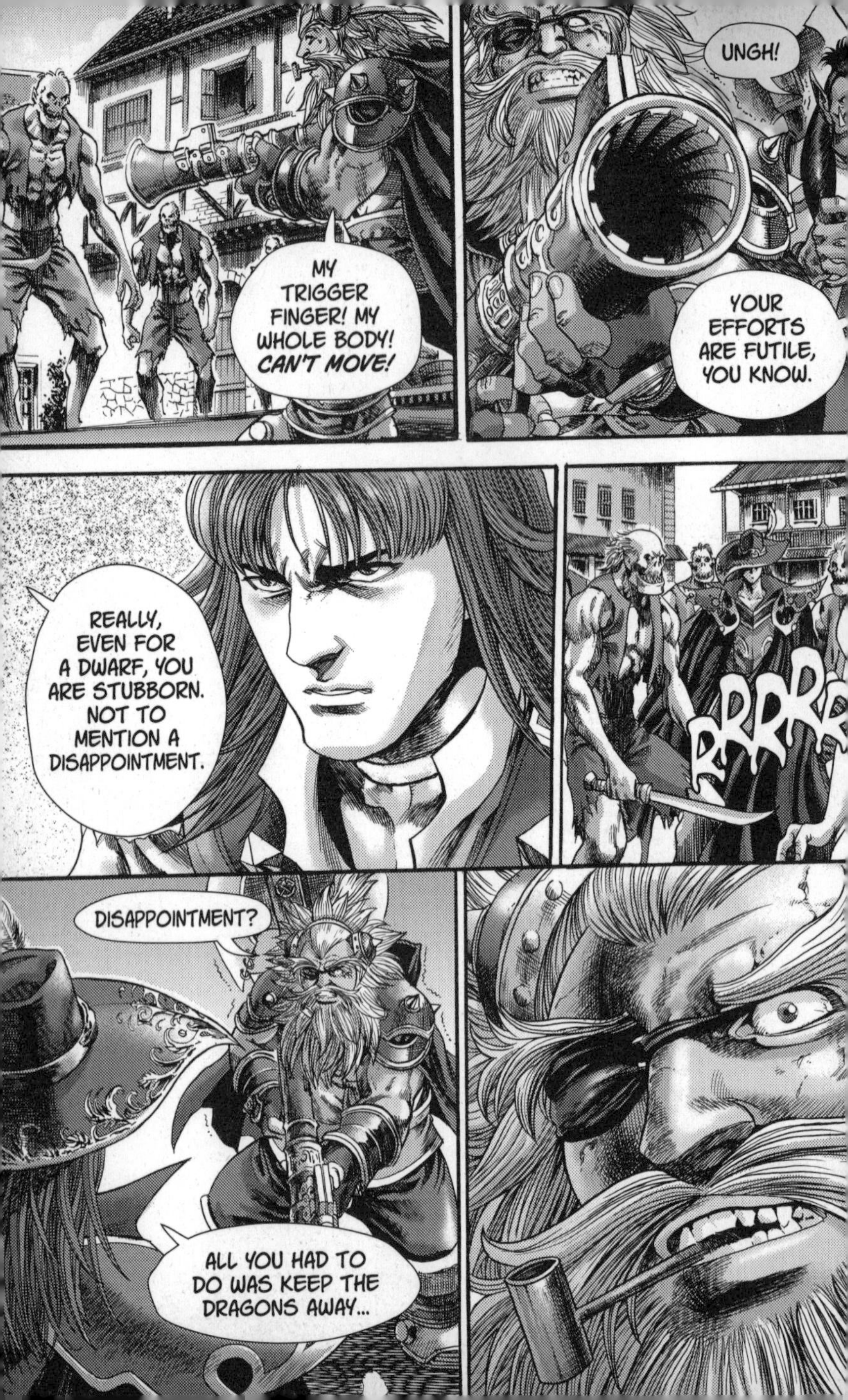

MY TRIGGER FINGER! MY WHOLE BODY! *CAN'T MOVE!*
UNGH!
YOUR EFFORTS ARE FUTILE, YOU KNOW.
REALLY, EVEN FOR A DWARF, YOU ARE STUBBORN. NOT TO MENTION A DISAPPOINTMENT.
RRRRR
DISAPPOINTMENT?
ALL YOU HAD TO DO WAS KEEP THE DRAGONS AWAY...

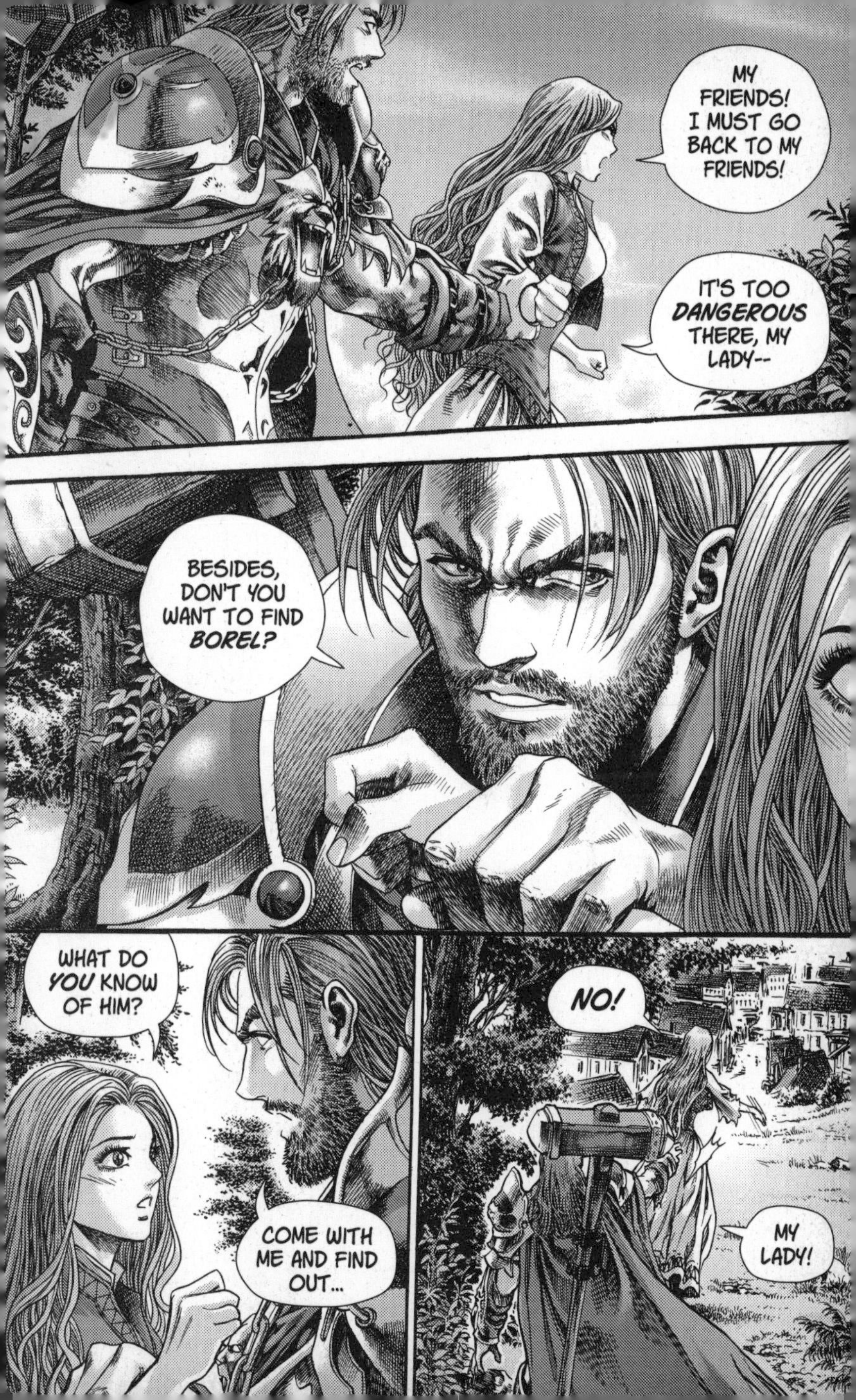
MY FRIENDS! I MUST GO BACK TO MY FRIENDS!
IT'S TOO *DANGEROUS* THERE, MY LADY--
BESIDES, DON'T YOU WANT TO FIND *BOREL?*
WHAT DO *YOU* KNOW OF HIM?
COME WITH ME AND FIND OUT...
NO!
MY LADY!

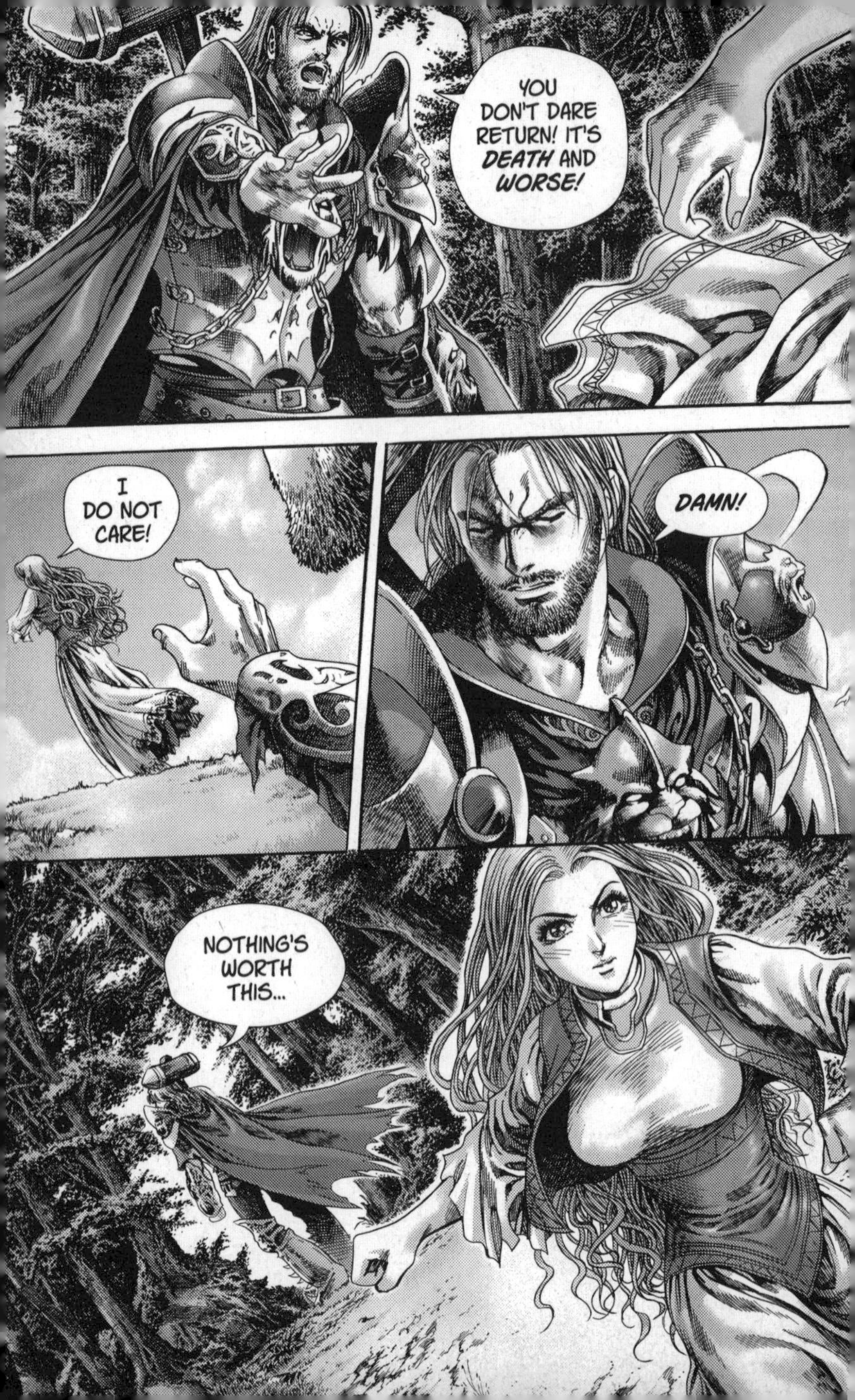
YOU DON'T DARE RETURN! IT'S *DEATH* AND *WORSE!*
I DO NOT CARE!
DAMN!
NOTHING'S WORTH THIS...

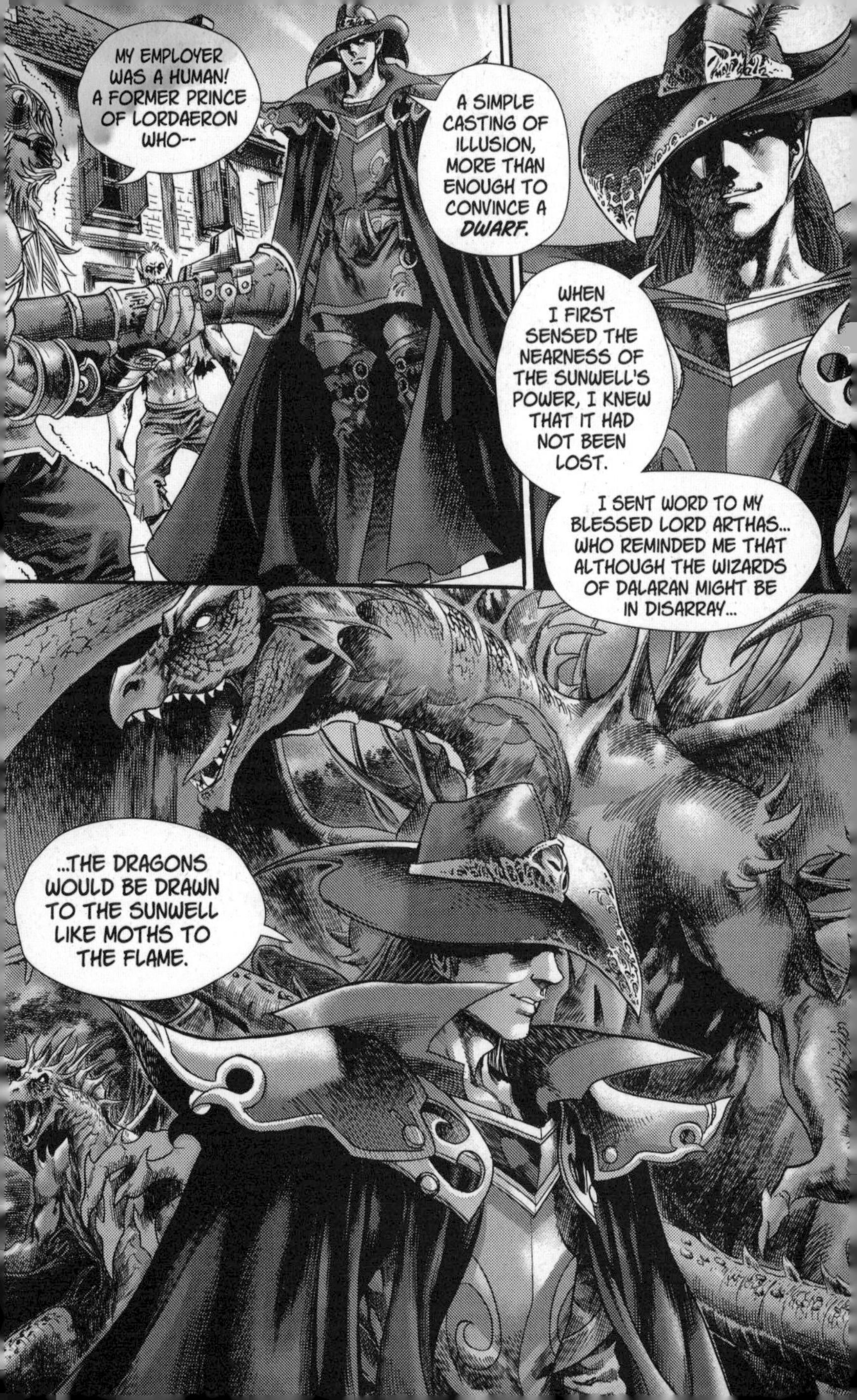
MY EMPLOYER WAS A HUMAN! A FORMER PRINCE OF LORDAERON WHO--
A SIMPLE CASTING OF ILLUSION, MORE THAN ENOUGH TO CONVINCE A *DWARF*.
WHEN I FIRST SENSED THE NEARNESS OF THE SUNWELL'S POWER, I KNEW THAT IT HAD NOT BEEN LOST.
I SENT WORD TO MY BLESSED LORD ARTHAS... WHO REMINDED ME THAT ALTHOUGH THE WIZARDS OF DALARAN MIGHT BE IN DISARRAY...
...THE DRAGONS WOULD BE DRAWN TO THE SUNWELL LIKE MOTHS TO THE FLAME.

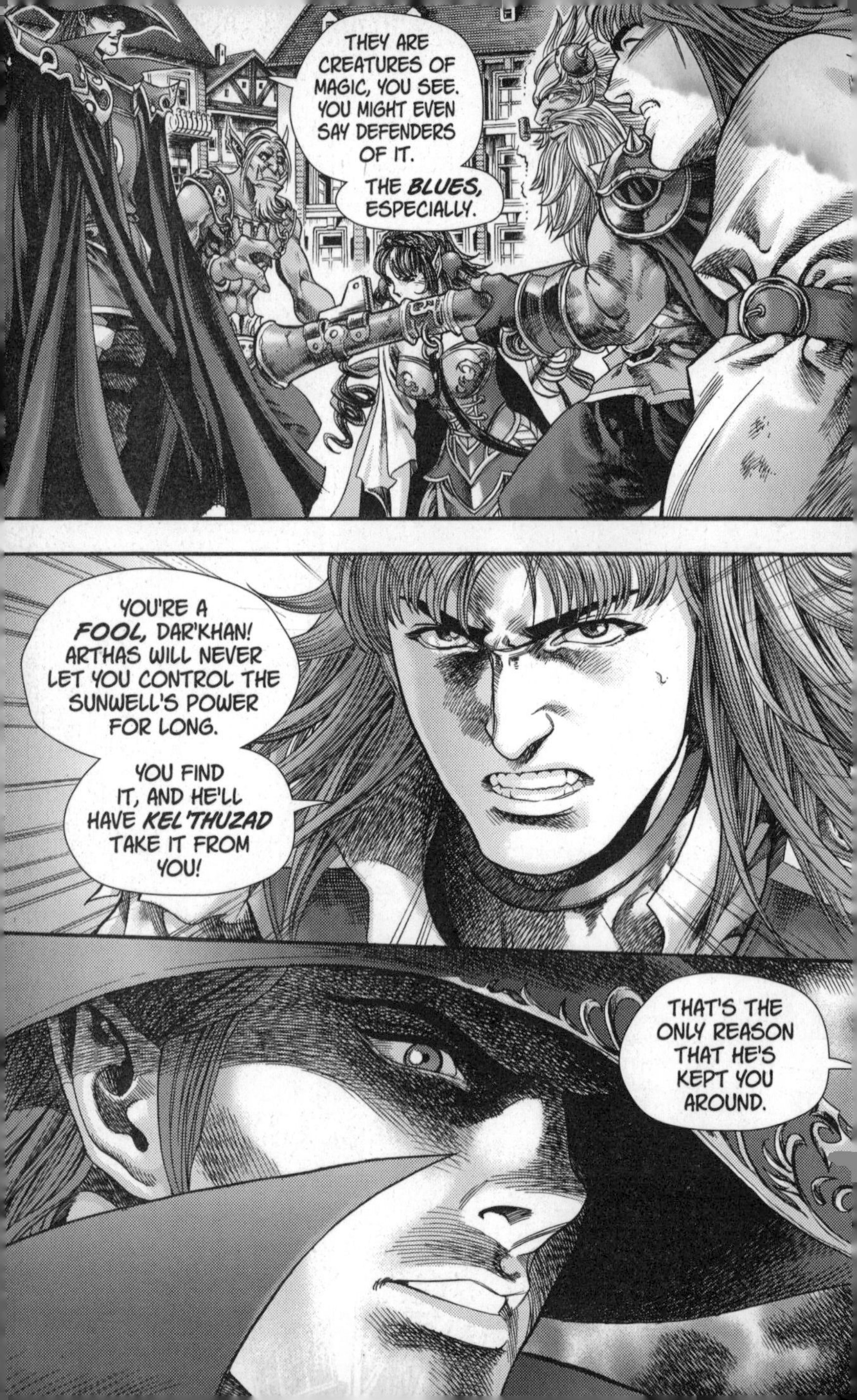
THEY ARE CREATURES OF MAGIC, YOU SEE. YOU MIGHT EVEN SAY DEFENDERS OF IT.
THE *BLUES,* ESPECIALLY.
YOU'RE A *FOOL,* DAR'KHAN! ARTHAS WILL NEVER LET YOU CONTROL THE SUNWELL'S POWER FOR LONG.
YOU FIND IT, AND HE'LL HAVE *KEL'THUZAD* TAKE IT FROM YOU!
THAT'S THE ONLY REASON THAT HE'S KEPT YOU AROUND.

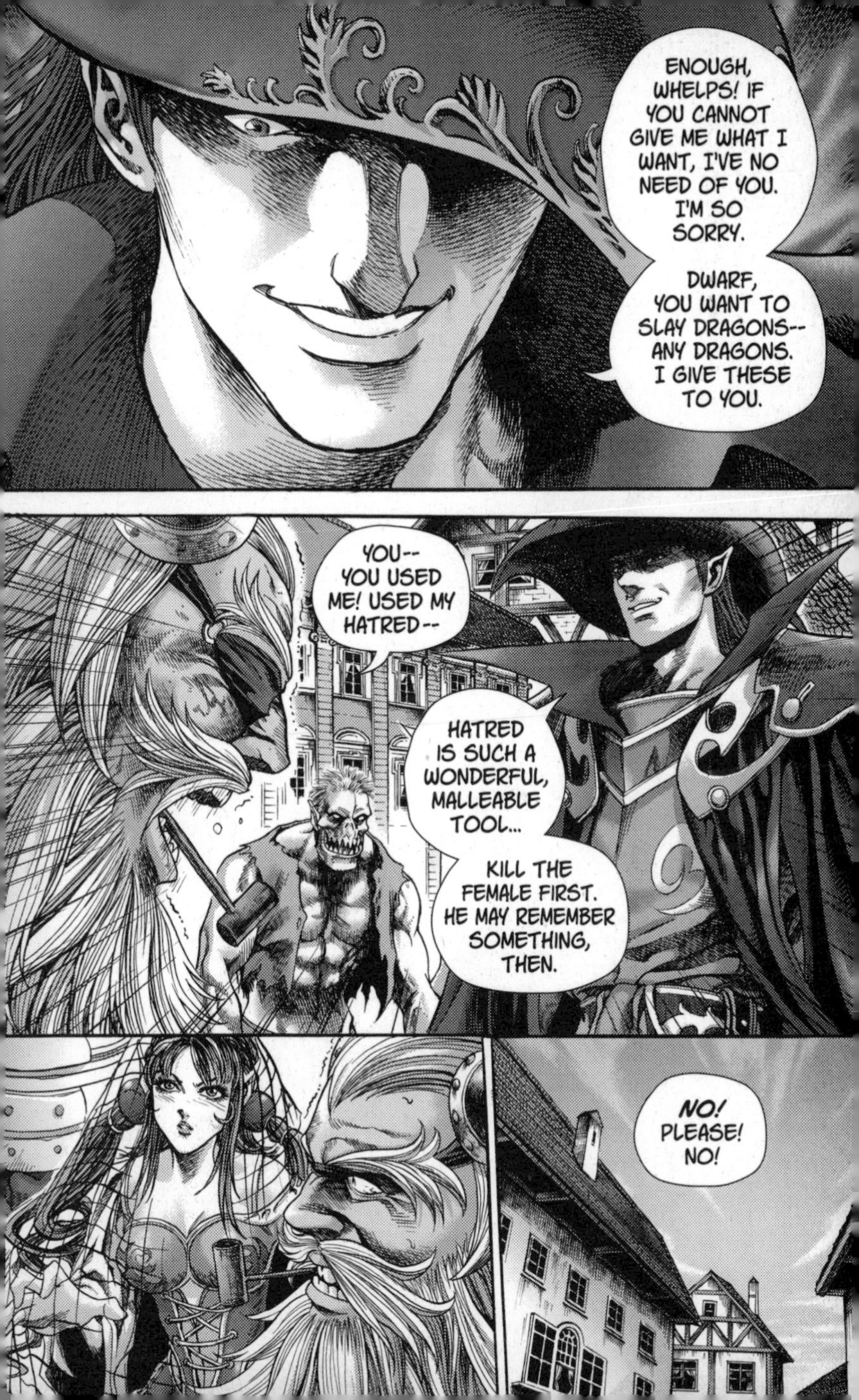
ENOUGH, WHELPS! IF YOU CANNOT GIVE ME WHAT I WANT, I'VE NO NEED OF YOU. I'M SO SORRY.
DWARF, YOU WANT TO SLAY DRAGONS-- ANY DRAGONS. I GIVE THESE TO YOU.
YOU-- YOU USED ME! USED MY HATRED--
HATRED IS SUCH A WONDERFUL, MALLEABLE TOOL...
KILL THE FEMALE FIRST. HE MAY REMEMBER SOMETHING, THEN.
NO! PLEASE! NO!

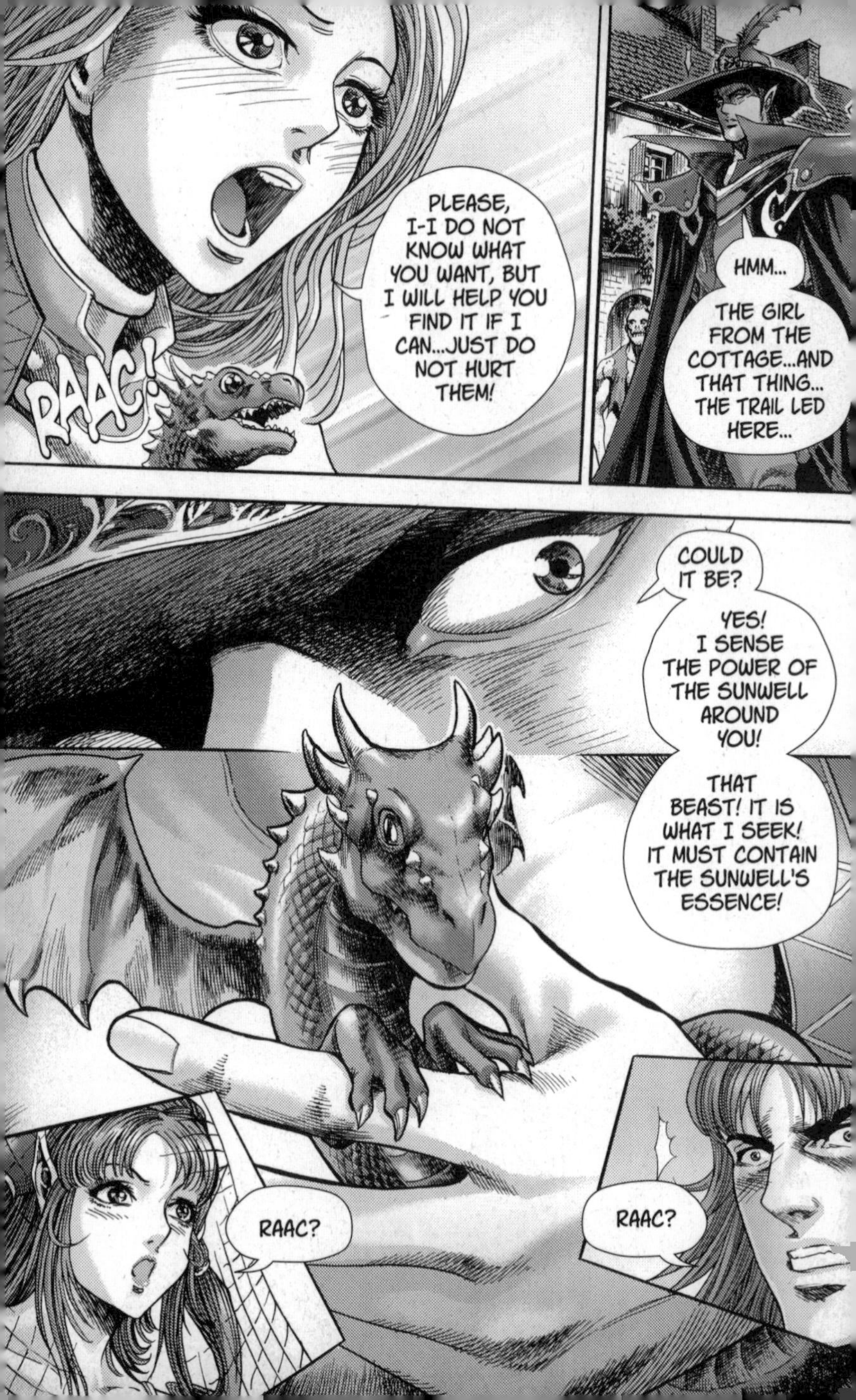
RAAC!
PLEASE, I-I DO NOT KNOW WHAT YOU WANT, BUT I WILL HELP YOU FIND IT IF I CAN...JUST DO NOT HURT THEM!
HMM...
THE GIRL FROM THE COTTAGE...AND THAT THING... THE TRAIL LED HERE...
COULD IT BE?
YES! I SENSE THE POWER OF THE SUNWELL AROUND YOU!
THAT BEAST! IT IS WHAT I SEEK! IT MUST CONTAIN THE SUNWELL'S ESSENCE!
RAAC?
RAAC?

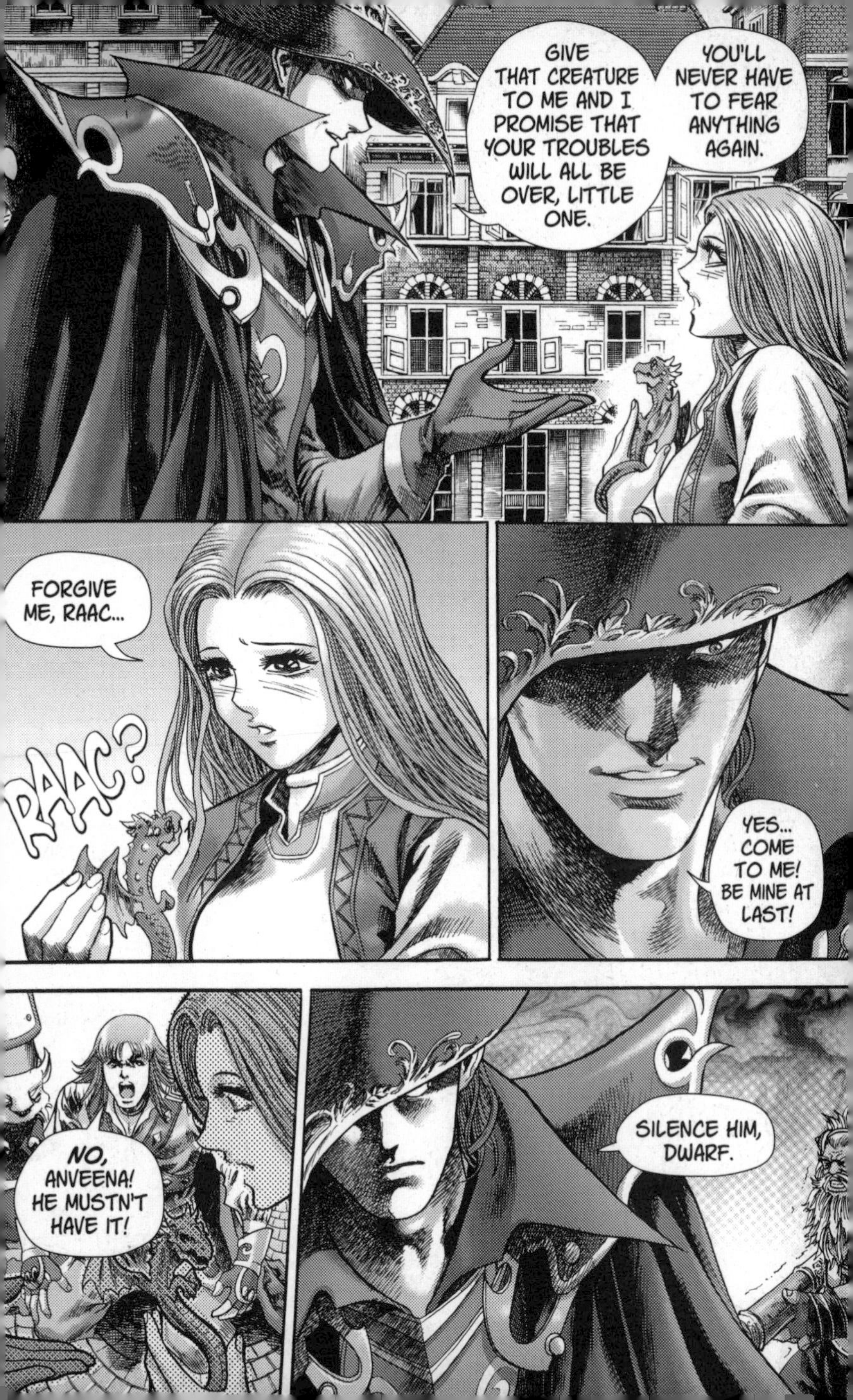
GIVE THAT CREATURE TO ME AND I PROMISE THAT YOUR TROUBLES WILL ALL BE OVER, LITTLE ONE.
YOU'LL NEVER HAVE TO FEAR ANYTHING AGAIN.
FORGIVE ME, RAAC...
RAAC?
YES... COME TO ME! BE MINE AT LAST!
NO, ANVEENA! HE MUSTN'T HAVE IT!
SILENCE HIM, DWARF.

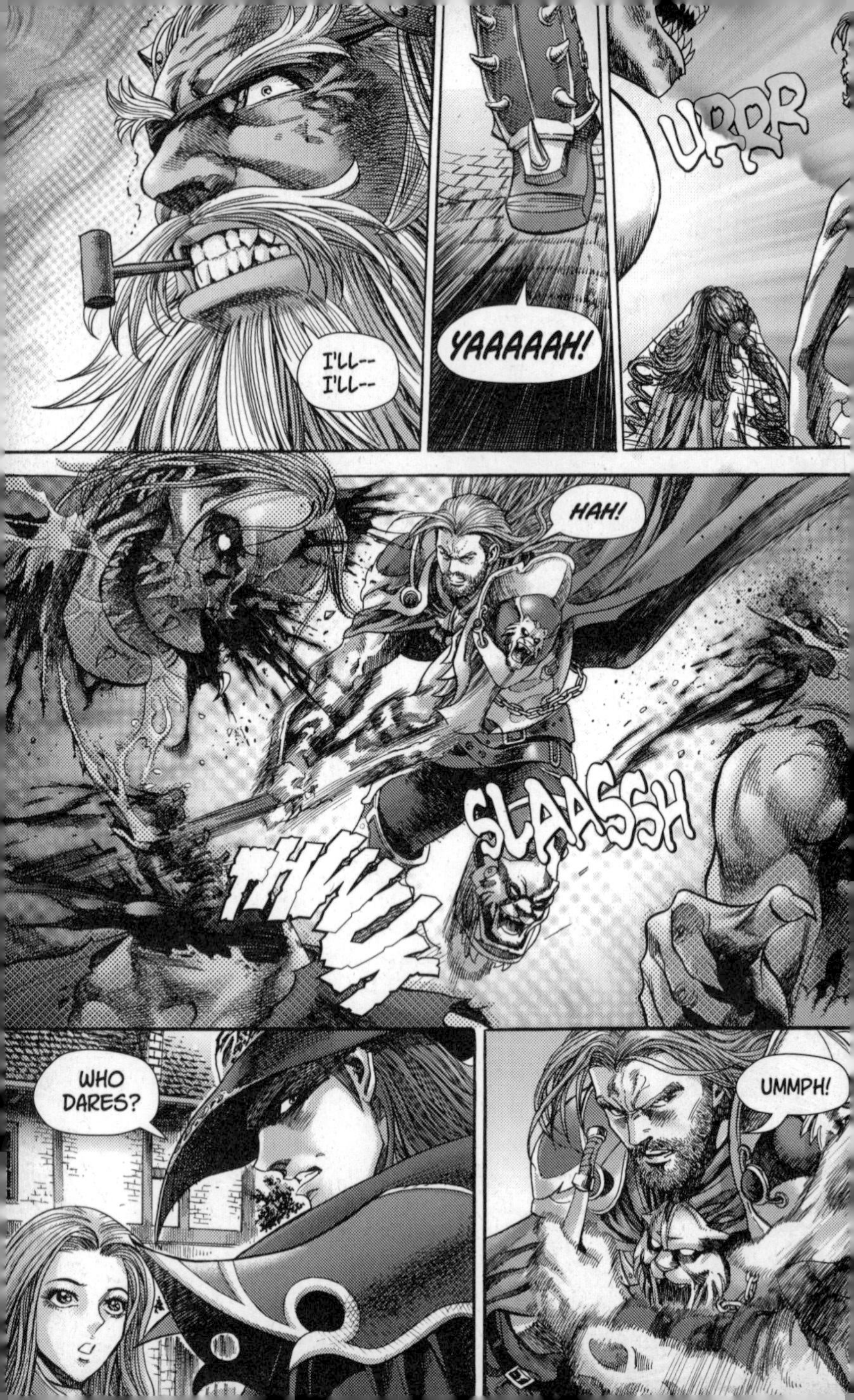
I'LL-- I'LL--
YAAAAAH!
URRR
HAH!
SLAASSH
THWK
WHO DARES?
UMMPH!

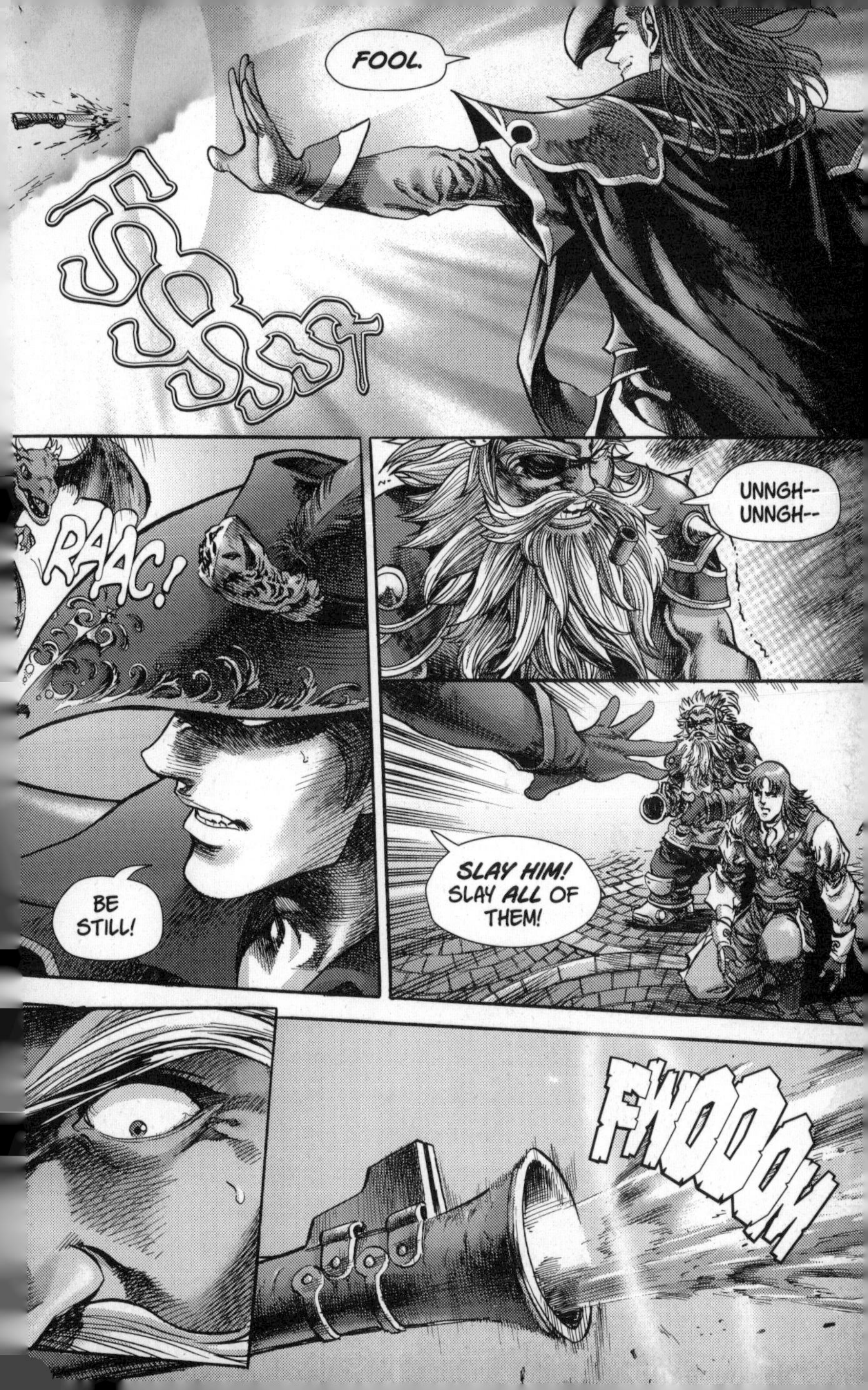
FOOL.
FSSSSSST
RAAC!
BE STILL!
UNNGH-- UNNGH--
SLAY HIM! SLAY ALL OF THEM!
FWOOOM

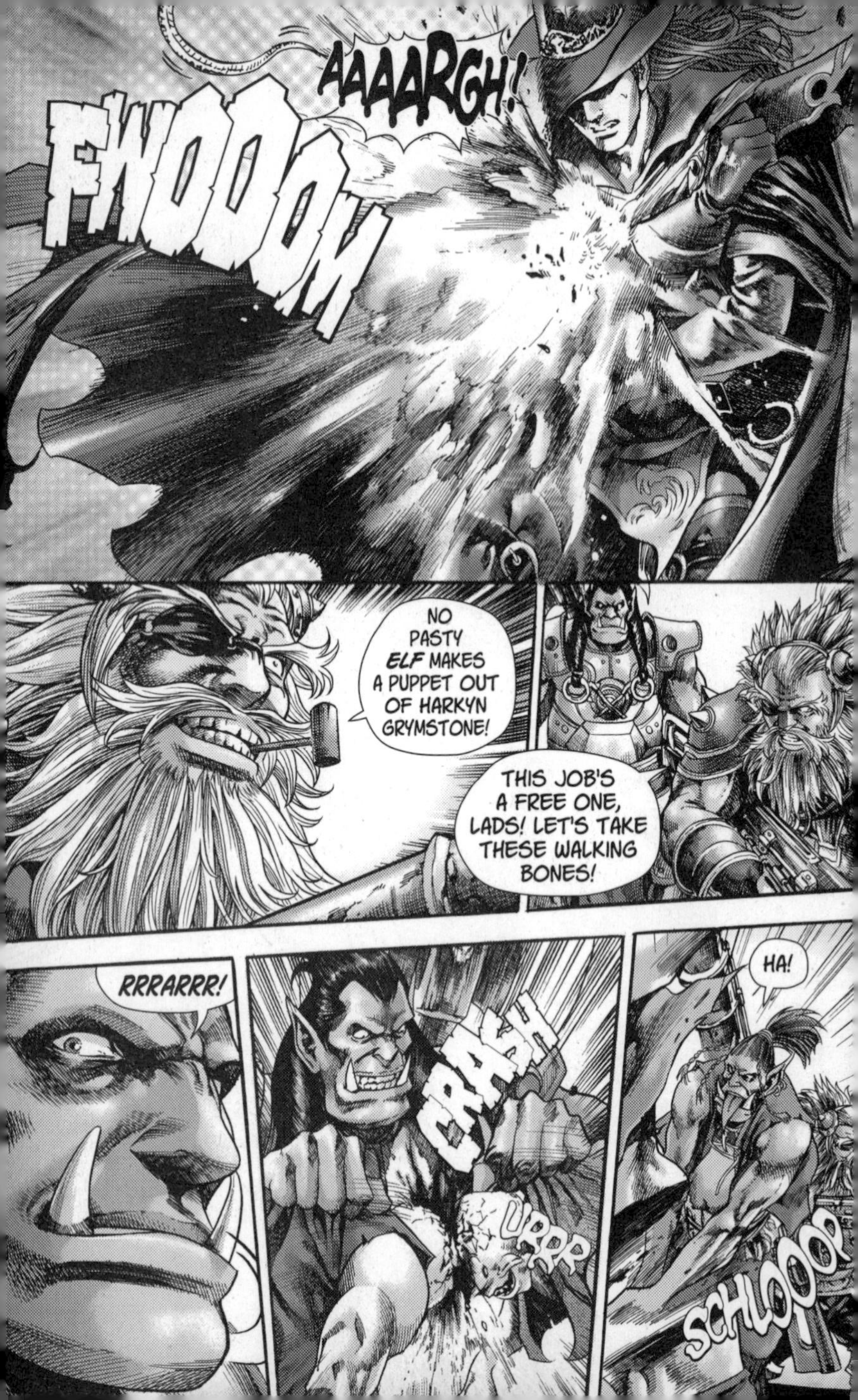
AAAARGH!
FWOOOM
NO PASTY ELF MAKES A PUPPET OUT OF HARKYN GRYMSTONE!
THIS JOB'S A FREE ONE, LADS! LET'S TAKE THESE WALKING BONES!
RRRARRR!
CRASH
URRR
HA!
SCHLOOOP

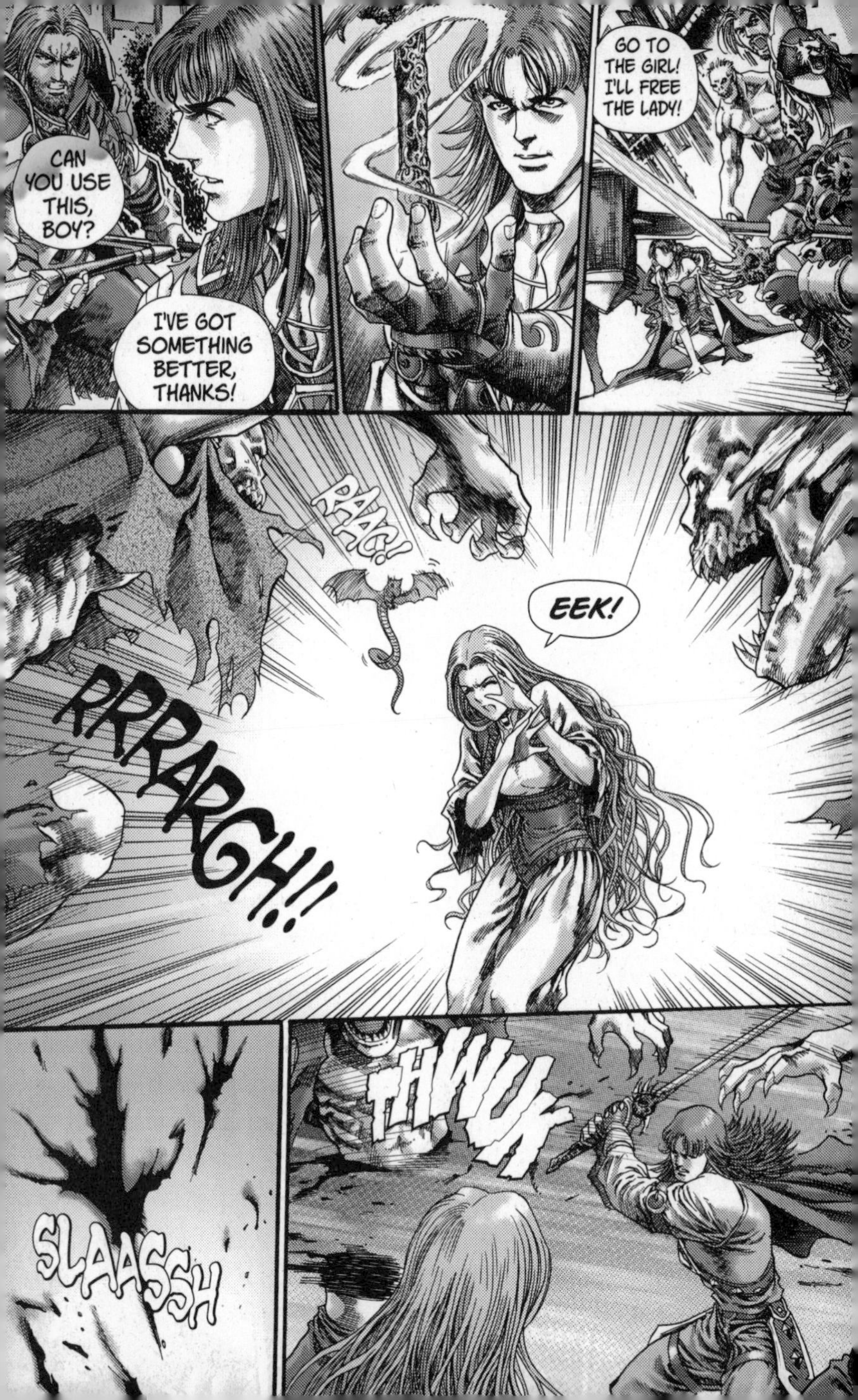
CAN YOU USE THIS, BOY?
I'VE GOT SOMETHING BETTER, THANKS!
GO TO THE GIRL! I'LL FREE THE LADY!
RAAG!
EEK!
RRRARGH!!!
SLAASSH
THWUK

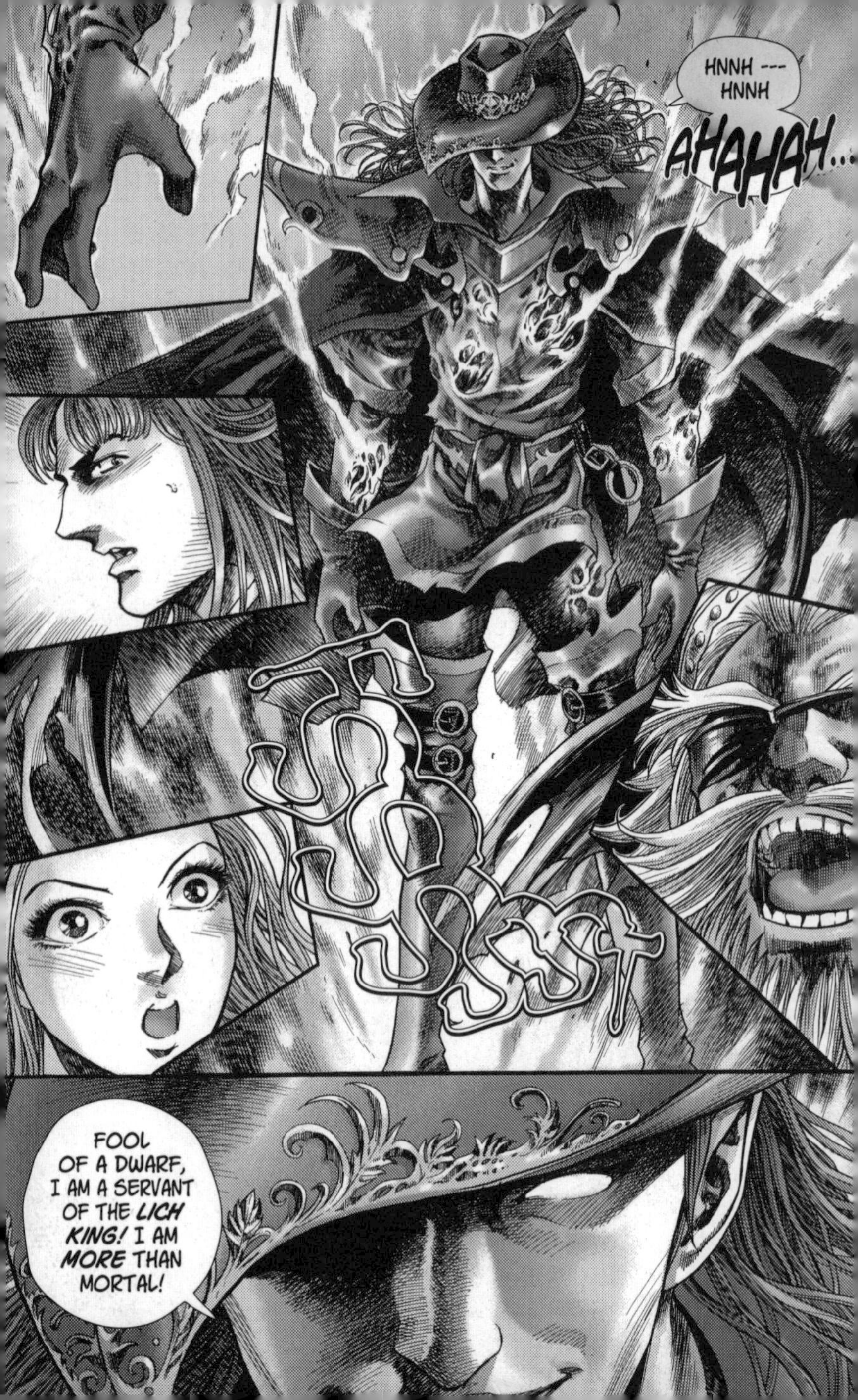
HNNH --- HNNH
AHAHAH...
FOOL OF A DWARF, I AM A SERVANT OF THE *LICH KING!* I AM *MORE* THAN MORTAL!

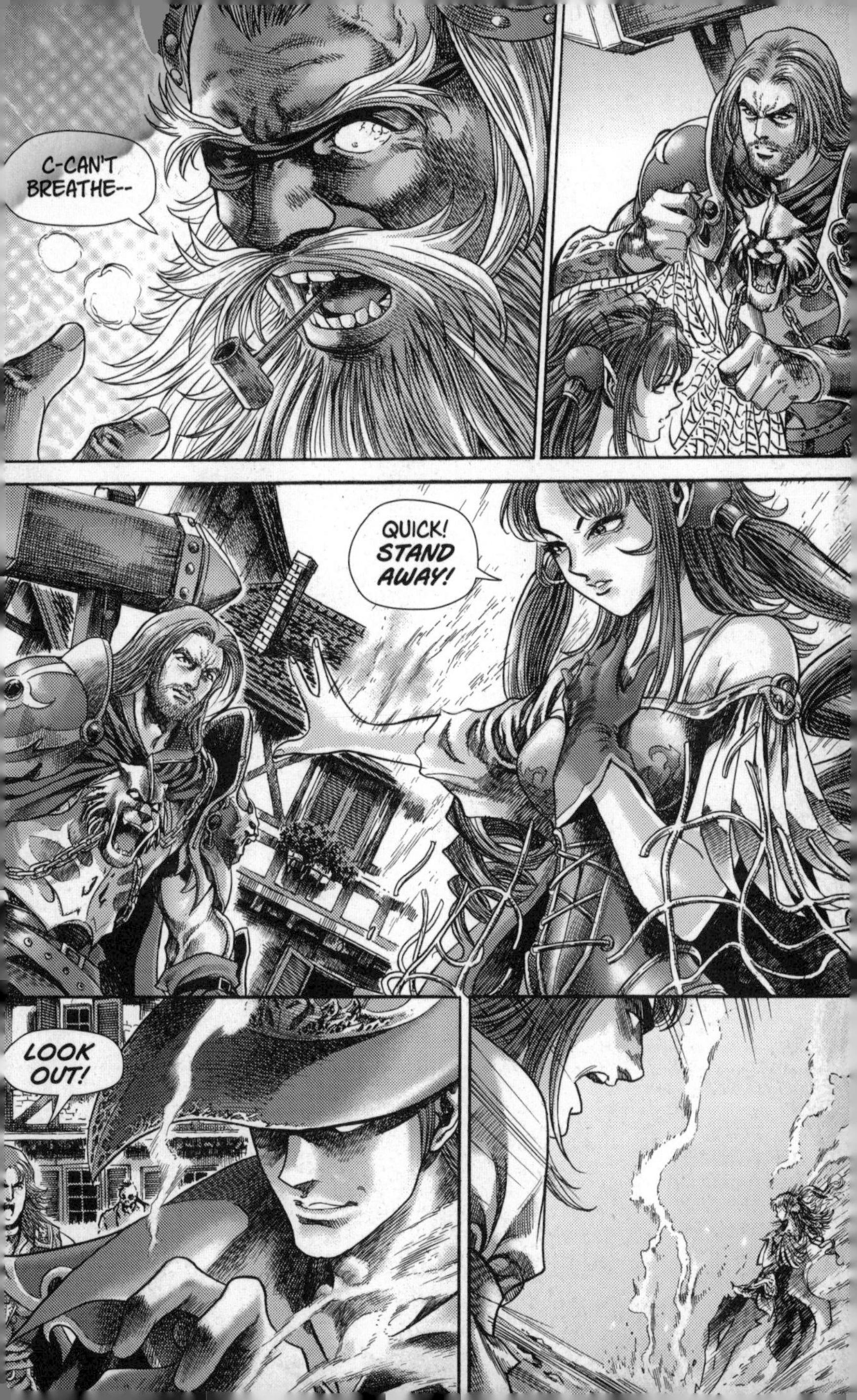
C-CAN'T BREATHE--
QUICK! STAND AWAY!
LOOK OUT!

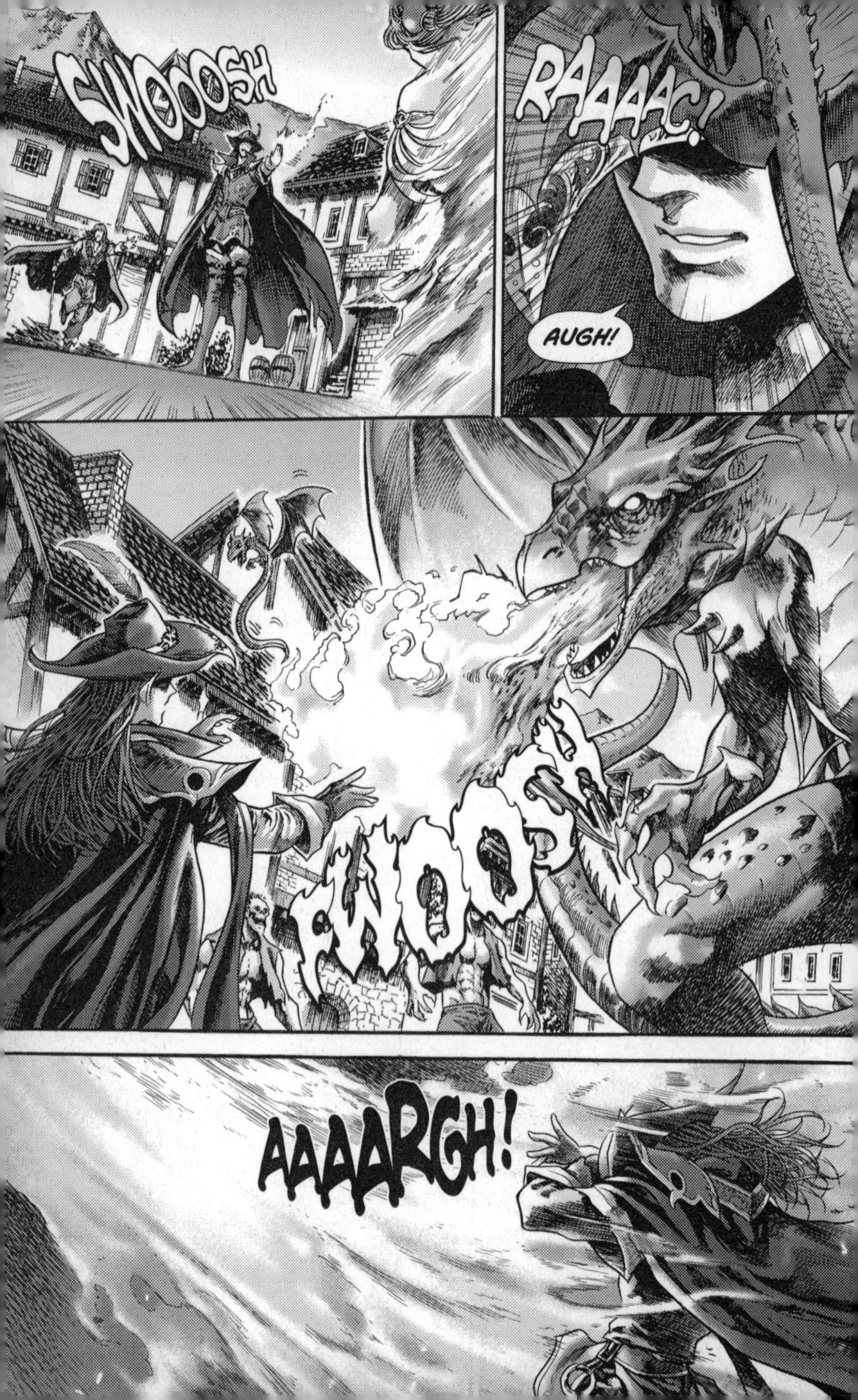
SHOOOSH
RAAAAC!
AUGH!
FWOOSH
AAAARGH!

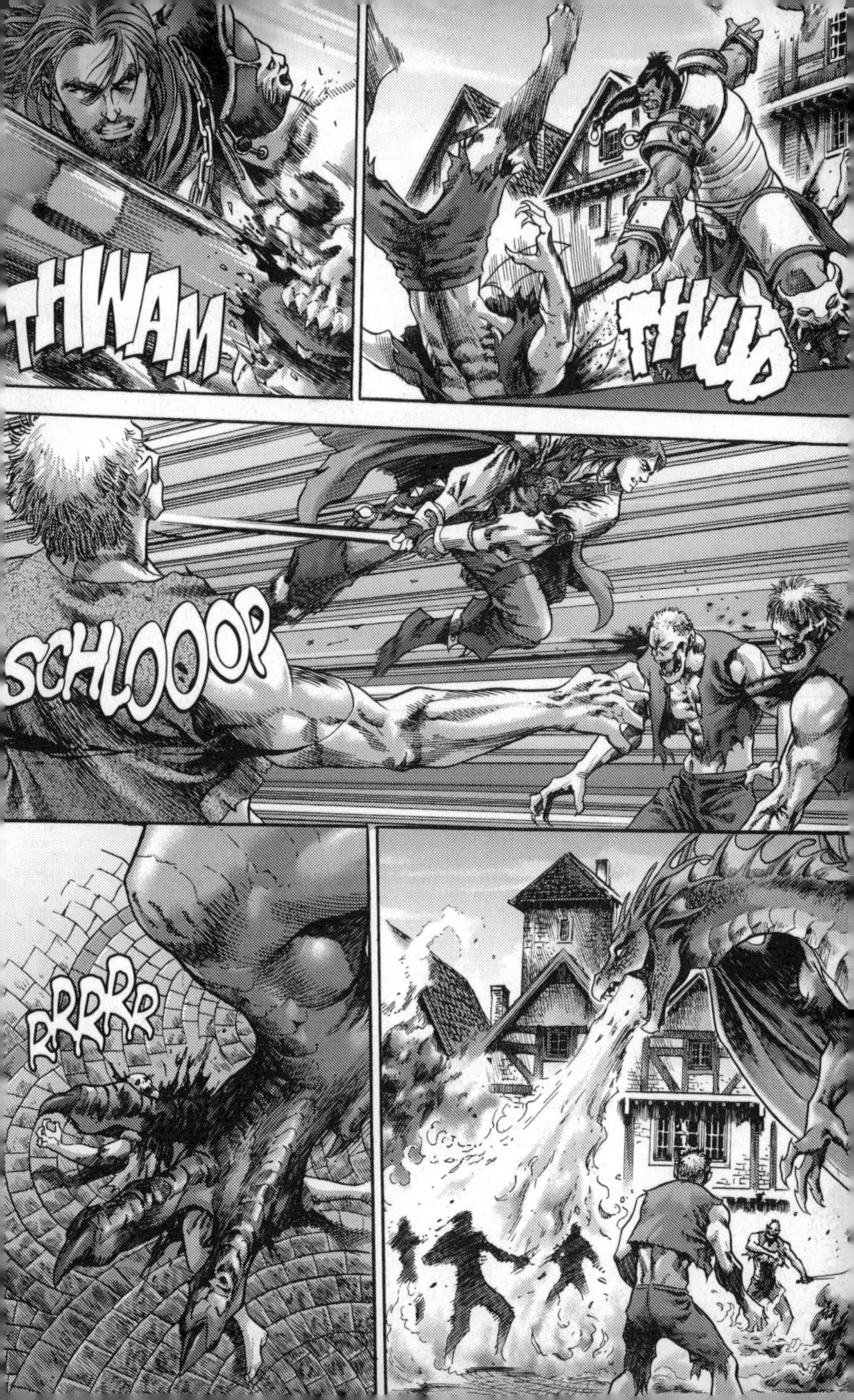
THWAM
THUD
SCHLOOOP
RRRRR

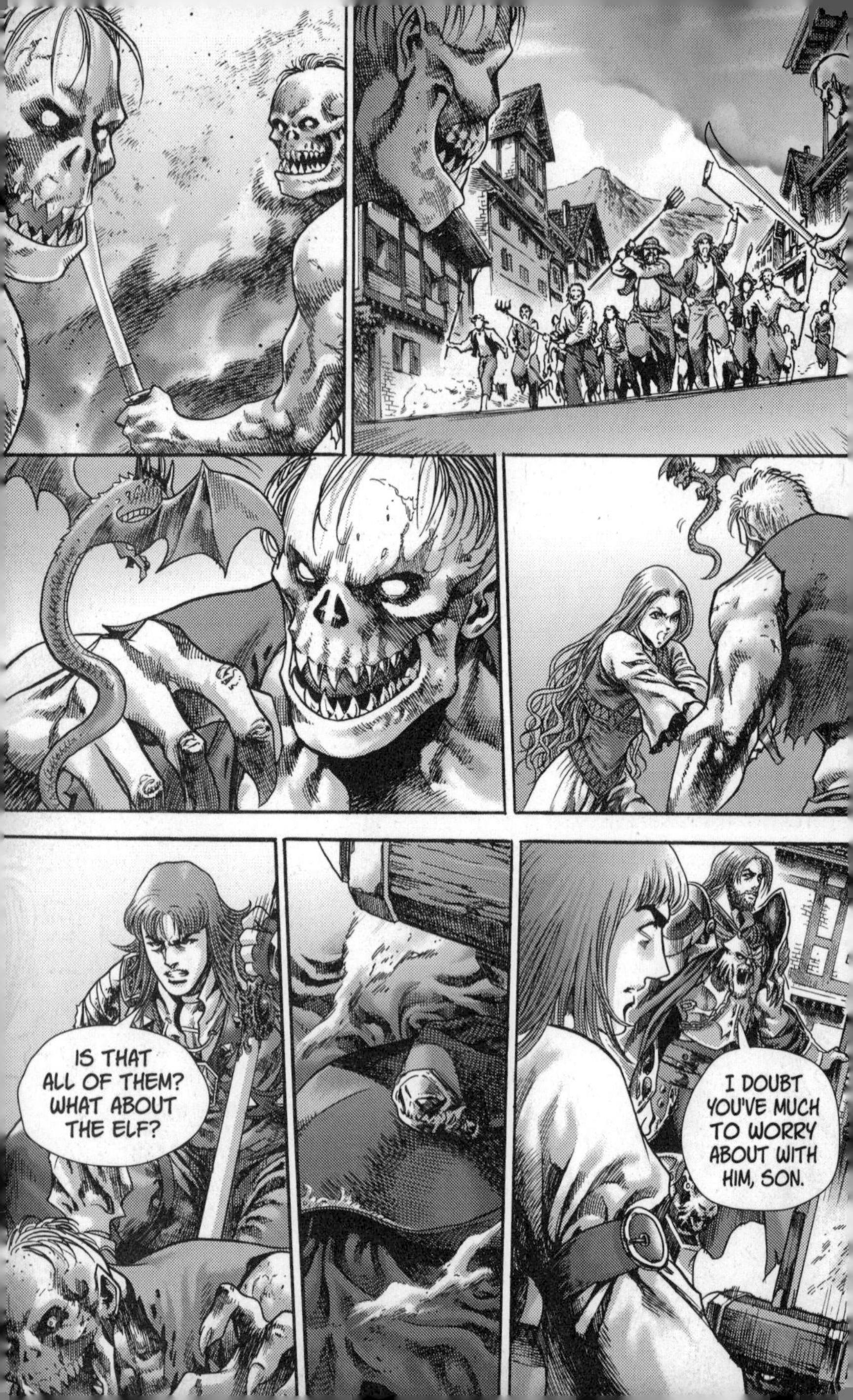
IS THAT ALL OF THEM? WHAT ABOUT THE ELF?
I DOUBT YOU'VE MUCH TO WORRY ABOUT WITH HIM, SON.

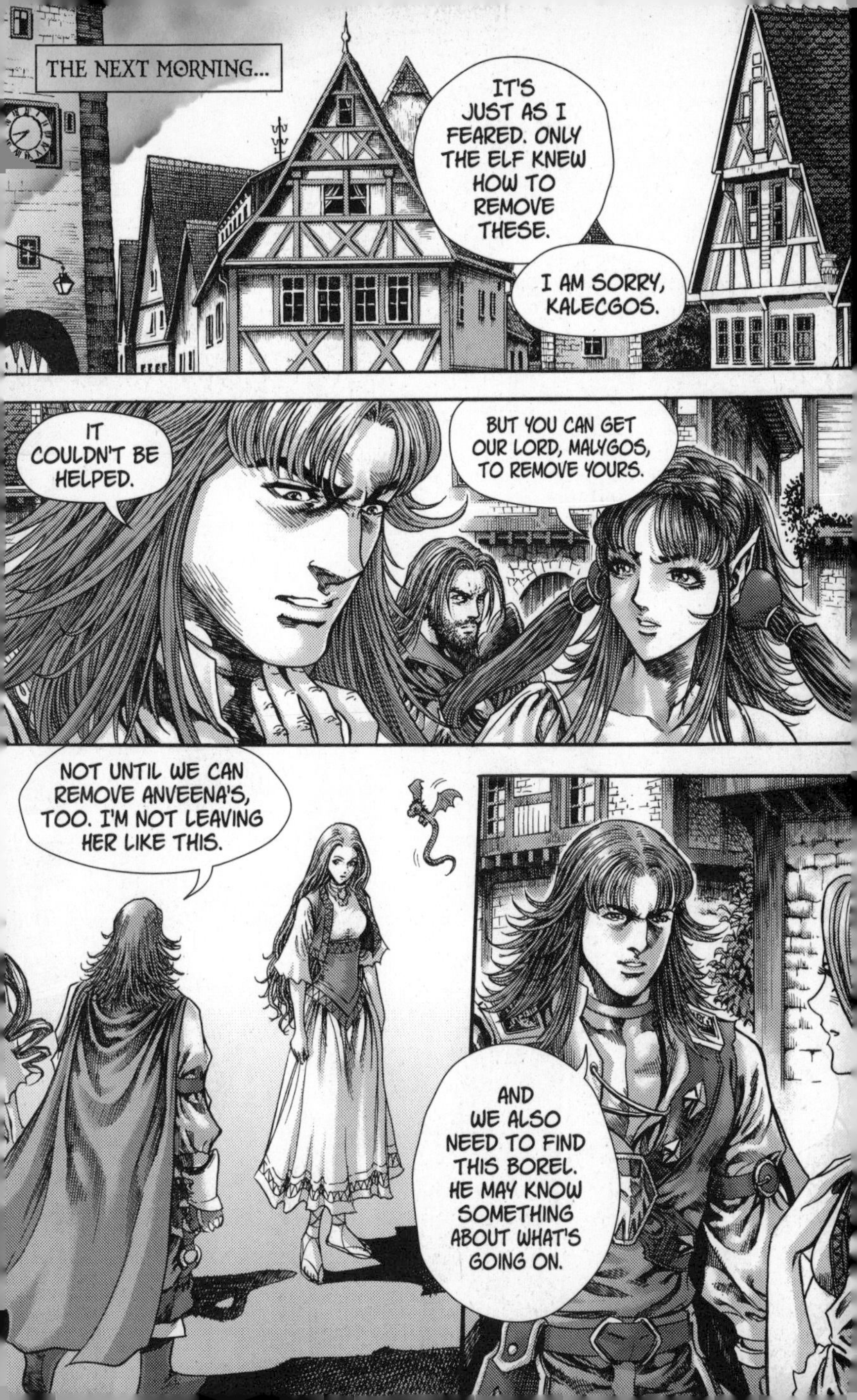
THE NEXT MORNING...
IT'S JUST AS I FEARED. ONLY THE ELF KNEW HOW TO REMOVE THESE.
I AM SORRY, KALECGOS.
IT COULDN'T BE HELPED.
BUT YOU CAN GET OUR LORD, MALYGOS, TO REMOVE YOURS.
NOT UNTIL WE CAN REMOVE ANVEENA'S, TOO. I'M NOT LEAVING HER LIKE THIS.
AND WE ALSO NEED TO FIND THIS BOREL. HE MAY KNOW SOMETHING ABOUT WHAT'S GOING ON.

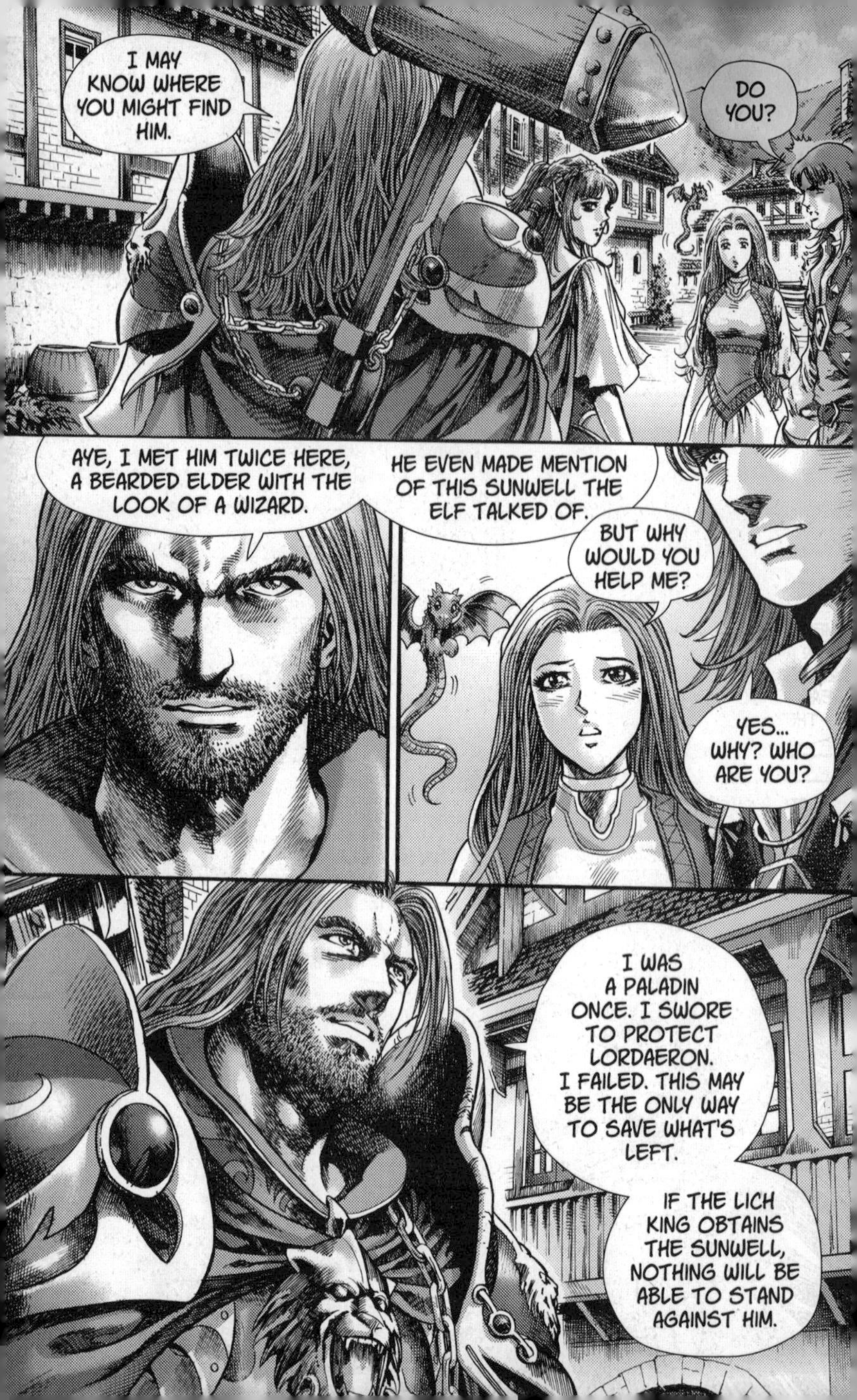
I MAY KNOW WHERE YOU MIGHT FIND HIM.
DO YOU?
AYE, I MET HIM TWICE HERE, A BEARDED ELDER WITH THE LOOK OF A WIZARD.
HE EVEN MADE MENTION OF THIS SUNWELL THE ELF TALKED OF.
BUT WHY WOULD YOU HELP ME?
YES... WHY? WHO ARE YOU?
I WAS A PALADIN ONCE. I SWORE TO PROTECT LORDAERON. I FAILED. THIS MAY BE THE ONLY WAY TO SAVE WHAT'S LEFT.
IF THE LICH KING OBTAINS THE SUNWELL, NOTHING WILL BE ABLE TO STAND AGAINST HIM.

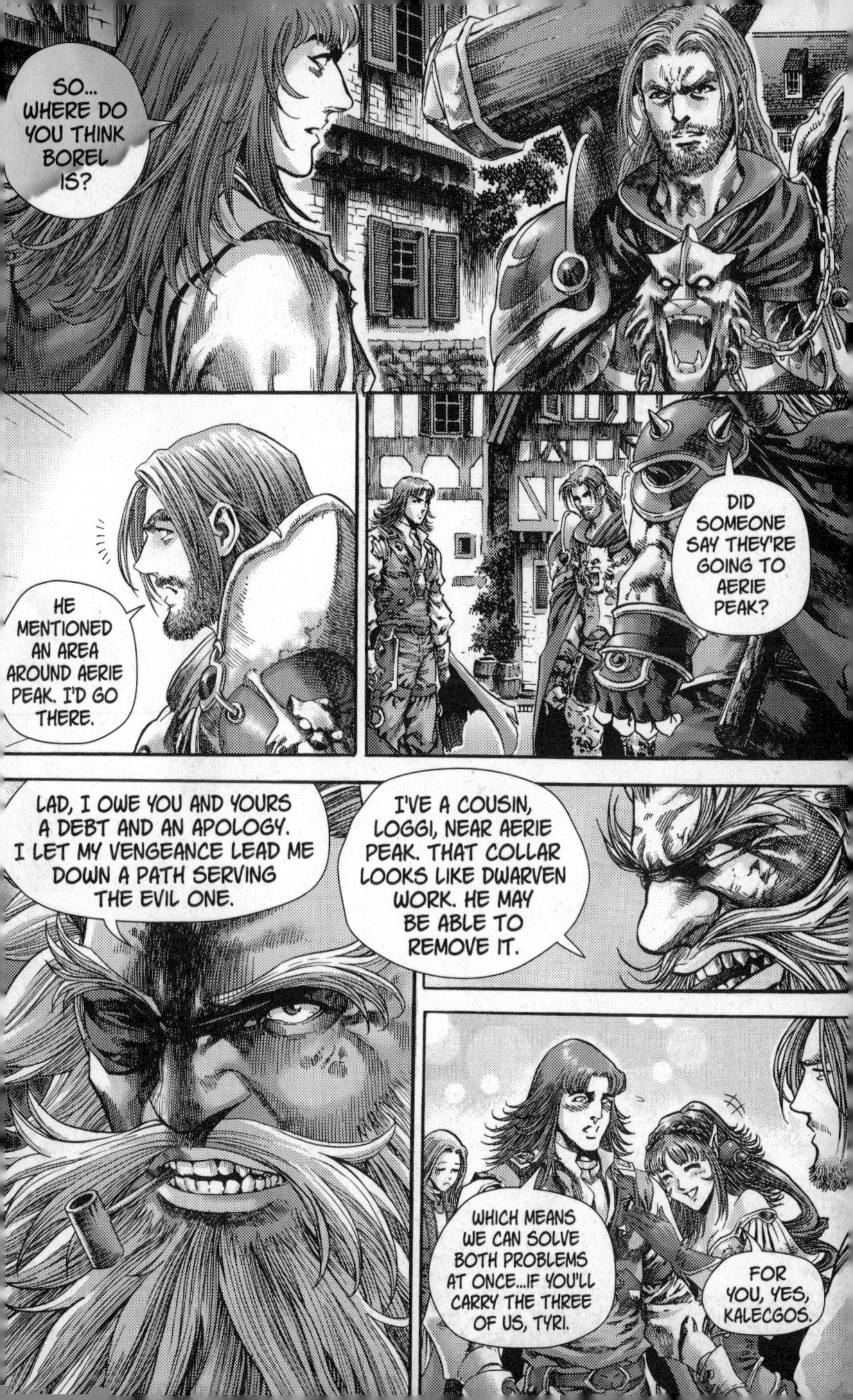
SO... WHERE DO YOU THINK BOREL IS?
HE MENTIONED AN AREA AROUND AERIE PEAK. I'D GO THERE.
DID SOMEONE SAY THEY'RE GOING TO AERIE PEAK?
LAD, I OWE YOU AND YOURS A DEBT AND AN APOLOGY. I LET MY VENGEANCE LEAD ME DOWN A PATH SERVING THE EVIL ONE.
I'VE A COUSIN, LOGGI, NEAR AERIE PEAK. THAT COLLAR LOOKS LIKE DWARVEN WORK. HE MAY BE ABLE TO REMOVE IT.
WHICH MEANS WE CAN SOLVE BOTH PROBLEMS AT ONCE...IF YOU'LL CARRY THE THREE OF US, TYRI.
FOR YOU, YES, KALECGOS.

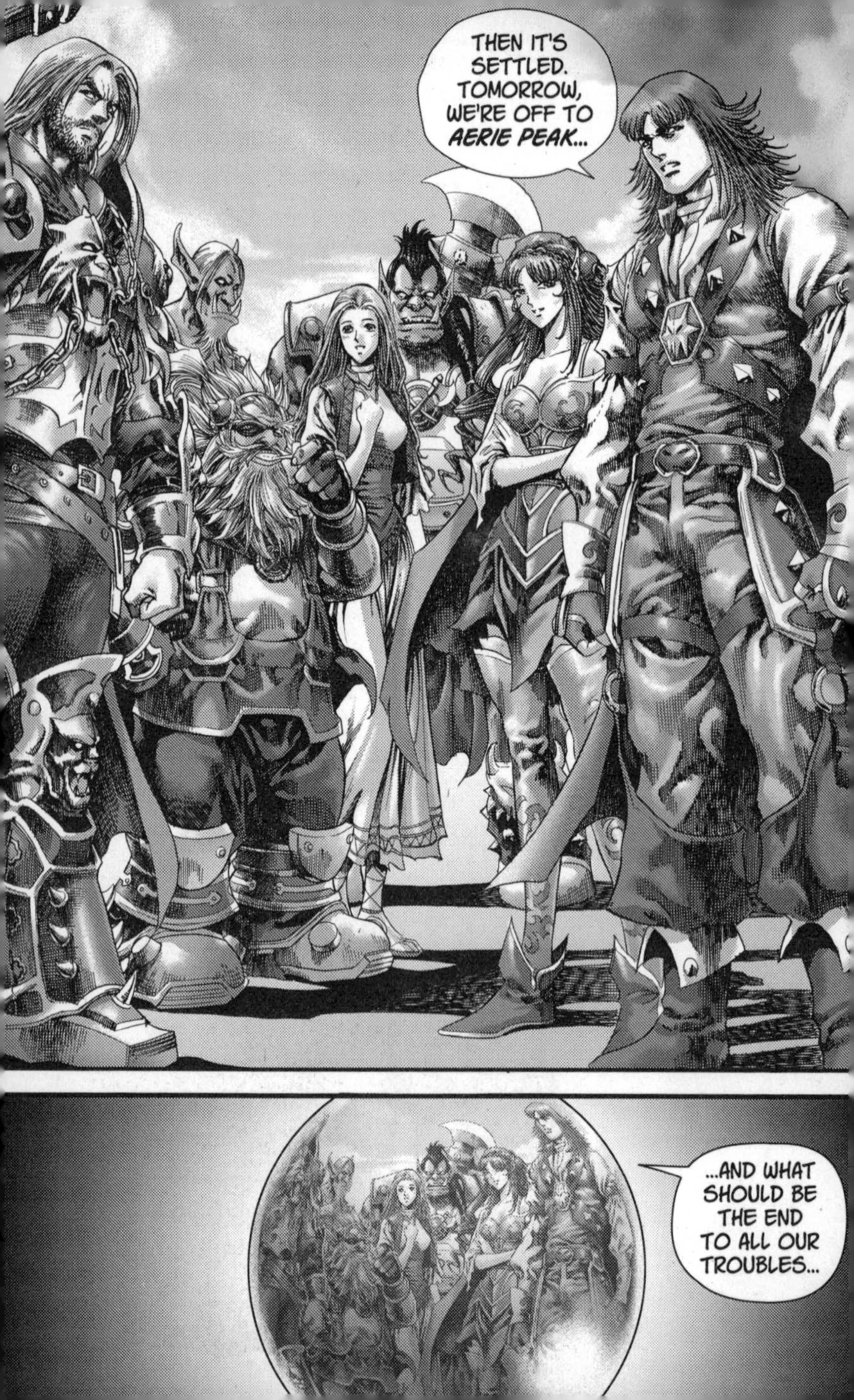
THEN IT'S SETTLED. TOMORROW, WE'RE OFF TO AERIE PEAK...
...AND WHAT SHOULD BE THE END TO ALL OUR TROUBLES...

To be continued in

Warcraft®
The Sunwell Trilogy™

Volume 2

Shadows of Ice

The action heats up in the frigid wastelands as Kalec, Anveena, Tyri, and Jorad make their way to Aerie Peak.

They go seeking the dwarf known as Loggi, but they find much, much more.

As more fantastic and frightening denizens of the world of Warcraft are revealed, the mystery of Raac deepens and the dragons face a frozen and furious foe!

Can't wait for volume 2? Go to tokyopop.com and check out our online manga player for some see sneak peeks at what's to come!

About the Creators

In addition to his work on *Warcraft: The Sunwell Trilogy* and *Ragnarok* (also by TOKYOPOP), Richard A. Knaak is the NY Times bestselling fantasy author of 27 novels and over a dozen short pieces, including *The Legend of Huma* and *Night of Blood* for Dragonlance and *The Demon Soul* for Warcraft. He has also written the popular Dragonrealm series and several independent pieces. His works have been published in several languages, most recently Russian, Turkish, Bulgarian, Chinese, Czech, German, and Spanish. In addition to *Warcraft: The Sunwell Trilogy*, he is at work on *The Sundering*, the third

volume of *War of the Ancients*, and *Empire of Blood*, the final book in his epic Dragonlance trilogy, *The Minotaur Wars*. All are due out in 2005.

Future works include a third Diablo novel and the *Aquilonia* trilogy, based on the worlds of Robert E. Howard. His most recent hardcover, *Tides of Blood,* the sequel to *Night,* was just released by Wizards of the Coast.

To find out more about Richard Knaak's projects or to sign up for his e-mail announcements, visit his website at http://www.sff.net/people/knaak

Jae-Hwan Kim was born in 1971 in Korea. His best-known manga works include *Rainbow*, *Combat Metal HeMoSoo*, and *Majeh*. Jae-Hwan currently lives and works in Thailand.

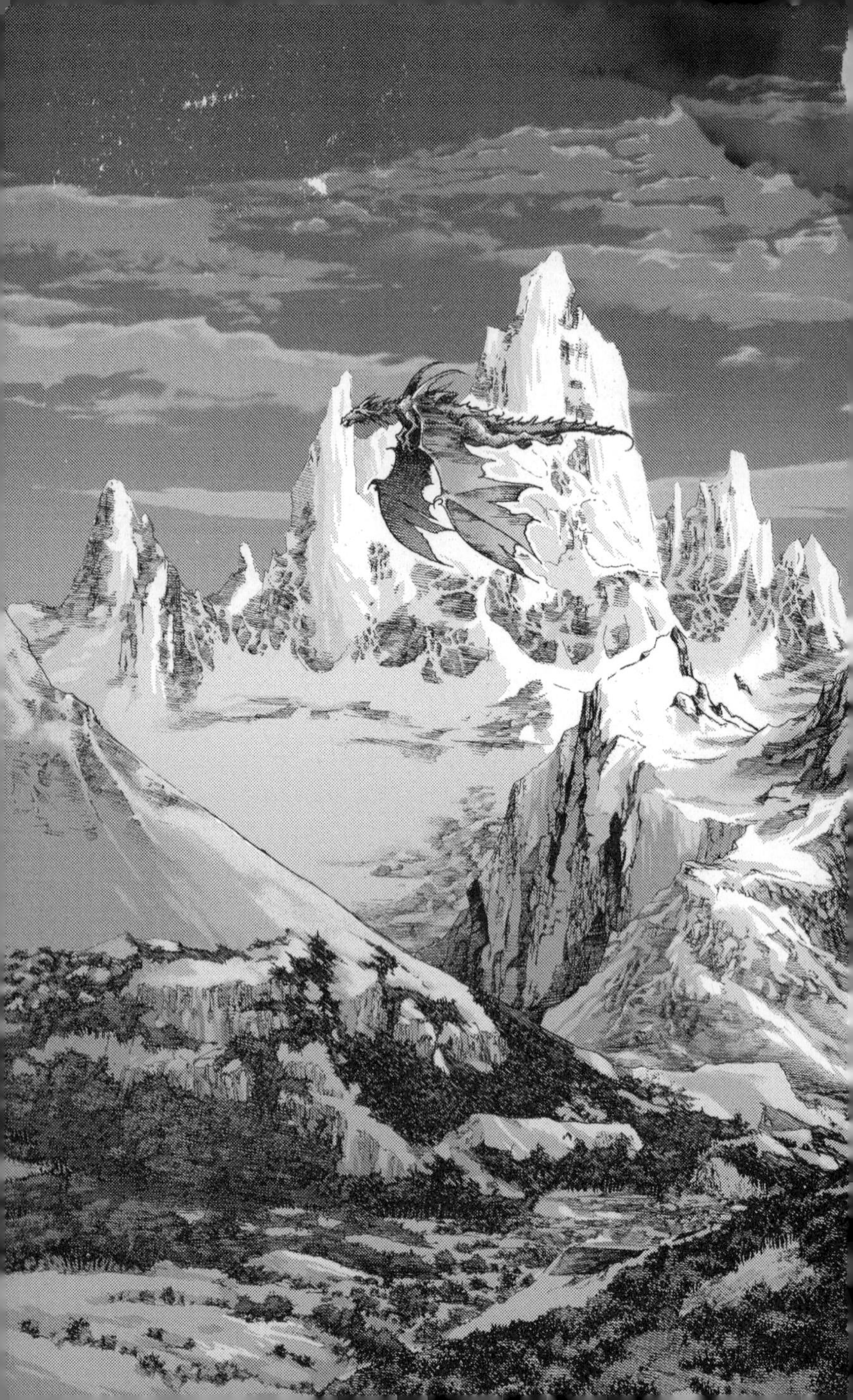